The Elephant in the Fridge

GUIDED STEPS TO DATA VAULT SUCCESS THROUGH BUILDING BUSINESS-CENTERED MODELS

John Giles

Technics Publications
BASKING RIDGE, NEW JERSEY

2 Lindsley Road
Basking Ridge, NJ 07920 USA
https://www.TechnicsPub.com

Cover design by Lorena Molinari

Edited by Lauren McCafferty

First Edition

First Printing 2019

ISBN, print ed. 9781634624893
ISBN, Kindle ed. 9781634624909
ISBN, PDF ed. 9781634624923

Library of Congress Control Number: 2019930218

Contents

Table of Figures

Table of Tables

Foreword

It was one year ago this month that I first met John Giles. I knew almost immediately that I had met a kindred spirit—a lover of nature and of data. I was in Canberra, Australia to participate in Steve Hoberman's Data Modeling Zone conference and had the pleasure of visiting the Tidbinbilla Nature Reserve with John, Steve, and Andrew Smailes. Even in the midst of a unique nature experience (we saw wallabies, koalas, platypus, many colorful birds, and much more) we slipped into data discussions. That's the mark of true data geeks!

Later in the week I attended a session presented by John and based on his first book, *The Nimble Elephant*. Here I saw the innovative style with which John approaches data management. Systematically applying data model patterns and commercially available data models within a defined process, he makes a compelling case that enterprise modeling and agility are not at odds, and illustrates how agile enterprise data modeling really is possible. The real magic, however, is his ability to clearly explain a complex topic in a way that makes it easy to understand and apply.

Now John has done it again. This time the complex topic is Data Vault modeling. I first learned about Data Vault from its inventor, Dan Linstedt, several years ago. Data Vault is a powerful way to design adaptable and highly resilient data structures. But with power comes complexity. Building a Data Vault isn't easy and there are many ways to get it wrong. Linstedt routinely warns about the pitfalls and common mistakes, and John revisits some of those warnings in this book.

But the book doesn't focus on warnings, pitfalls, and mistakes. Instead it provides a step-by-step approach to getting it right where enterprise view and business-centric design are critical elements. Along with a four-step design process, John describes Data Vault with easily understood explanations and examples. With a look inside the architecture you'll understand the roles and relationships of hubs, links, and satellites. You'll see the difference between a raw data vault and a business data vault and fully grasp the importance of business-oriented design and business-centric models.

Business orientation is a recurring theme throughout the book with discussion of enterprise views, enterprise models, ontologies, taxonomies, etc. Reading between the lines, it seems that the implicit message is "Business before Data." This is an especially important message about the design process: start with business needs, not with the data that you have. Working from the business focus, you'll get in depth explanation of how to go from enterprise view to Data Vault design, with details and examples of modeling hubs, links, and satellites. All of the business modeling takes place first, driven by enterprise perspective. Then it is time to turn attention to the data that you have, mapping sources to the data model and reconciling gaps and conflicts.

The weird title notwithstanding (what is it about John Giles and elephants?), I'm happy that this book is not called *Data Vaults Made Easy* because they are not easy. I'm glad it isn't called *Data Vault for Dummies* because they are too vital a part of data management ecosystems to be built by dummies. The book is just exactly what we need—Guided Steps to Data Vault Success—with careful attention to data modeling for the vault.

For data management professionals, Data Vault is an important tool in the toolbox. In this age of data lakes, many pundits are quick to declare the data warehouse dead. But we practitioners know better. The data warehouse is not dead. My recent research shows a majority of companies (approximately 90%) operating multiple data warehouses. Today's focus is on data warehouse modernization—improved scalability, cloud migration, and handling of non-relational data—and Data Vault is a practical solution to these challenges.

For data architects and data engineers, data modeling is an essential skill. NoSQL technology gave rise to a mistaken belief that data modeling is obsolete. Nothing could be further from the truth. Data models are needed initially to support the basic principle of design before you build. They continue to be necessary throughout the data lifecycle, providing essential metadata and mapping for maintenance, troubleshooting, change management, and impact analysis.

In a nutshell, we need Data Vaults, we need data models, and we need them to work together. Thank you, John Giles, for showing us how to meet those needs.

Dave Wells
Director, Data Management Practice
Eckerson Group

Seattle, WA, March 2019

Introduction

Why "The Elephant in the Fridge"?

The "*Elephant …*" bit ties back to my previous book, "*The Nimble Elephant: Agile Delivery of Data Models using a Pattern-Based Approach*". The theme of "Agile" development of pattern-based models most certainly has applicability when generating Data Vault models.

But why "*… in the Fridge*"? It's got nothing to do with the rather lame jokes from the middle of last century (Question: "How do you know there's an elephant in the fridge?" Answer: "Elephant footprints in the butter"). Rather, it's an alternative to the word "vault".

A bank vault is something that is relatively easy to put things in. You want to store your jewelry there? Fine. Leave it with us, says the bank. But you want to get it out again? Sorry, that's harder. Forms to be filled in, identification to be performed, permission to be granted, and declarations of consent to be made.

Unfortunately, that's how some people have mistakenly portrayed Data Vault – easy to get data in, harder to get it out. It shouldn't be like that, and it doesn't have to be that way. Instead, what if we portray an image of a fridge? Easy to put food in, easy to get it out, even at midnight when hunger pangs strike. Pity about the diet.

So my light-hearted joke is to refer to a Data Fridge instead of a Data Vault. I'm not being critical of the correct phrase – I just want to be a little cheeky and suggest there may be some ways to make it easier for the business to get out what they want, when they want it. Even at midnight!

Acknowledgments

Rob Barnard is a good friend and mentor. He was the first to introduce me to the wonderful world of Data Vault, and has continued to expand my horizons. Without him, this book would not have happened.

Later on my journey I had the privilege of working with Natalia Bulashenko and Emma Farrow. They brought their own distinctive enrichment to my journey.

Roelant Vos is a fellow Aussie, but is respected internationally, both for his pragmatic approach and for his delightful personality. His generosity in sharing with the world-wide community, and with me, is gratefully noted. His detailed review of my "top down" papers on TDAN.com helped shape many of the ideas in this book.

There are many front-line developers whose support has been appreciated, but I wish to spotlight Johnny Mackle and Peter Dudley. It is wonderful when work colleagues become trusted friends.

Then there is the huge circle of friends from the wider data modeling community, including the quiet behind-the-scenes encouragement from Larry Burns. And then there's Steve Hoberman who is not only the publisher of this book, but a massive supporter of all things "data".

Last but not least, I am sure I am one of many who recognize the impossibility of tackling projects such as writing a book were it not for the loving support of their family. My wife is the hidden gem behind this book.

CHAPTER 1

Setting the Scene

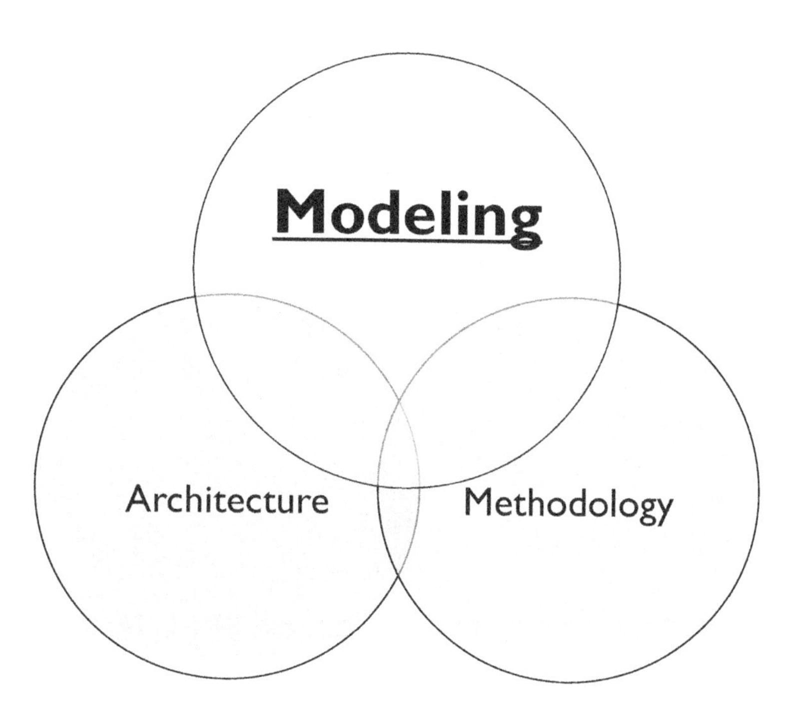

Figure 1: Data Vault 2.0 components

The core aspects of Data Vault 2.0 are depicted in Figure 1. Perhaps you already have a good grasp of these Data Vault fundamentals. If so, I am genuinely pleased because it is essential to have these foundations. If not, don't despair – this book includes an optional primer for those new to the wonderful world of Data Vault, though as the picture suggests, the focus for this book is on how to shape the model for overall Data Vault success.

Whether you come to this book with a commendable prior knowledge, or if you are on a steep learning curve and about to acquire foundational knowledge, the fundamentals are essential. However, there's a serious warning: Data Vault project experience suggests that just understanding the basics will most likely not be sufficient to drive a project to success.

Data Vault projects can have the methodology and architecture topics well covered, but they can run aground nonetheless due to modeling challenges. Modeling can sound so easy – there are only three components (Hubs, Links, and Satellites), and they can be learned relatively quickly. They're not the problem.

Dan Linstedt, the founder of Data Vault, has clearly warned of some of the danger zones, yet there are still shipwrecks, which is really sad, given the enormous potential of the Data Vault approach.

This book intends to assist in achieving Data Vault success by erecting a few lighthouses around the Data Vault modeling shoals, and by providing a few navigation maps (to push the sailing analogy a bit harder). By avoiding some of the known dangers, it is my sincere desire that you get to deliver measurable business value from your Data Vault investment.

An "owner's manual" is a good start, but ...

There's a story of a good-hearted country lad who lived in isolation from the so-called modern world. One of his jobs was to cut firewood, using a cross-cut saw and an axe. On one of his rare visits to the big smoke, a salesman convinces him that buying a chainsaw will massively increase his productivity. The salesman is willing to lend him a chainsaw to try it out.

On the next visit to town, the country lad returns the chainsaw. He got nothing like the productivity promised. The salesman notices that the chain is blunt, and asks how often he sharpened it. The answer? "Never." OK, please try it again, this time performing regular sharpening.

Next visit, the disappointed lad's had enough, but the salesman is persistent. He takes the lad out the back to see if they can work out what the problem is. The salesman fires up the chainsaw, and is stunned by the lad's question, "What's that funny noise?" The kid had been using this modern contraption as a hand-saw, not realizing it had an engine!

OK, that's a bit of a tall story. Now I'll make it a bit more personal. In the 1990s I bought a four-wheel drive (4WD) for getting to some out-of-the-way places. It came with an owner's manual, and that was a good start. For a bit extra money, I also got a workshop manual so that if I broke down in a remote place, my more mechanically minded friends had a better chance of getting me going again.

But all of these manuals still made one assumption – that I knew how to *drive* the vehicle in off-road conditions.

I still remember the tragedy of a tourist who hired a 4WD here in Australia and headed out to see Lake Eyre, which is a massive salt lake below sea level.

He got bogged in sand, and couldn't get his vehicle moving again. He died of thirst. When his vehicle was later found, the recovery crew simply let some air out of the tires to allow them to spread the vehicle's load over a wider area of sand, and drove straight out. Simple if you know that trick, and dangerous if you don't.

It's a crude analogy, but Data Vaults are a bit like a chainsaw or a 4WD. They're very capable, and designed beautifully for a purpose. And yes, you can buy technical manuals or attend training on some aspects (and I would encourage you to do just that), but if you don't know how best to "drive" your lovely new Data Vault, you may be sadly disappointed.

Did I hear a warning?

I also love driving my four-wheel drive in the Aussie outback – somewhere that's flat, dry, hot, and remote – which is most of Australia! One of our desert areas is called the

Nullarbor. For the IT types reading this, the "Null" in Nullarbor means the absence of things, and the "arbor" bit tells the careful map reader what this area is missing – trees (an arborist is a person who works with trees).

So imagine one of the world's longest straight roads, with not a tree in sight. The drive might be boring, but at least you're pretty safe, as there is plenty of traffic to help you if you get in trouble. ("Plenty" is a relative term.)

I've driven the Nullarbor, but I've also ventured well off the beaten track, and you need to heed the warnings as there's no-one likely to come your way for a long time if you're stuck. Such as the time my wife and I and some friends were heading along one of my infamous "shortcuts". We could have gone the long way round, but why tackle dirt roads that are corrugated from all of the traffic (at least one car a day, apart from the wet season when the roads are totally impassable)? So we tackled my shortcut.

It was really nothing more than a disused track in the middle of nowhere. There were two major problems. Some of the time we couldn't even find the track, so we had to stop the cars and fan out looking for the next visible hint of where it might be. And when we did find it, it was obviously a number of years since anyone last came along, as there were small trees that had grown between the wheel ruts – we had to push them over just to get through. One stretch of 70 kilometers (40 miles) took a full two days. My shortcuts haven't made me popular with most of my travelling companions.

Finally we got to the end of the track and pulled up on a picture perfect beach that I'd assured my friends would be wonderful. What could be better than sun, surf, sand, and the whole beach to ourselves – apart from the resident salt-water crocodiles. I wasn't popular. Again.

Here's the message. Australia has some great places, and many visitors who have ventured beyond the cities have loved the experience. But there are very real dangers. Heed the warnings, and you'll have a great time. Ignore the warnings, and things can go badly wrong.

Dan Linstedt, the founder of Data Vault, has also issued a number of warnings. Not about the Aussie outback, but about how to build a Data Vault. Some people ignore travel warnings about the Aussie outback, and come unstuck (or stuck as the case may be). Some people ignore Dan's warnings, too, and wonder why things don't go so well.

So what does Dan say? Amongst other things, he's said[1]:

- *"Data Vault modeling was, is, and always will be* **ABOUT THE BUSINESS.** *And if the Data Vault you have in place today* **is not currently about the business,** *then unfortunately you've hired the wrong people, and those people need to go back to school and re-learn what Data Vault really means. OR you've built the wrong solution, and you need to fix it – immediately."*

- *"Ontologies are a very very important asset to the corporation – if built at the enterprise level,* **you must focus on ontologies** *while you are building the Data Vault solution, or the full value of the … Data Vault cannot be realized."*

To put it in my own words, Dan's saying that the model behind the Data Vault design must be business-centric, and the way to achieve this is to start with an enterprise

---

[1] https://danlinstedt.com/allposts/datavaultcat/datavault-models-business-purpose-data-as-an-asset/.

ontology. The term "enterprise ontology" may be a frighteningly unfamiliar phrase for some, but please don't shy away, as it's really not that complicated. One way of seeing an enterprise ontology is that it can be represented as a data model that describes business concepts, their inter-relationships, and their major attributes. For practical purposes in this book, I suggest that an enterprise ontology is pretty much the same as a top-down, big-picture enterprise data model. I go into more detail on this topic later in "Before we go any further, what is an 'enterprise data model'?", but for now, that might be enough.

And it is important.

OK, so an enterprise ontology appears to be central to success. We're hearing your warning loud and clear, Dan, and unlike some travellers in outback Australia, we want to heed your warning, but:

- What on earth is an "enterprise ontology", 'cause I won't know if I've got one if I don't know what I'm looking for.
- If I can't find one, and Dan says I need one, how do I get my hands on one, or create one?
- And even if I have one of these wonderful things, how do I apply it to get the sort of Data Vault that Dan recommends?

We're going to be answering those questions in this book.

A vital context

It's easy to get lost in the detail of any book, and wonder how all the pieces are going to fit together. To maximize your pleasure, and the value you get from reading this book, I want to quickly lay out the roadmap. It's not too hard, really. Perform 4 tasks and you are on your way to Data Vault success. Well, at least that's the goal.

Seeding the Data Vault project

We start by collecting knowledge that hopefully is freely available within our organization.

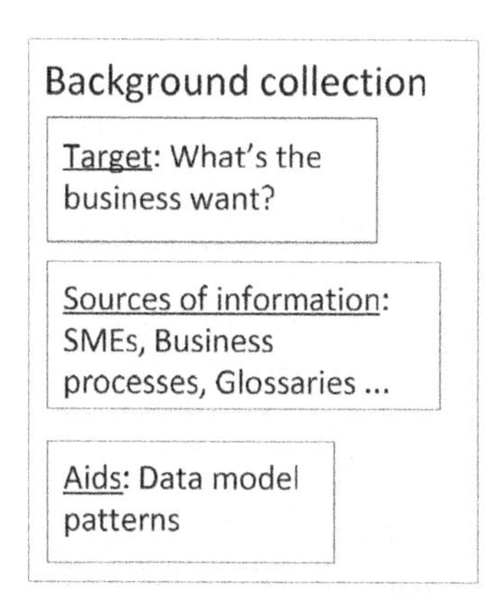

Figure 2: Collecting background knowledge

I suggest we start with defining the target of our project? Or to put it another way, if we talk to the stakeholder who is funding our project, what does he or she want to get for their money? Behind broad-brush statements of intent, we might also collect some details of the intended data marts and the like that will require our new Data Vault to feed them.

Next we act like sponges. We can seed our knowledge base from all sorts of sources of information. We can chat to the subject matter experts (SMEs) across the business. We can collect and analyze business process documentation. We can go through business glossaries to find definitions for business object such as Customers, Assets and so much more.

Last but not least in preparing to launch out, I encourage participants to gain familiarity with data model patterns. Len Silverston calls his patterns "universal" data model patterns for a very good reason. They provide proven, generic ways of structuring data, and fit most situations – hence the "universal" title. Yes, you will need to specialize them to tune them for your particular needs, but that's what we will look at in "Step #5: Assemble a lightweight Enterprise Framework (in days)" later in this book.

OK, we're on the starting blocks. What's the first task?

Task #1: Define how the business sees their data

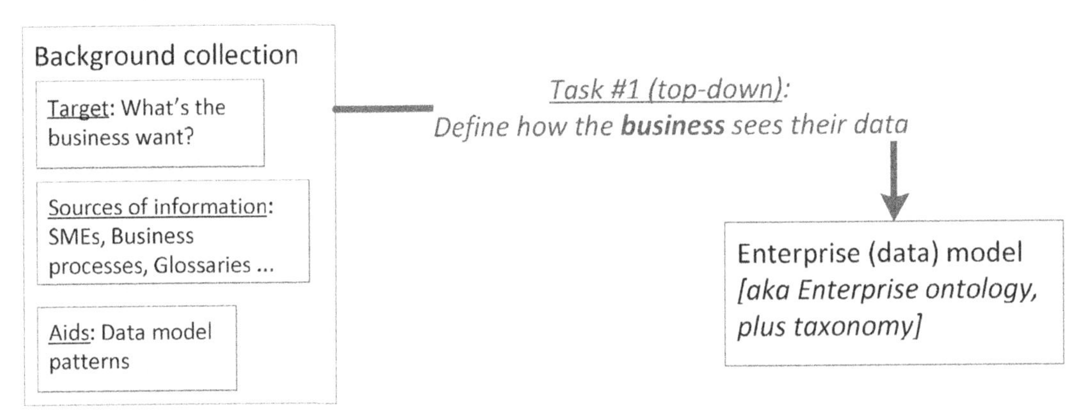

Figure 3: Building the "enterprise ontology"

This is at the heart of top-down design for a Data Vault. Dan quite correctly says we need an "enterprise ontology" to shape the design. Many data model professionals will talk of enterprise (or "business") data models, enterprise conceptual models, or enterprise logical models. David Hay, in "*Achieving Buzzword Compliance*", provides precise definitions, and even goes so far as to identify three types of conceptual models! Here, I am going for something simpler. And for the sake of this book, I am pretty flexible as to what we call this thing. Yes, it has an enterprise-wide view, and it's a model of the data we're interested in. I guess that makes it an enterprise data model.

But what does it look like? For us, it's got two simple parts.

- I like to start with a one-page diagram identifying the major data subject areas of the enterprise, with an icon for each, typically based on generic data model patterns.

- I then do a drill-down from the generic data model patterns into the specifics of the organization. This includes what some will refer to as the "taxonomy" – the hierarchy, from supertypes (that represent the patterns but often are too generic to represent the business directly) down to subtypes (that do represent the business).

It's a light-weight framework, and it can be assembled in weeks (or even days), assuming you've got a working familiarity with the patterns.

Task #2: Design the Data Vault, based on the business view

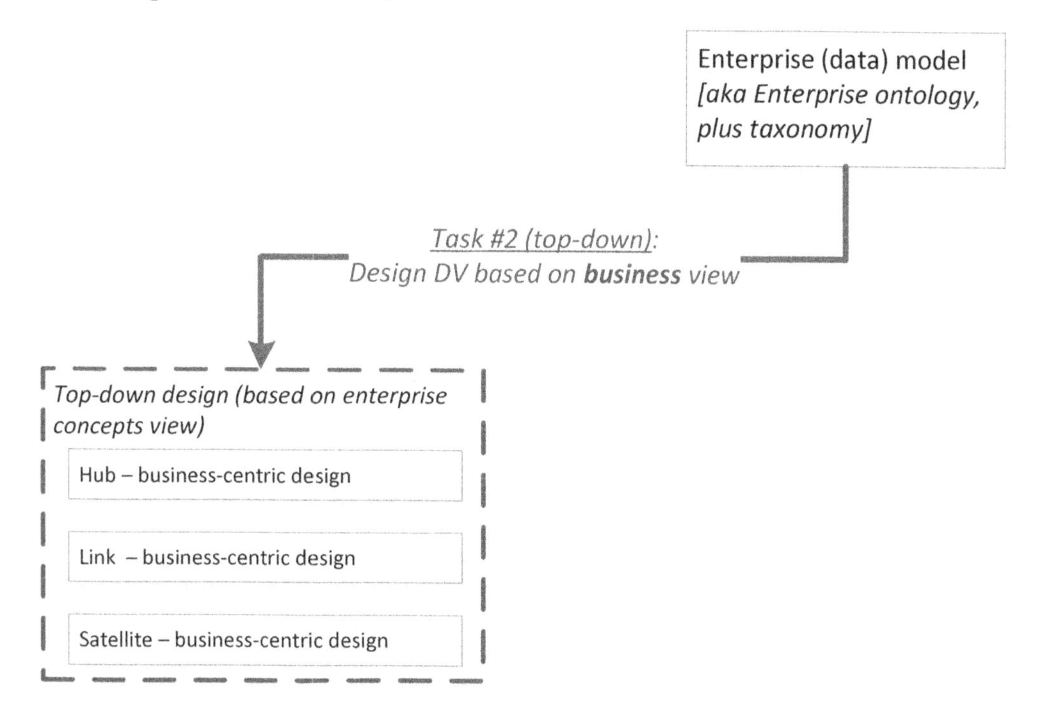

Figure 4: Design a business-centric Data Vault

We've now got a light-weight view of how the *business* sees their data. Next we want to map that into our Data Vault design. Again, it's top-down.

- Hubs are selected from a sweet-spot on the supertype / subtype hierarchy – the taxonomy
- Links are constructed based on business Links between business Hubs!
- Business Satellites specify how the business wants to see their data attributes, not how the source systems name and hold the data items. These business-centric Satellites are likely to become conformed Satellites, used to drive Data Marts a bit later. At this stage, they are a first-cut capture of the target information the business wants.

Please note something very important. For these two tasks, we haven't even spoken about source systems. We don't want to build a "source system Data Vault". We want to deliver tangible value to the business, and we want the Data Vault to reflect their business view, not a technology-based view, so we start with the business, then of course we must move to the hard reality of what data is available to us – the next task.

Task #3: Bottom-up Source-to-Data Vault mapping

We've already got business-centric Hubs, Links and Satellites defined. This is where business-centric Data Vault design distinguishes itself from source-centric Data Vault design – we want to map to the business objects, not to source-centric Hubs or Links unless we absolutely have to. Satellites are a little different.

We will go into a lot more detail later, but let's look quickly at this topic.

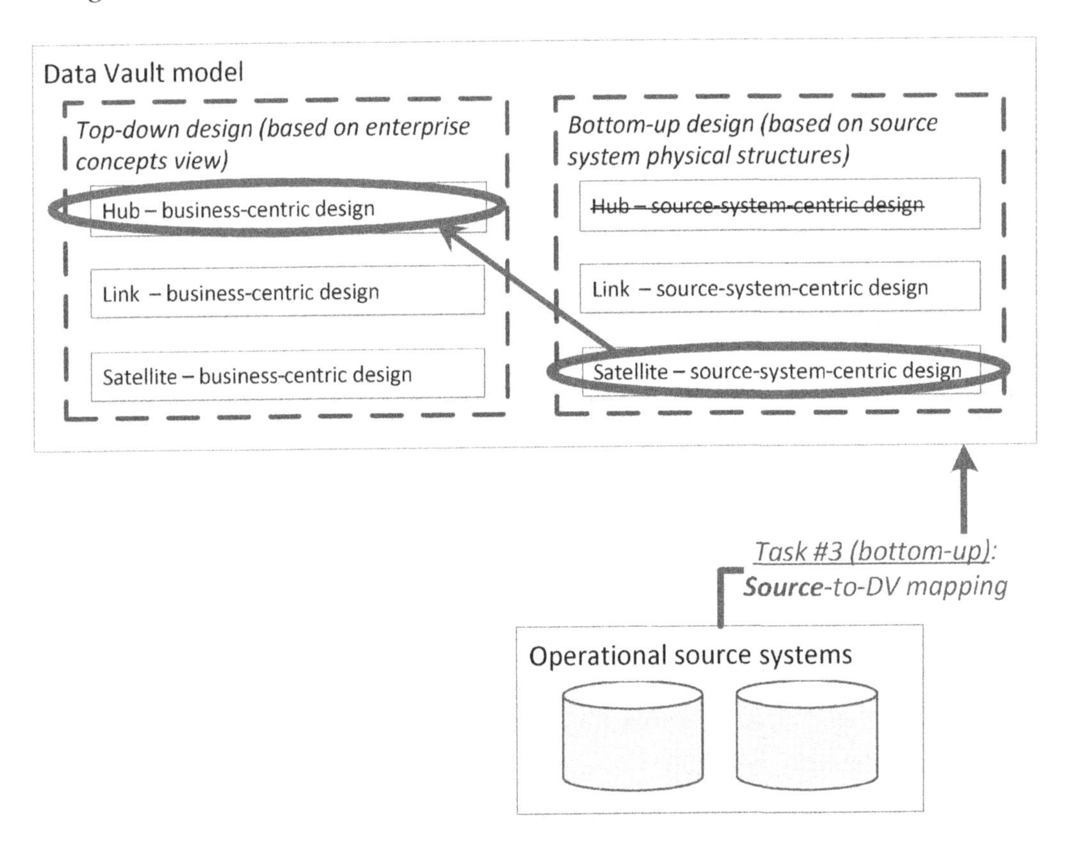

Figure 5: Source system mapping to Data Vault Hubs

If we've got 50 source data feeds with Customer data, we don't want 50 Customer Hubs, one per source, with one Satellite each! Instead, we can create Source-specific

Satellites, attached to just one ***business***-centric Hub. You'll notice that I've crossed-out the Hub in the source-centric box. It's something we rarely if ever want.

Links can be a bit more tricky. The short story version is that if the source feed has Links that map neatly to the business-centric Links that have already been identified, that's where they map. However, you will often encounter Links that represent transactions / events as presented by source system data feeds, and these may require construction of their own Links. (And these Links may require Satellites, too, but that's a separate and sometimes contentious topic.)

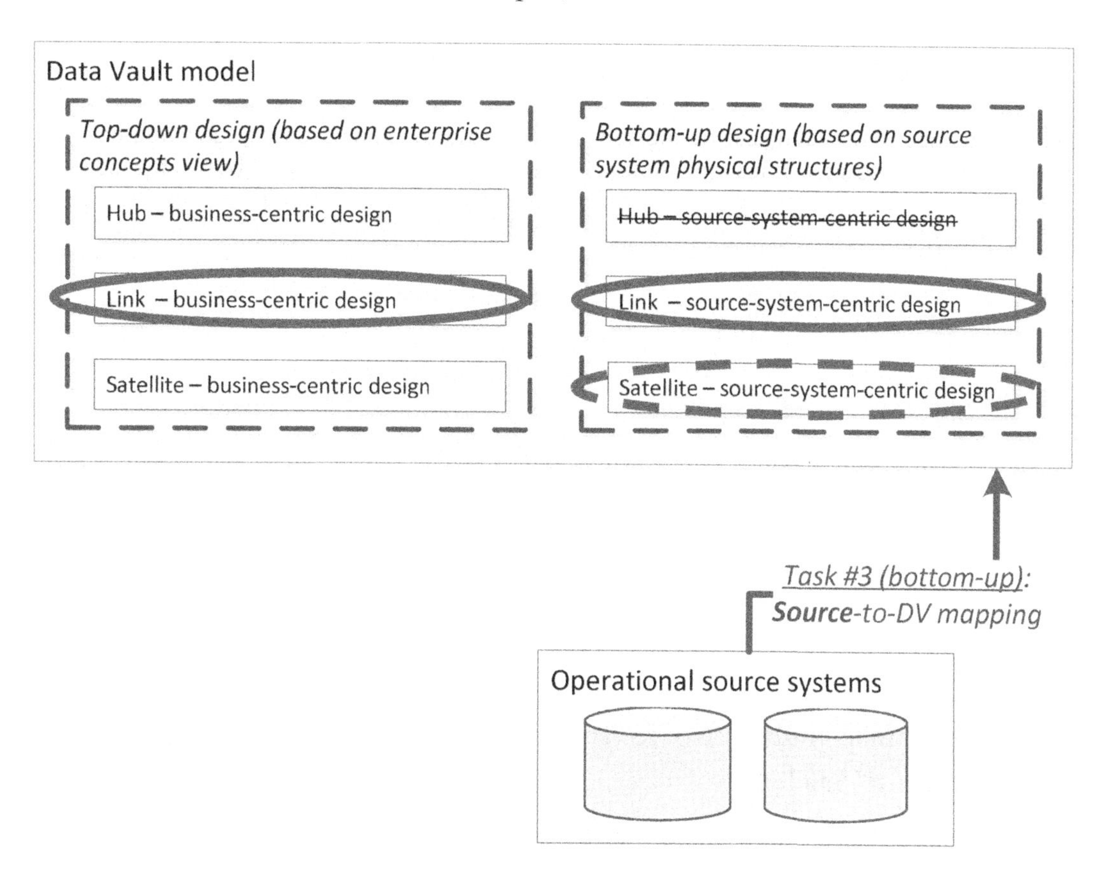

Figure 6: Source system mapping to Data Vault Links

At this point we've done the mapping to populate probably all we can from direct source feeds. I say "probably", because, for example, we might have a source-system feed whose data attributes match directly to the business-centric Satellite design the information consumers want. If that's true, you should consider yourself lucky. Most of the time, we need a little bit of data transformation to shape our data ready for consumption, and that's the next task.

Task #4: Define business rules

We've designed the business-centric Hubs, Links and Satellites as our targets in Task #2, and we've done mapping to populate the Data Vault in Task #3, but not all of the target objects have been included. There are some gaps, and we need business rules to fill them.

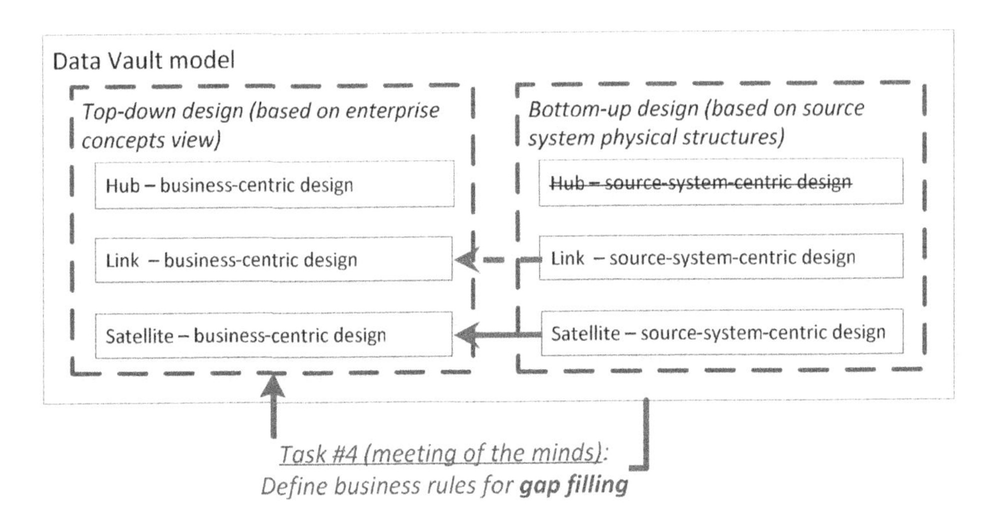

Figure 7: Source-to-Business transformation rules

The two most common forms of business rules are:

- Rules to map multiple source-specific Satellites into one consumption-ready "conformed" Satellite
- Rules to map source-specific "Event / Transaction" Links to their Hubs, Links &/or Satellites

There are other types of business rules, and one example relates to de-duplication of instances in a Hub. Maybe you've got 1,000 Customer instances, but you've identified some duplicates. In such cases, the business may want the duplicates consolidated so as to present a de-duplicated view ready for consumption.

In summary

If we pull those four tasks together we have a roadmap for end-to-end design of a Data Vault.

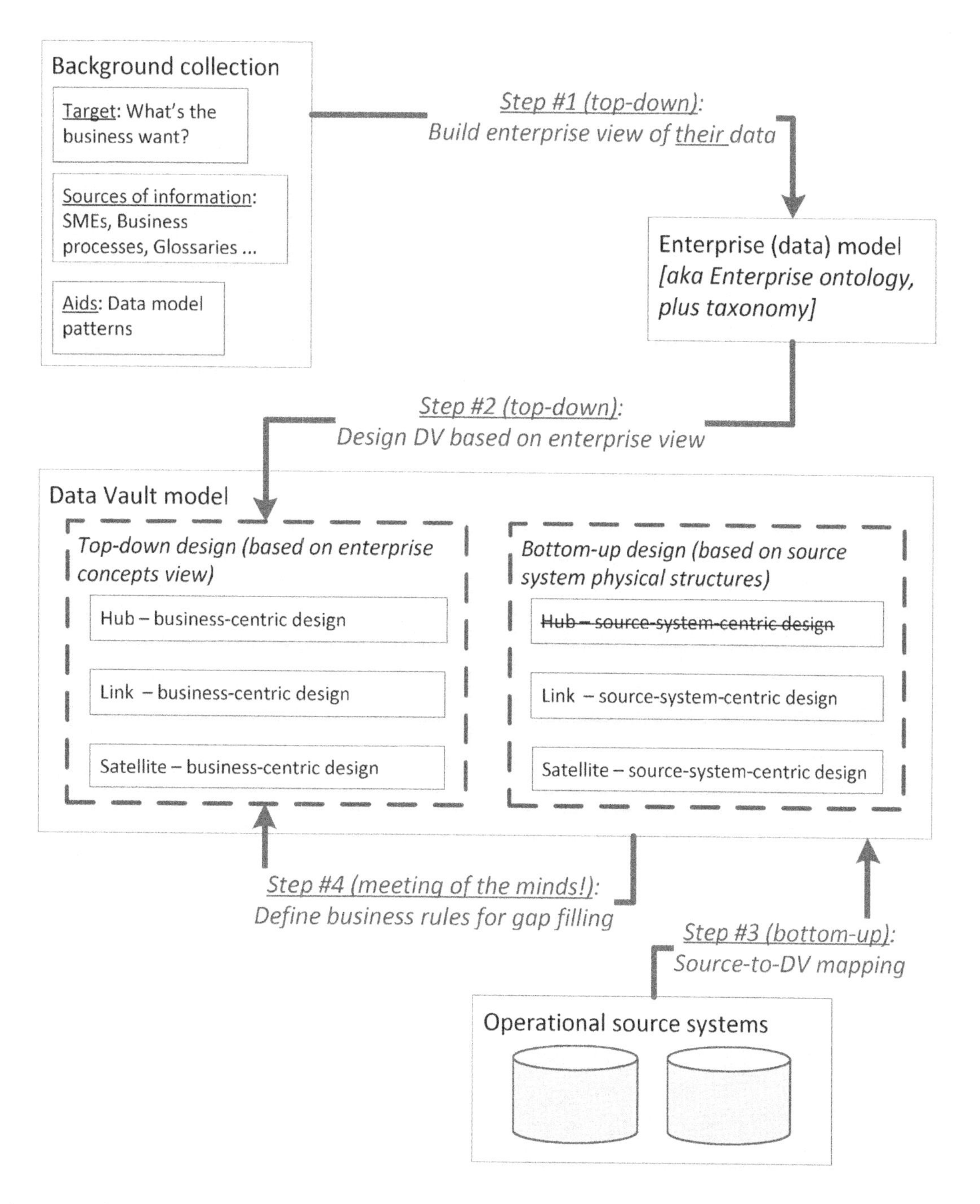

Figure 8: The Data Vault design roadmap

The diagram presents the essence of sound Data Vault design. With that preparation as a foundation, the book now presents:

- A primer on the Data Vault elements.
- Details on the four tasks introduced above.
- A deeper dive into some details of Data Vault.
- An appendix to introduce you to several common data model patterns that may help you perform Task #1.

CHAPTER 2

A Data Vault Primer

For those not yet familiar with the marvelous world of Data Vaults, first let's kick off with a Data Vault primer. For those already well acquainted with where Data Vault fits in relation to the other data warehousing approaches of Ralph Kimball and Bill Inmon, and who are comfortable with the Data Vault modeling fundamentals, you may prefer to go straight past this entire Data Vault primer and get your teeth into Dan's "ontology" stuff in the next major section, "Task #1 – Form the Enterprise View".

A bit of data warehouse history

What follows is a massive oversimplification of what's happened in the data warehouse world, but it might do to set Data Vault in context.

First, we look at Ralph Kimball's work. You may hear people talk of Dimensional Modeling, Star Schemas, Cubes, and Data Marts. If we take a registry of health practitioners (doctors, nurses, chemists ...) as a case study example, we can look at the essence of how Kimball's approach works.

Transaction-processing systems run the day-to-day operations of the business – they're shown on the left. They may be well designed for operational purposes, but often struggle to support business reporting.

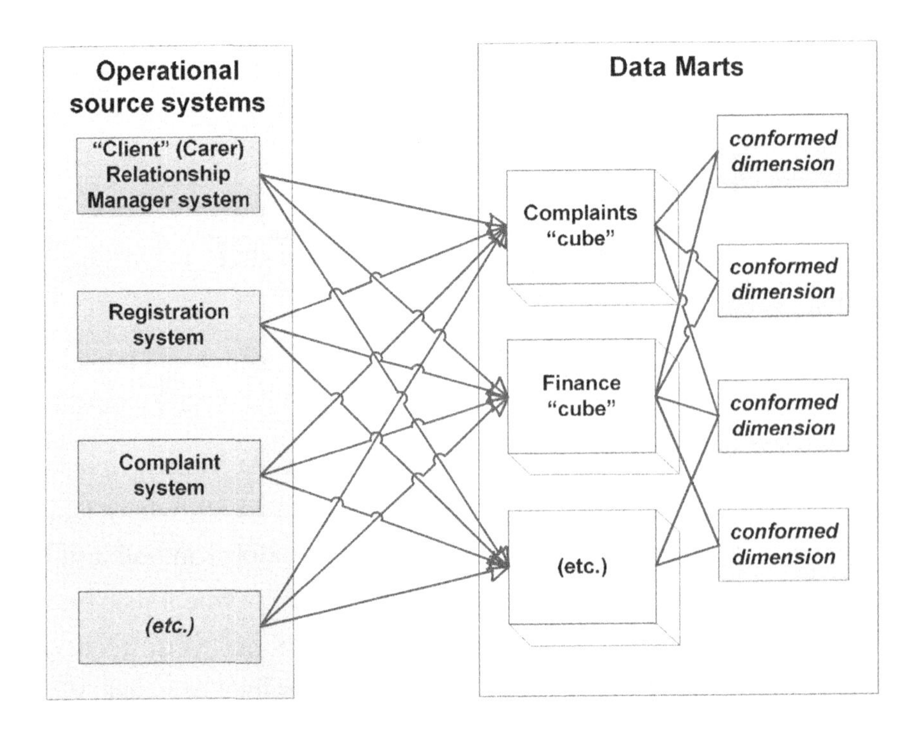

Figure 9: Ralph Kimball schematic

On the right-hand side of the diagram are purpose-built data marts. Each has a focus on just one set of "facts", such as complaints made against medical practitioners, classified by "dimensions" such as the practitioner, the type of complaint, and dates. A level of enterprise-wide integration can be achieved by using common, shared dimensions across multiple data marts, known as "conformed dimensions". These data marts are very well suited for slicing-and-dicing the data in a multiplicity of ways.

An advantage of this approach is the ability of the first data mart to relatively quickly and easily be built. Also, there is a good choice of tools for non-technical people to visualize the data.

One perceived disadvantage may emerge over time – as more and more operational systems source data for more and more data marts, and as existing data marts and their conformed dimensions are extended to meet new demands, complexity can increase.

Enter Bill Inmon and his Third Normal Form (3NF) Data Warehouse, a centralized approach for supporting organization-wide reporting:

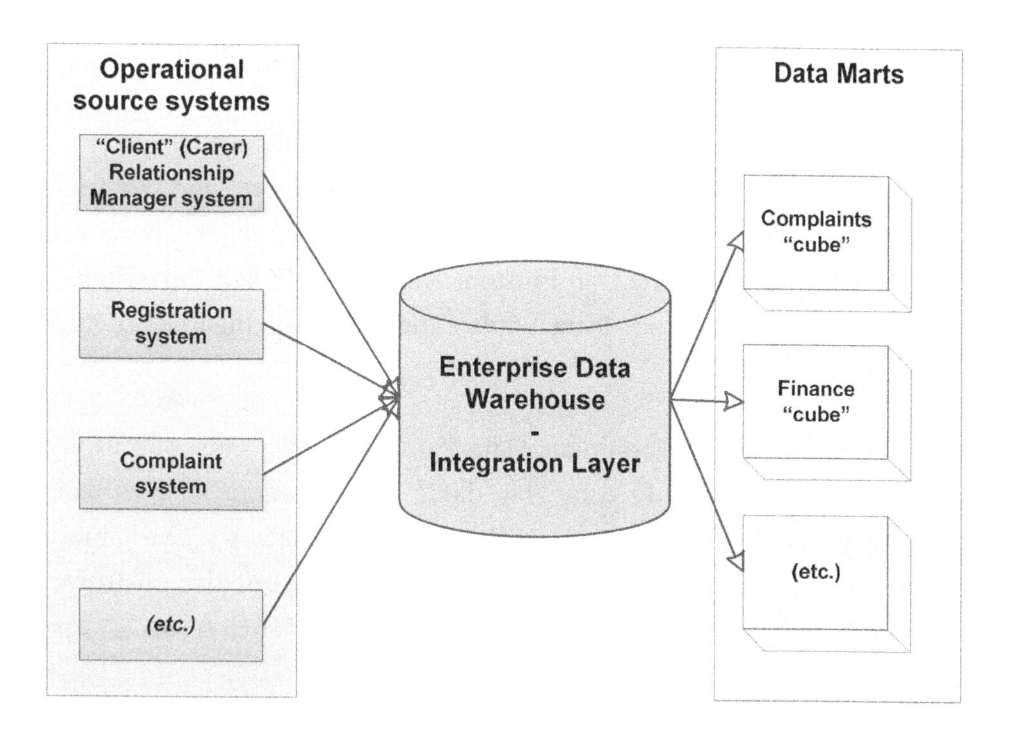

Figure 10: Bill Inmon schematic

The same operation systems all feed into one central "normalized" repository. Data from there is then pushed out in forms ready for easy consumption, including, of course, Data Marts.

One advantage of this approach is consistency – all reports are sourced from one, clean, uniform version of the "truth". Another advantage appears over time – the data supplied from each single source feed can potentially be reused to support multiple Data Marts. But this approach does have a price tag. The first Data Mart to be supported has an overhead not needed by the Kimball approach.

Then along comes Dan Linstedt with his Data Vault architecture. Some may say, "We've already got turf wars between the followers of the Kimball versus Inmon approaches, so why on earth do we need a new player in the field?" Perhaps we can answer that by looking at the origins of Data Vault.

They say that necessity is the mother of invention. Dan had a client in the 1990s whose demands pushed the boundaries of Data Warehousing. I understand that they wanted to store petabytes of data. That's thousands of gigabytes if you're not familiar with the term. Storing that much data is one thing; getting timely results from queries is another. Hence, Data Vault was born.

A more recent Data Vault implementation is at Micron, the computer chip manufacturer. They add billions of rows to their Data Vault each day. It's probably fair to say that the title of the book by Dan Linstedt and Michael Olschimke highlights one of the many reasons people adapt Data Vault – they're in the business of "Building a Scalable Data Warehouse ..."

But scale is only one reason for looking at Data Vaults. Frankly, most of my clients have very modest requirements if judged by "big data" considerations such as volume and velocity, but they may be interested in another of the big data V's - variability. When you're required to ingest not just predictable structured data, but also unstructured and semi-structured data, Data Vaults' ability to accommodate all such forms is impressive.

Then there's agility and extensibility. Wouldn't we all love it if we could quickly incorporate changes, or even better, if we got things "right" the very first time? Data Vault isn't some silver bullet that solves all problems, but it certainly eases the pain we will all face. For example, the philosophy that we always insert new stuff and never update what's gone before is a breath of fresh air, avoiding tedious reloading.

The "sales pitch" for Data Vault goes on and on, and reflects the ever changing demands. Some want real-time feeds. No problem. Some want a service-oriented architecture that interacts dynamically with operational systems and the Data Warehouse. Data Vaults can accommodate that. Many people want full traceability of the data lineage, going from the view presented to data consumers, right back to the operational systems that sourced the data. And again, Data Vault supports this need.

Some batch processing approaches are based on ETL (extract-transform-load), while others adopt ELT (extract-load-transform). The ETL approach often aims to clean up the data on the way into their data repository. In contrast, Data Vault has the goal to load "all the data, all the time" into the Data Vault, *and then* apply business rules to clean it up. If we later decide we got the rules wrong, we can change them and regenerate the derived Data Vault artifacts. We hadn't discarded the "dirty" data on the way in. What's more, the dirty data often is very instructive.

Enough of the "sales pitch". Let's take a very brief look at some of the Data Vault architectural components and their context:

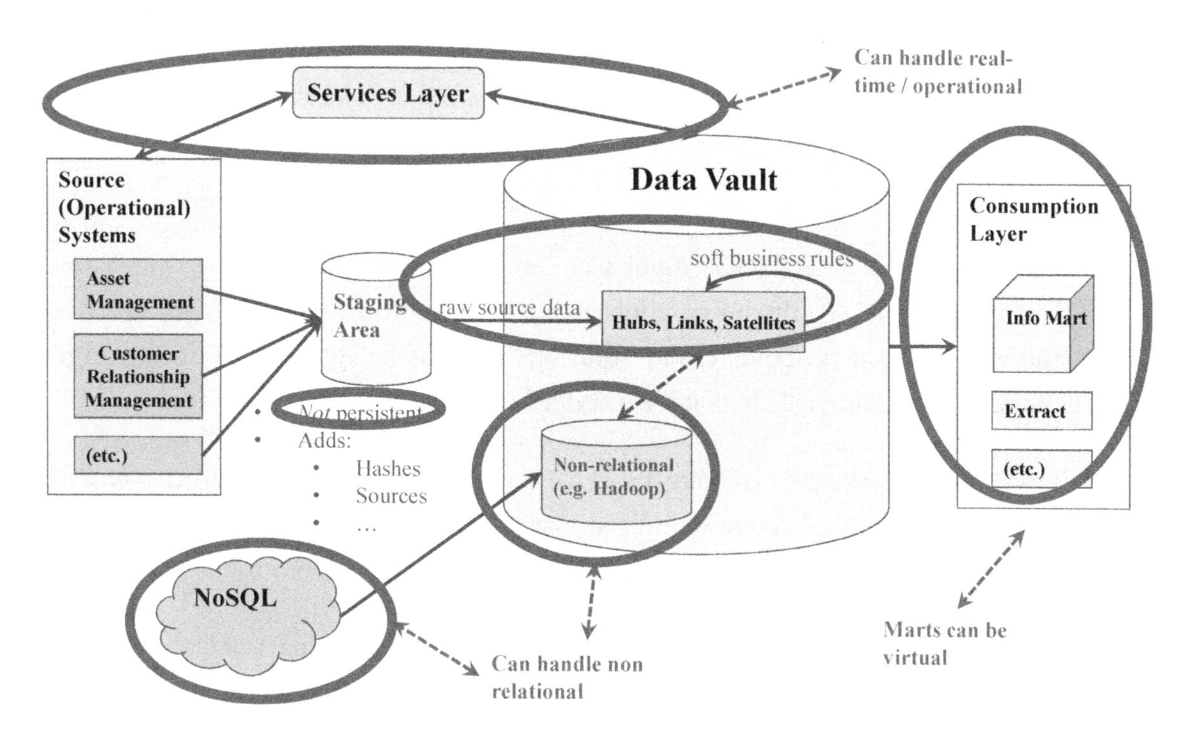

Figure 11: An interpretation of Dan's Data Vault schematic

Across the middle, we've got something that looks somewhat similar to Inmon's style. We've got operational systems feeding data via a staging area into the centralized Data Warehouse, which in turn feeds Data Marts, flat extracts, and so on.

A few things are worth noting:

- The staging area does not need to persist (store) all the data that ever goes through it. The Data Vault is capable of recording these details (though if your organization already has persistent staging area mechanisms in place, some people argue that this role can continue).

- The one Data Vault holds data from two distinct sources. It has "raw" data that faithfully captures all of the data as it was presented from operational source systems. Some of this "raw" data is ready to go for direct consumption by end users, while other data needs a bit of transformation. This transformation, such as renaming attributes or computing derivable values, is accomplished by executing explicitly declared business rules, generating "business" data in Data Vault.

- The consumption layer can be virtual, as can the objects in the Data Vault generated by business rules. This enables fast construction, and reconstruction, as needs change.
- Technologies such as NoSQL databases can be an integral part of the Data Vault. In fact, the Data Vault can be constructed in a platform such as Hadoop. And though not shown above, cloud solutions such as Snowflake are increasingly playing an exciting role in Data Vault deployment.
- Last but not least, you can have a services layer in two-way communication with both the operational systems and the Data Vault. For example, a data load into the Data Vault may trigger an alert to be managed by an operational system.

Now time for me to declare that my passion is about the modeling part of Data Vault. A bit like my story of buying a workshop manual for my 4WD, if you want to get into the detail of the inner workings of these technology aspects of Data Vault, there are people with far more knowledge than me. I have only included the above to try and set Data Vault in context.

So now let's swing our focus to the data model components inside a Data Vault.

Data Vault made (too) easy

One position on Data Vault standards

Before we launch into modeling a Data Vault, I probably need to comment on Data Vault standards.

These standards, like any standards, can and do change over time. Perhaps the most notable change was when Dan Linstedt introduced Data Vault 2.0 as an upgrade to the original Data Vault. Of course, over time I expect Dan and others will refine these, too.

Others in the wider community have their own adaptations for Data Vault modeling standards. One light-hearted joker once said to me, "That's what I love about standards – there's so many to choose from!" But all jokes aside, it can get confusing.

This book is arguably not the best platform for resolving any differences between the voices across the Data Vault community. Dan encourages people to challenge his standards, but he does suggest that any proposed variation be thoroughly and objectively debated before being adopted. This book is but one voice, and delivery of objective evaluation involving multiple parties is not possible with my one-way-only conversation.

I recognize the existence of alternative views, and each variation may have strengths and weaknesses in certain circumstances, but for the sake of simplicity and consistency, I will seek to follow the modeling standards as published in "*Building a Scalable Data Warehouse with Data Vault 2.0*".[2] I may also from time to time make some passing comments on some of the other variations I have encountered. Towards the end of the book, I will also explicitly present some aspects of alternative views. But until then, can I please suggest that for the sake of progressing the wider discussion on how an enterprise view can (and should) contribute to a Data Vault design, we all might find it simpler to assume Dan's perspective, at least for now? Thanks.

A case study

I talk of "hypothetical" scenarios such as emergency response to fires, floods, earthquakes and the like, but unfortunately in many parts of the world these scenarios are far from hypothetical.

---

[2] Linstedt D. & Olschimke O. (2016) "*Building a Scalable Data Warehouse with Data Vault 2.0*".

It still raises deep emotions in me when I recall the day I knew my children were threatened by a severe firestorm and there was nothing I could do. This was before mobile phones, and the telephone land lines were down. I was at work, safely in the city, and they were possibly trapped at school and under threat, or maybe the school had shut down and they were at home and even more threatened, or worse still, they didn't make it home, and never would. I simply didn't know. Thankfully, as it turned out, all was OK for them, but not so for many others that day.

I have worked on IT solutions for emergency response organizations, and believe me, I am passionate about using technology to protect the community. A tiny subset of some data involved in managing wildfires is shown below:

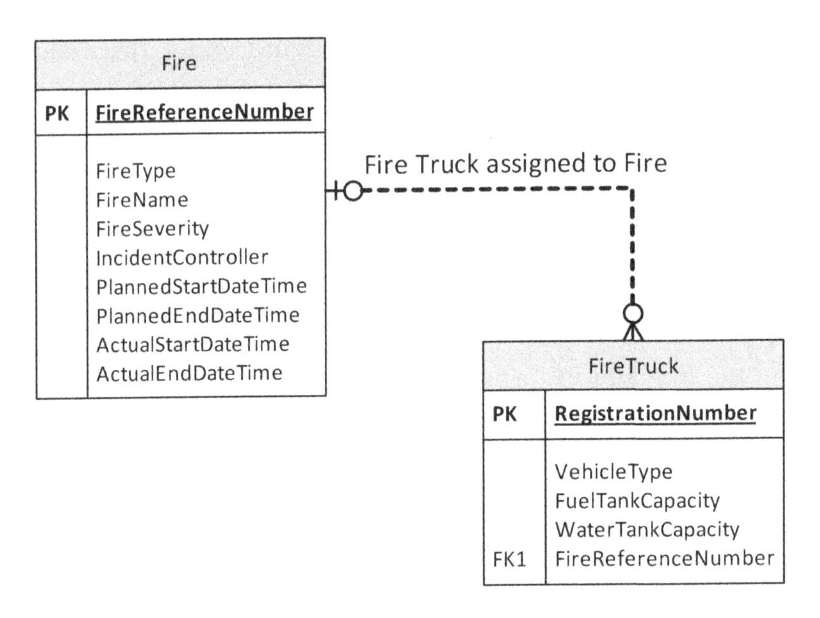

Figure 12: "Fire" data model – Operational source system

Using one form of Entity-Relationship Diagram (ERD) notation, this portrays information such as:

- Each fire is uniquely identified by a business key known as the Fire Reference Number.
- Each fire truck is uniquely identified by a business key known as the Registration Number.
- At any given point in time, each fire truck may be assigned to only one fire, while each fire may have zero, one or more fire trucks assigned to it.

I highlight the phrase "point in time", because many operational systems hold the current values, but not history. Keeping a record of past data values is one of the reasons people consider a Data Warehouse, of which Data Vault is one more modern form. If the only data ever to be loaded to our Data Vault was sourced from those two tables, we could do a fairly mechanistic transformation of the data and end up with a Data Vault structure something like this:

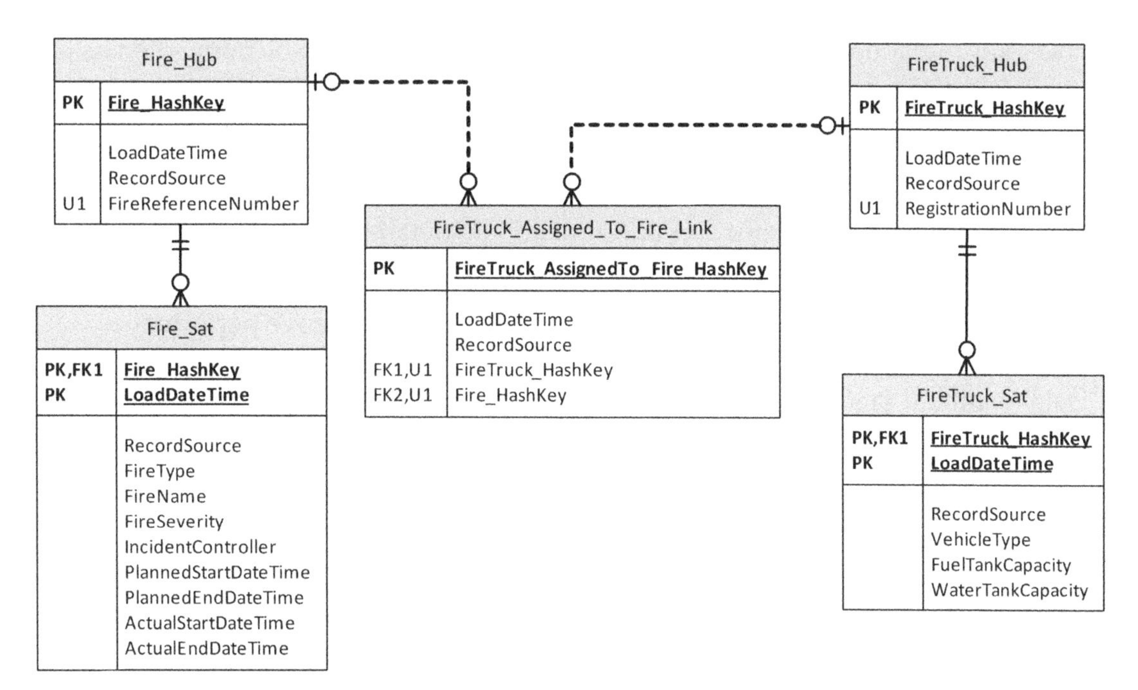

Figure 13: "Fire" data model – Data Vault

Hubs

We start with Hubs. Like the name suggests, they are at the center of data structures in a Data Vault. They are based on business concepts, and hold business keys. The word that appeared twice in the previous sentence was "business". More on that later, but I do want to draw your attention to the fact that building a Data Vault is not just a technical exercise; it must involve the business.

For the sake of simplicity, we will assume that a Fire is a recognized business concept, with a business key of Fire Reference Number. Likewise, let's assume that a Fire Truck is a recognized business concept, with a business key of Registration Number.

So now we've got two Hubs, and they've both got a unique index for the nominated business key. Relational databases typically expect a single key to be nominated as their "primary key". Every row in the table must have a unique value for its primary key. We could obviously make the business key the primary key for the table. After all, it is unique. However, in Data Vault, we may choose to use another mechanism, often called a "surrogate key". We probably don't need to go into details of this style here. Sufficient to say that it's typically a unique but meaningless number generated by some software. Here, in a Data Vault, one reason for using a surrogate is to improve performance.

In Data Vault 2.0 (again, I am using the standard as published in *"Building a Scalable Data Warehouse with Data Vault 2.0"*, and I recognize that standards may be challenged and changed over time), this "surrogate primary key" is a hash key – another technical artifact. Put simply, the text string value of the natural business key is thrown into a mathematical algorithm, and out pops some number. The important thing is that the same text string will always produce the same hash key value. The previous version of Data Vault had a sequence number that served a similar purpose. But please note that whether your Data Vault is Data Vault 1.0 or 2.0, the Hub's surrogate key is for Data Vault internal use only. It should not be used as an alternative business key. In reality, I doubt that anyone looking at the big, ugly structure of the value generated for a hash key would want to use it that way!

Some may ask why we might use a hash key, and there may be several good reasons. Put simply, this approach helps deliver good performance in several situations. It may help for loading data (including facilitating massive parallel processing if we need to go that far), or with relational join performance on data retrieval, and, as a bonus, assist with the joining of relational and non-relational data. The last point on non-relational data is all a bit technical, and not my area of strength, so I am happy to accept that there are sound computer science reasons for this stuff, and then get back to my modeling!

We've still got two more columns in the Hub tables. The Record Source column notes the source system that *first* presented the business key value to the Data Vault, and the Load Date / Time notes the precise date and time that this occurred. These columns may prove useful for audit and diagnostics purposes, but please don't get side-tracked; a Hub table fundamentally exists to hold the set of business keys for a given business concept, and nothing more.

Let's look at the attributes and their values that one instance in the Fire Hub table (as shown in Figure 13) might have:

- Fire Reference Number: "WF2018-123" (Wild Fire number 123 in the year 2018).
- Fire Hash Key: "27a3f042…", being a hexadecimal representation of the hash key generated by presenting the text string "WF2018-123" to some hashing algorithm.
- Load Date / Time: "10/10/2018 12:34:56.789" being the very moment (to a nominated level of precision) the row was loaded into the Data Vault table, *not* the moment when the row was created in some source operational system.
- Record Source: "ER/RA", being an acronym ("ER" for the Emergency Response IT operational system, and "RA" for Resource Acquisition, the data feed providing load data for the Data Vault). Note that the "source" can be a multi-level hierarchy, and is typically finer-grained than just the IT system.

Instances in the Fire Hub never change after they are created. No matter how many of the fire's descriptive attributes such as Fire Type (grass fire, forest fire ...), Fire Name, Fire Severity, and so on change, the Hub instance is rock solid. The Hub instance says that the Data Vault *first* saw Fire "WF2018-123" on 10/10/2018, and that this visibility of the nominated fire was provided by the Resource Acquisition data feed from the Emergency Response IT operational system. These facts will never change, nor will the instance in the Fire Hub table. So where do we hold the Fire Type, Fire Severity and other attributes? In a Satellite!

Satellites (on a Hub)

While most people think of satellites as things that zoom around in the sky, the term is used in Data Vault for a very different purpose.

Typically, at the same time a Hub instance is created, we want to capture the related attribute values as they existed at that first-seen point in time for the business key. The first instance in the Fire Satellite table (refer to Figure 13) might have values such as:

- Fire Hash Key: "27a3f042...". This is the Foreign Key, relating the Satellite to its "parent" Hub for Fire Reference Number "WF2018-123". Of course, we *could* have designed the Hub to have the natural business key (the Fire Reference Number) as its Primary Key, and simply used that natural business key value here in the Satellite as the Foreign Key. That might be easier to understand, but it's not the Data Vault 2.0 standard, and there are reasons for using the hash key construct.

- Load Date / Time: "10/10/2018 12:34:55.555" being the very moment (to a nominated level of precision) the row was loaded to the Data Vault table. Note that the load time for the Satellite is not the same as the load time for its "parent" Hub. While as human beings we might think that a Hub and its Satellite values are loaded together, particularly as they may come from exactly the same data feed, there might be one code module for loading Hubs, and a separate code module for loading Satellites. If one load succeeds and the other fails until a restart the next day, the time difference can be significant, and that's OK – the Load Date / Time provides an audit of when the load actually occurred, not when we might have expected it to occur. In this example, the load time for the "child" Satellite is actually before the load time for its "parent" Hub. For the more technically minded raised with relational databases, they might have expected to have referential integrity enforced between the Hub and its Satellite, meaning that the "parent" Hub *had* to be created first. On the entity-relationship diagram I have presented in Figure 13 above, we could quite rightly state that is in fact what I am implying, but in the Data Vault world, we can have a "child" Satellite created before its "parent". It is to be noted, however, that when the entire data load is completed, there should be no "children" without "parents". This approach may be a real bonus if we want to perform Massive Parallel Processing (MPP) to handle vast volumes of data.

- Record Source: "ER/RA" as an acronym, with "ER" for Emergency Response (the IT operational system) and "RA" for Resource Acquisition. In this example, this value is the same as the Record Source value in the related Hub, as one source feed of data provides data for the Fire Hub and the Fire Satellite, though they may be processed in separate load modules as noted above.

- Satellites primarily exist to hold a copy of data values for the Hub's non-business-key values. In this example, the data values at the time of initial creation of the Hub could be:
  - Fire Type: "Forest Fire"
  - Fire Name: "Black Stump"
  - Fire Severity: "2"
  - Incident Controller: "Alex Anderson"
  - Planned Start Date of "NULL" in this case, as we didn't plan to have this fire. Where I live in Australia, we do have deliberate burns in the

cooler weather to reduce the fuel load, but this hypothetical fire might have been started by a lightning strike.

- Planned End Date is also "NULL" at this stage, but will later be set to a target date once we've worked out how big the fire is and what our plan of attack is to be.
- Actual Start Date: "10/10/2018"
- Actual End Date is also "NULL" at this stage.

The example above follows the Data Vault 2.0 standard, with its use of hash keys. In contrast to Data Vault 2.0 where the "child" Satellite can be created before its "parent" Hub, in Data Vault 1.0, the Satellite load program might have to look up the "parent" Hub table by doing a search against the natural business key and then find the sequence number before the Satellite instance can be created.

OK, so our Satellite now has the snapshot of values for the fire at the time of creating the matching Hub instance. That's great, but values change over time. A few hours after first reporting the fire, its Fire Severity drops to "1", and the Incident Controller is now "Brooke Brown". These new values are presented to the Data Vault. What happens?

It's simple, really. A new instance in the Fire Satellite is created for the same "parent" Hub, but with a different Load Date / Time, and of course the data values as they now apply. We're starting to build up the history we need.

Note that each instance in the Satellite is a *complete* snapshot of all data values active at the time. Even if the Fire Type and Fire Name haven't changed, the new Satellite instance will hold their (unchanged) values, alongside the changed values for Fire Severity and Incident Controller.

> *[One little side note: In the above example, all the attributes from the source were held in one Satellite. It is possible to split a Satellite so that, for example, attributes whose values frequently change can go in one Satellite, and attributes with relatively static values can go in another.]*

Links

Hubs represent *business concepts*, such as a Fire and a Fire Truck. One of the roles of a Link is to represent *business relationships* such as the assignment of a Fire Truck to a Fire.

Hub instances are identified by a *business key*, such as the Registration Number of a Fire Truck or the Fire Reference Number for a Fire. Link instances are identified by *sets of business keys*, such as the combination of a Fire Truck's Registration Number and the Fire's Fire Reference Number.

If we look at the Entity-Relationship Diagram for the Data Vault in Figure 13, we see that there is a table named Fire-Truck-Assigned-To-Fire Link, which is the short-hand way of saying we've got a Link table that associates a Fire Truck with the Fire to which it is Assigned. Taking just the association between Fire Truck "ABC-123" and the Fire "WF2018-123" to which it is assigned as an example, the instance in the Link table might have attribute values such as:

- Fire Truck Hash Key: "f0983ba7…". This is a Foreign Key, relating the Link to one of the Hubs that participate in the Link's relationship. In this scenario, the Foreign Key points to Hub for a Fire Truck with Registration Number "ABC-123".

- Fire Hash Key: "27a3f042…". This is a Foreign Key, relating the Link to one of the Hubs that participate in the Link's relationship. In this scenario, the Foreign Key points to Hub for a Fire with Fire Reference Number "WF2018-123".

- Load Date / Time: "10/10/2018 12:44:55.555" being the very moment (to a nominated level of precision) the row was loaded to the Data Vault table, not the moment when the row was created in some source operational system.

- Record Source: As we continue with this example, we are assuming that the data feed is the same as that of the two Hub instances that are participating in this Link instance. The value is, again, "ER/RA".

- Fire-Truck-Assigned-To-Fire Hash Key: "12ab34cd…", being a hexadecimal representation of the hash key generated by presenting a text string that is itself formed by concatenating the business keys of the participating Hubs (Fire Truck and Fire). The text string to be hashed might, in this example, be "ABC-123|WF2018-123". Note that it is recommended that the text string formed by concatenation of the Hub's business keys have a separator (such as the so-called pipe symbol, "|") between the component parts. Consider a Fire Truck with Registration number "ABC-432" and a Fire with a Fire Reference Number "10-Black Stump". Without a separator, the concatenated string would be "ABC-43210-Black Stump". If we then consider the admittedly unlikely scenario of a Fire Truck with Registration number "ABC-43" and a Fire with a Fire Reference Number "210-Black Stump", then concatenate them without a separator, we would get the same result as a text string, and hence exactly the same hash key, which we don't want – the same identifier for two distinct relationships. Conversely, with a separator, the first string would be "ABC-432|10-Black Stump", and the second "ABC-43|210-Black Stump". To the human eye, they look almost the same; to a hashing algorithm they are totally different and will produce totally different hash results. Job done.

The formation of the text string combining the Hub's business keys must always follow the same order of concatenation. If one time, for the relationships between a given Fire Truck and a Fire, we put the Fire Truck business key first, then later for the exact same intended relationship we reverse the order, we will not get a matching hash key.

In a similar manner to Hubs, instances in the Fire-Truck-Assigned-To-Fire Link never change after they are created. The Link instance we've been studying says that the Data Vault *first* saw the relationships between Fire Truck "ABC-123" and Fire "WF2018-123" on 10/10/2018, and that this visibility of the nominated relationship was provided by the Acquisition data feed from the Emergency Response IT operational system. These facts will never change, nor will the instance in the Fire-Truck-Assigned-To-Fire Link table.

Also like Hubs, a Link can have associated information that does change over time, and again this can be stored in a Satellite belonging to the Link. This requirement is not shown in the diagram, but it's not uncommon for Links to have attributes such as the relationship start date-&-time and the relationship end date-&-time. By now we're unfortunately getting into some territory where there are differing views on Data Vault modeling approaches. Just for a moment, let's stick with Dan's Data Vault 2.0 standard, and later we'll discuss some other opinions.

Please note that in this very simple example of a Fire Truck assigned to a Fire, there are only two Hubs involved. However, life isn't always that simple. Maybe the assignment transaction also required nomination of the Employee authorizing the assignment. In such a case, the Link may involve the Fire Truck Hub, the Fire Hub, and an Employee Hub. A Link can have as many participating Hubs as are required, but must always have at least two (or in the case of self-referencing relationships, two or more Foreign Keys can point to the same Hub table).

A drill-down into cardinality on Links

If we look back to Figure 12 at the Entity-Relationship Diagram for the operational system that is the source for this hypothetical Data Vault, at any point in time a Fire Truck can only ever be at one Fire. That makes a lot of sense in this case study example. However, over time, the same Fire Truck, say Registration Number "ABC-123", can be assigned to many Fires. At some time in the past it was at Fire "PB2018-012" – a "Prescribed Burn" fire deliberately lit to reduce fuel load. Today it's at the Fire "WF2018-123" and in the future it may be assigned to Fire "WF2018-456".

Now if we look back at Figure 13 for the Entity-Relationship Diagram for the Data Vault, those of us with a data modeling background may notice that the structure for the Link is a many-to-many resolution entity – that's a technical term that says this particular Link entity can accommodate the Fire Truck Hub and the Fire Hub being in a many-to-many relationship. The Data Vault can record all of the relationships over time, which is what we want.

This flexibility has another important feature; the ability of the Data Vault to absorb changes in the cardinality in the operational systems without having to have the Data Vault reconstructed. Let's say we want to record marriage relationships between people. I recognize there are diverse and changing views about what constitutes a "marriage", but let's look at a hypothetical country that has some interesting twists and turns in the attitudes of its people and the law-makers. I also recognize that there may be a difference between what the medical profession records as a child's sex at birth compared to the gender an individual may later nominate for themselves, but for the sake of simplicity, this hypothetical country only recognizes males and females as declared at birth. My simple request is that we put aside personal views as to what relationships should or should not be recognized, and please let's inspect the hypothetical as that country's views change over time (maybe too much for some, and too little for others).

In this made-up scenario, the laws of this country originally defined marriage as not only being between one man and one woman at any point in time, but they went one step further. In their country, each individual could only be married once in their entire lifetime. If your partner left you, or even died, sorry, but you could not enter into another legally recognized marriage. If this "business rule" was enforced in the operational system, you would have a one-to-one relationship between a man and a woman. Using the UML notation so we don't have to get into debates on primary keys and foreign keys, the operational system might be represented as below.

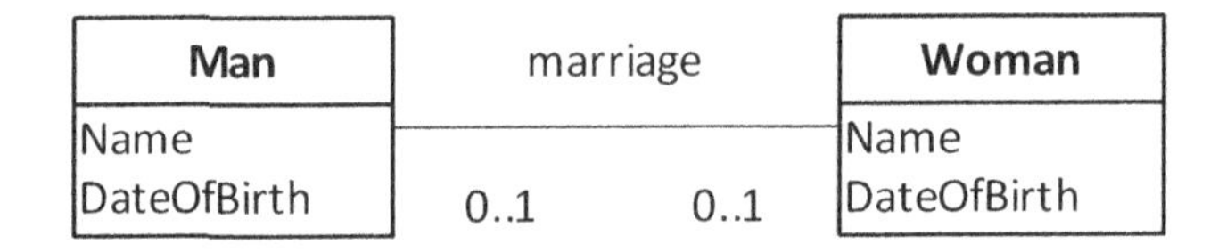

Figure 14: Marriage scenario #1

Again using the UML notation, and suppressing all of the Data Vault attributes (Load Date Time, Record Source, and keys), we might have a Data Vault model as shown in Figure 15. We've got a "Man" Hub and a "Woman" Hub in the Data Vault. And at this point, the "Marriage" Link between these two Hubs only needs to handle a one-to-one cardinality, even though the Data Vault can happily cope with many-to-many.

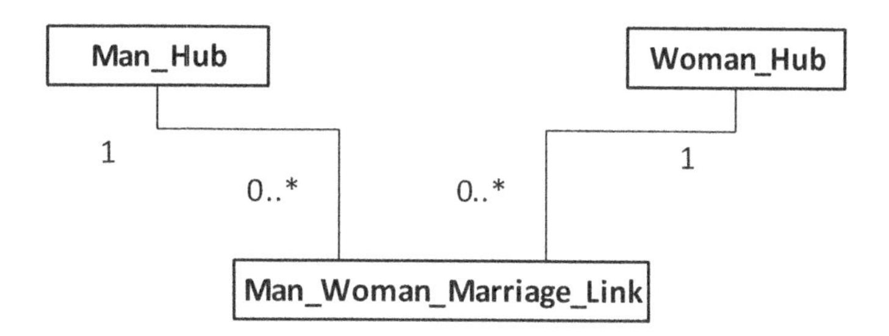

Figure 15: Man-&-Woman Marriage in a Data Vault

Let's pretend the country's rules are loosened a little. Remarriage after death of a spouse is now permitted. The operational system might not need any change if it only records current status (still one-to-one), but the Data Vault needs to accommodate many-to-many over time. But it already can, so no change there either.

Have you ever seen the film, "Paint your Wagon"? There was a man with multiple wives who passed through a gold-mining frontier town. If this hypothetical country likewise allowed a man to have more than one wife, the UML representation changes in the operational system.

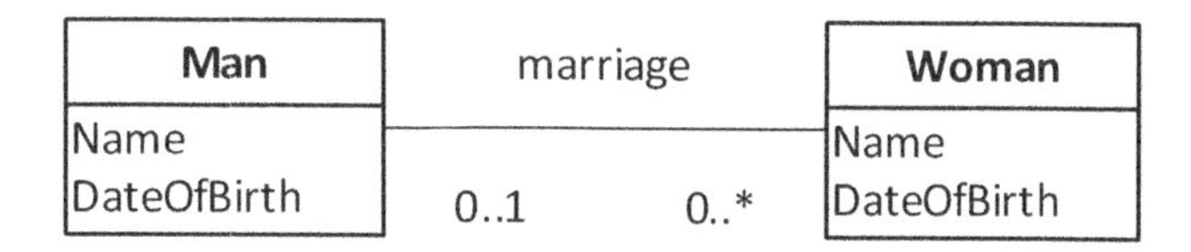

Figure 16: Marriage scenario #2

It's only a subtle change with the asterisk representing "many". Think of it a bit like a crows foot in an entity-relationship diagram if you prefer. The operational system changes, but again, the Data Vault model remains unchanged.

Back to "Paint your Wagon". There was a shortage of wives for the miners. Some figured that if one man can have more than one wife, why can't a woman have more than one husband? And that was the eventual outcome. If we stretch our hypothetical scenario this little bit further, we've now got a many-to-many relationship on the point-in-time view of the operational system. It requires changes. Again!

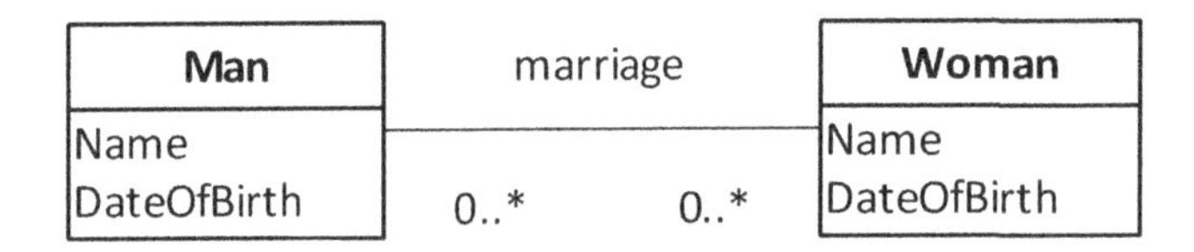

Figure 17: Marriage scenario #3 (many-to-many)

We've now got a many-to-many relationship in the operational system. In a relational implementation, this is likely to become a resolution entity as follows.

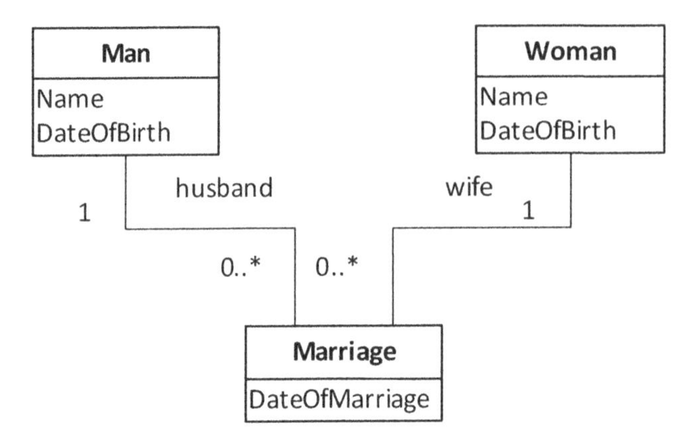

Figure 18: Marriage scenario #3 (resolved)

The core message is that the Data Vault implementation hasn't changed across any of these scenarios. It continues without a glitch. But now we challenge the Data Vault model.

The Link is robust as long as the Hubs are stable, too. But if we introduce same-sex marriage, we might need some Data Vault changes. One option is to add a self-referencing Link for the Man Hub, and another for the Woman Hub. Another is to challenge the Hubs themselves. Maybe we could have started with a Person Hub with a self-referencing Link?

If that's the model we had used from the outset, all of the incremental changes in the country's laws would have been absorbed in the initial Data Vault model. We will spend a lot more time on Hub design in "Well-formed Hubs: Getting the right foundations", but for now, the focus is on Links. This example was a bit artificial. Now I'll take a real-life story from my own experience on the changing cardinality of relationships.

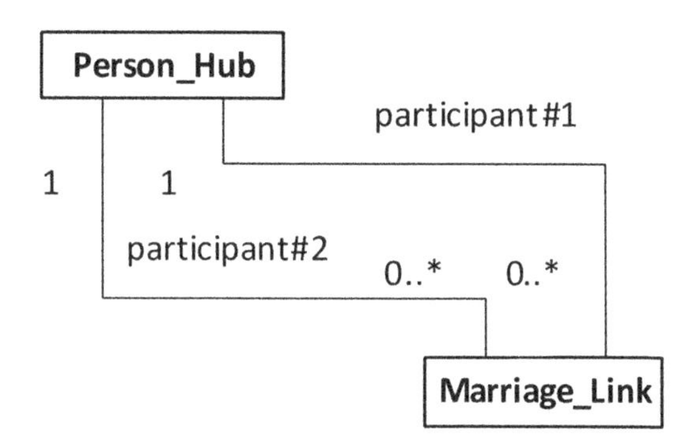

Figure 19: Person-to-Person Marriage in a Data Vault

Wind the clock back to the late 1970s. Projects were run using waterfall approaches. Find the requirements, document them, and get them signed off. Do a solution design, and get it signed off. Do development, and document it. Do testing and write up the results. Finally, put the system into production and train the users. Of course, if any mistakes were made in analyzing the requirements, but they weren't detected until the solution was in production, there can be costly rework.

I'm the project lead, and in those days, that meant being a jack-of-all trades – OK, I know how that phrase finishes! I'm the analyst, the solution designer, a programmer, the lead tester, the trainer, and I could make coffee for the team when needed. But here's the first problem. The client is sited at the other side of Australia. If I had my own private jet, it might be a quicker trip, but on commercial routes hopping around the coast, it's nearly 4,000 kilometers (well over 2,000 miles), and with poorly connecting flights, it took the best part of a day.

Now here's the next problem. There's no Internet, and no such thing as video conferencing. If I want to do waterfall-style analysis, I have to fly up to the remote mine site. If I want to do further interviews, or present the solution for sign-off, I have to fly up again. So during the analysis stage, I try really hard to absolutely pin down cardinality. Each mine-site project has only one prime supplier. Sure, that same supplier can be the successful bidder for several projects, but each project must have one and only one supplier that takes overall responsibility.

We designed it that way, and at the end of the project, I fly up again to do the training and handover. Thankfully, I take one of my best developers, Dianne, with me. That's a story in its own right. When we got to the mine site, Di stayed in the single women's quarters – she was single. She temporarily raised the population of single women by 33% - from three women to four. And single men? A few thousand. Needless to say, her presence was noticed. But back to the project. I start training, and one of the students says our system will never work. Great! What's the problem? I'm now told that there are plenty of projects where the prime responsibility is shared. Each project can have more than one "prime" supplier. Thankfully Di was a brilliant developer. We paused the training, and she made the changes over a couple of days, at the mine site. A bit of testing, and it's back in production and we are ready to go again.

The point is that the tightest of specifications on cardinality can prove to be false. Changes can be challenging in the operational system, especially if you don't have a Di on the team. But a Data Vault doesn't flinch as it's always capable of handling all cardinalities.

Satellites (on a Link)

Some people in the Data Vault community advise against having Satellites on Links. They typically concede that maybe holding effective-from and effective-to dates for the relationship are a valid use of Link Satellites, but beyond that, they shy away from this construct. We will look at the relative merits of such alternative modeling approaches in "Modeling a Satellite on a Link?", but for now I suggest we get a shared common understanding of just one position, namely that represented as the Data Vault 2.0 standard. From that foundation we might be better able to evaluate other options.

The good news is that a Satellite on a Link is just a normal Satellite. It is the same as a Satellite on a Hub, other than the Foreign Key to a Link Satellite's "parent" points to a Link instead of a Hub. And the other bit of good news is that there's no bad news.

While not shown in this hypothetical example, if the assignment transaction between a Fire Truck and a Fire recorded the assignment-from-date, and the assignment-to-date, the attributes of the Satellite might look something like this:

- Fire-Truck-Assigned-To-Fire Hash Key: "12ab34cd…" This is a Foreign Key, relating the Satellite to its "parent" Link for the text string "ABC-123|WF2018-123", being the concatenation of the Fire Truck and Fire business keys.
- Load Date / Time: "10/10/2018 12:44:32.100" being the very moment (to a nominated level of precision) the row was loaded to the Data Vault table.
- Record Source: "ER/RA" as an acronym, with "ER" for Emergency Response (the IT operational system) and "RA" for Resource Acquisition. In this example, this value is the same as the Record Source value in the related Hubs, as one source feed of data provides data for the Fire Hub, the Fire Truck Hub, the Link between them, and the Fire Satellite, though they may be processed in separate load modules as noted above.
- Data values at the time of initial creation of the Link could be as follows.
    - Assignment Start Date: "10/10/2018"
    - Assignment End Date: "11/11/2018"

Untangling "raw" and "business" Data Vault

You may encounter people talking about "raw Data Vault" (RDV) and "business Data Vault" (BDV), the latter sometimes shortened to "Business Vault". Unfortunately, some think these are physically separate databases, and that's what they actually build. At best, they are logical parts of the one Data Vault.

I say "at best" because there are two somewhat interrelated concepts at play here – data structures that reflect raw source system thinking versus data *structures* that reflect business thinking, and data *instances* that were sourced from raw source systems versus data instances that were sourced as the result of applying business rules. Confused?

You're not alone, but I think we can untangle the confusion. And I think it's important. Let's take these two concepts one at a time.

Firstly, a central theme in this book focuses on whether the Data Vault objects have their data *structures* designed to reflect business-centric thinking or source-centric thinking. A simple example can be seen in Satellites. Good practice suggests that each source data feed maps to its own source-centric Satellite structure. Additionally there is likely to be a business-centric "conformed" Satellite structure, holding data ready for consumption by the business users. Maybe I might have an Employee Hub with data for it and its Satellites sourced from a Payroll system and a Human Resource (HR) system. In this case, we might have one Employee Payroll Satellite whose structure is shaped by the raw source feed from the Payroll system source, one Employee HR Satellite shaped by the raw source feed from the HR system, then finally a "conformed" Satellite whose structure is shaped by how business sees their world.

The second consideration as to what's "business" and what's not relates to the *sourcing* of every instance of data in the Data Vault. Every Hub, Link and Satellite has a "Record Source" attribute that tells us where a given instance (e.g. one row in a relational database table) came from. For example, you might pick up just one instance in the Employee Hub, inspect its "Record Source" attribute, and determine that this discrete Employee's business key data came from the nightly batch extract from the Payroll system. The very next instance (another Employee) might have as its source a Change-Data-Capture (CDC) feed from the Human Resource system. In both of those cases, the source of that data is a "raw" data feed, coming from some operational source system.

Now let's look a bit further. Let's say we've got some business rule that looks at raw source transactions containing timesheets for contractors who never appear in either the Payroll system or the HR system. If the business deems them to be "employees", it is possible that a business rule may be applied to transform data in the raw timesheet transaction and add contractors to the Employee Hub. These instances would then have an entry in the "Record Source" attribute that claims their source is a business rule.

The Employee Hub itself isn't a "raw Data Vault" Hub, nor a "business Data Vault" Hub. It has instances that are "raw", and instances that are "business"!

The conclusion? I suggest we try and avoid the phrase "raw Data Vault" or "business Data Vault", and instead note whether:

- the structure of a Hub, Link or Satellite reflects a business view or a raw source system view, and
- the "Record Source" for an instance stored within a Hub, Link or Satellite claims it was sourced from a raw source-system data feed or from the execution of a business rule.

With that as a foundation, let's work our way through 4 Tasks that (1) articulate the business view, (2) use it to define the structure of our business-centric Data Vault objects, (3) map raw source data feeds to this framework, and (4) use business rules to close any gaps.

CHAPTER 3

Task #1: Form the Enterprise View

Or *"When things look better top-down instead of bottom-up"*

Setting our compass bearing

Is the enterprise view really that important?

Data Vault 2.0 most certainly has technical components, especially in its architecture dimension. It has to. Data Vault is pressed into service by some of its adherents to handle massive volumes (petabytes of stored data), with billions of new rows arriving each day to add to that base. The relatively frequent introduction of new technologies is also a challenge, too; big data, columnar data stores, schema-on-read ... The list goes on and on, and parts of today's list may be old hat by tomorrow.

There is absolutely no doubt that we need really sharp technical people to be able spot the trends and enable their prudent inclusion in Data Vault. The good news is that not every Data Vault client has to reinvent the wheel. I love it that those behind the Data Vault 2.0 architecture, including the technical vendors who've come on board, can do the hard yards and allow us to plug-&-play, at least to some extent. But even then, anybody implementing a Data Vault solution will need some technical expertise, be it internal or external. We sure need techos.

But I'm hearing people say that Data Vault isn't just about technology, that it also *must* focus on the business.

I remember chatting to Mike Magalsky from the massive computer chip manufacturer, Micron. He attributed one of the major reasons for a successful Data Vault implementation as being their creation of its foundational design based solidly on core business concepts.

Roelant Vos, a fellow Aussie, has earned an international reputation for his thoughtful and practical views on Data Vault. In a posting on his blog,[3] he states that the Data Vault approach supports "*...incremental, business focused and tightly scoped information delivery*" [emphasis mine].

Hans Hultgren's book on Data Vault modeling[4] has a section on his recommended steps involved in developing the Data Vault model, starting with identifying business concepts and business keys, then moving on to modeling the natural business relationships.

---

[3] http://roelantvos.com/blog/?p=1986.

[4] Hultgren H (2012) *Modeling the Agile Data Warehouse with Data Vault*.

Again, the emphasis is mine. But the message is clear. Data Vault is about the business. Just in case we're still in any doubt, we return to Dan Linstedt, and look again some of his quotes[5] presented earlier in this book.

- *"Data Vault modeling was, is and always will be* **ABOUT THE BUSINESS.** *And if the Data Vault you have in place today* **is not currently about the business,** *then unfortunately you've hired the wrong people, and those people need to go back to school and re-learn what Data Vault really means. OR you've built the wrong solution, and you need to fix it – immediately."*

- *"Ontologies are a very very important asset to the corporation – if built at the enterprise level,* **you must focus on ontologies** *while you are building the Data Vault solution, or the full value of the ... Data Vault cannot be realized."*

By the way, I have encountered some confusion as to what an ontology is, so I will briefly look at some definitions, then replace them with what I think may be a simpler term. Then we can leave the word "ontology" behind for most if not all of this book!

The Oxford dictionary[6] gives two definitions for the word "ontology". The first is its traditional, historical meaning: *"a branch of metaphysics dealing with the nature of being."* I'm not sure about you, but the first time I read that, I didn't feel overly enlightened. Thankfully, the second definition is closer to what we need if we want to build an enterprise view of an organization's data. An ontology is *"a set of concepts and categories in a subject area or domain that shows their properties and the relations between them."* [underlining mine]

Apologies to the Oxford Dictionary folk, but I am going to do a simple mapping of their second definition to an enterprise data model. Let's say that we've talked to the business and come up with a conceptual data model that has entities that represent the business concepts, major attributes (also known as properties) for each of the entities, and using an entity-relationship diagram (ERD) notation, we also have relationships between the entities. It looks like we've got ourselves an ontology.

---

[5] https://danlinstedt.com/allposts/datavaultcat/datavault-models-business-purpose-data-as-an-asset/.

[6] https://en.oxforddictionaries.com/definition/ontology.

Too easy! It may not be precise, and I am sure some may wish to debate with me, but when Dan asks for an "enterprise ontology", I am suggesting we can deliver an enterprise data model, and that will do the trick.

Tool vendors, and "source system Data Vault"

I don't know if you've come across Data Vault tool vendors who point their product at a source system, press what I call "the big green Go button", and automatically generate a Data Vault model, and populate it with data from the source? It's pretty impressive stuff, and many of these tools are wonderful. I do, however, have a serious caution.

Please hear me clearly. I'm not in any way challenging the quality of their products. Rather, my concern relates to the message these product demonstrations may convey.

Dan Linstedt directly warns against what he calls "source system Data Vault". However, in these tool demonstrations, instead of the Data Vault model being shaped by the business, the raw source data feeds are loaded to Hubs, Links and Satellites that are nothing more than simplistic reflections of the data structures in the source systems. Warts and all.

Let's say we've got a package for handling our customer details, and the central customer table is called Party Of Interest Object. That sounds pretty horrible, but I've seen worse, such as TABLE_00123. And while it's got a true Customer Number business key as a unique index somewhere in one of its columns, for possibly quite valid operational reasons, it uses a surrogate as the primary key, and it's called the Party Of Interest Object ID.

Now let's look at what an automated tool might generate. For starters, a Hub called PARTY_OF_INTEREST_HUB to represent the business concept of a Customer, with what pretends to be a "business key" of PARTY_OF_INTEREST_HUB_ID. Perhaps the business people simply wanted a Customer Hub, with a Customer Number as the recognized business key. It gets worse. Another operational system has a table named TABLE_PROSPECTS, with a PROSPECT_ID as its identifier. In this hypothetical, independent of how the source systems might see the world, the business sees prospects as no more than early-stage customers, and they want all of the customer data integrated, especially as the data values assigned to a PROSPECT_ID eventually become their Customer Numbers. But no, this source system Data Vault approach generates a TABLE_PROSPECTS_HUB (another horrible name), with its "business key".

If we see a product demonstration, the sample source data set probably won't include TABLE_00123 as one of the source tables. It will be cleaner. The source system table name is likely to be named Customer, and the primary key is probably Customer Number. Careful selection (or artificial creation) of a source system that aligns with what is wanted in the automatically-generated Data Vault more nicely show the tools' potential to operate with no human intervention.

I will say it again. I think we should all appreciate the fact that vendors are investing time and money bringing tools onto the market, but we shouldn't unquestioningly embrace the simplistic messages implied in some of their product demonstrations.

Consultants, and "source system Data Vault"

There are very good reasons why a tool vendor may choose to demonstrate some lovely features in an easy-to-understand way. But do Data Vault practitioners ever build source system Data Vaults, or even anything close to them? Unfortunately, yes.

I don't want to focus on the problems. Solutions are much more valuable! But maybe an awareness of how good people fall into traps can serve as a warning. It's better to have warning signs at the top of a cliff than have excellent paramedics at the bottom treating those who have fallen. And we must heed Dan's warnings when he says, *"If you build a* **source system Data Vault Model,** *the value of the solution drops to one tenth of one percent overall."*[7]

So why on earth would some people, if not building full-blown "source system Data Vault", walk so dangerously close to it?

---

[7] https://danlinstedt.com/allposts/datavaultcat/datavault-models-business-purpose-data-as-an-asset/.

One reason, I suggest, is an honorable desire to deliver value to the business quickly. These practitioners load data into source-centric Data Vault structures as hastily as possible, and have good intentions that at some time in the future they will worry about who will consume it, and what business rules need to be applied so the business *can* consume it. The business may admire these people for today's visible progress in getting data into the Data Vault, but may be bitterly disappointed when they try to get integrated, enterprise-wide information out of the Data Vault.

Another reason I suspect perhaps relates to their background and training. Some may have solid experience in other forms of data warehousing. They may have finely tuned expertise in extract / transform / load (ETL) techniques, and they want to hit the ground running.

However, they may not have been trained in the necessity of building an enterprise view before they just throw lots of source data into a source-centric Data Vault structure that doesn't yet have a vision for the end game. Or maybe they agree with the ideals of having an enterprise view, but they can't find one that already exists, or worse yet, the organization does have an enterprise model (or several versions, each claiming to be the single, unifying view!), but these models have a bad smell and the management explicitly mandate that these models must *not* be used to shape any design going forward! Have you encountered such scenarios? I have, several times.

So if we believe in the value of founding our Data Vault solution on the enterprise view, we may feel trapped unless we build a suitable enterprise data model ourself. Many fear that will take months or years, and to be fair, I have observed such mammoth projects. But it doesn't have to be that way, and I will shortly show you how we can build a framework that delivers "sufficient" quality, at the speed demanded by agile projects. So instead of asking *if* we can afford to assemble an enterprise view, I like to ask the question the other way around. Can we afford to *not* reflect the enterprise view?

I've seen first-hand the outworking of tensions over source-driven Data Vault design versus enterprise-centric design. I share some experiences from a particular client site to help turn the spotlight on how these tensions can adversely impact the overall Data Vault project. There were some great people involved at various times of the project, and some had impressive resumes with lots of experience. So why did the project flounder? This real-life case study highlights some of the undesirable side-effects of the Data Vault team having the wrong emphasis. Firstly, a number of the consultants erroneously focused on source systems, leaving business integration for another day.

And secondly, some of them were willing to accommodate ugly Data Vault designs because they just couldn't agree on a way to handle the diversity of business key structures. This is a technical issue, not a business issue, but it threatened the entire Data Vault initiative. It's a key issue in Data Vault (pun intended), and is tackled in quite a bit of detail in the section titled "Not only Semantics & Grain – now there's Key Values" later in this book.

For now, please join me in a quick look at some of the twists and turns experienced on this project so that you can feel some of the pain of a misguided approach. Hopefully it will provide you with sufficient incentive to avoid repeating these mistakes!

A case study in conflicting designs

There was one consultant who had started the Data Vault build. In my opinion, he'd done a brilliant job. He understood the importance of the business view, and welcomed me aboard to assist. Things began well.

There were many business-level Hubs required – Customers, Products, Accounts, Assets and more. Some of these high-level concepts needed breaking down into finer-grained business concepts, but the discussion had been held, and agreement reached, that "Customer" had the right semantics (meaning) and grain (subtype level) to be one Hub. For the sake of the following example, can we please assume that position was correct? Thanks.

The "Iteration #1" design was business-centric, simple, and elegant.

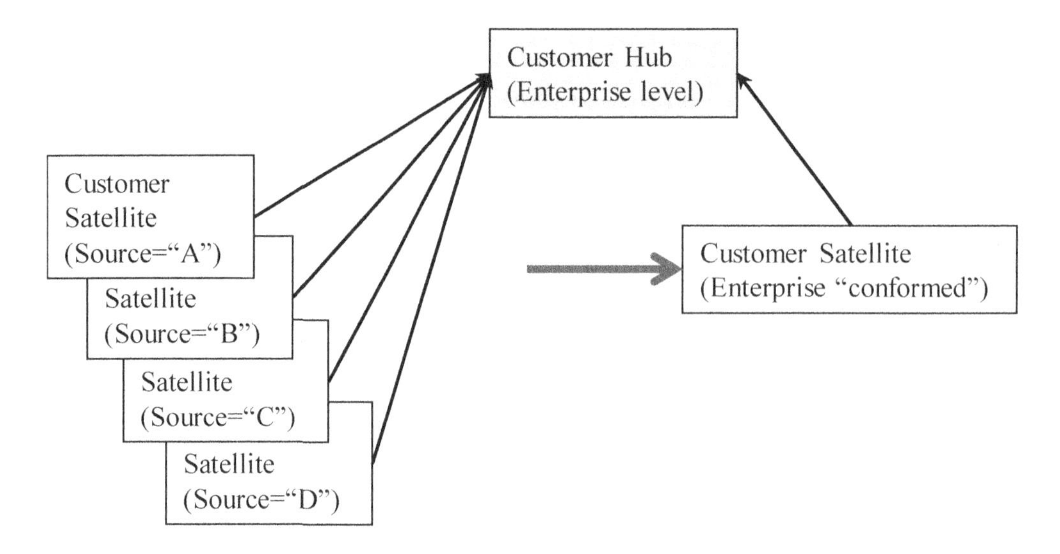

Figure 20: Customer Hub design, iteration #1

In essence, this design incorporated:

- One Customer Hub, reflecting what the *enterprise* saw as a "customer".
- Multiple source-related Satellites hanging off this one central Customer Hub.
- One conformed Satellite to hold the business view that consolidated selectively from the source-related Satellites. The arrow pointing to the conformed Satellite denotes the fact that it is a Data Vault object that is generated by the application of business rules to the myriad of source-centric Data Vault Satellites and their attributes.

It was what the business wanted, and it all looked rosy.

The diagram actually represents a subset. It displays only four source systems. One employee informed me that there were more like 50 source systems, but the approach portrayed remains stable, just with more Satellites, all hanging off one central Customer Hub. By default, each source system will be allocated its own Satellite, so this case study assumes that if there are 50 source systems, there will be at least 50 Satellites. That's not the problem; the issue which we will see shortly is more focused on whether there is one Customer Hub, or 50, or more!

The next notable milestone was the engagement of another consultancy. They had some really good people, but the team leader had a different approach to doing Data Vault than the preceding team. The client temporarily assigned responsibility for this project to the new consultancy, as the original team had some other pressing demands.

Iteration #2 was born, driven by the new team (Figure 21).

This design incorporated:

- Multiple Customer Hubs, and their matching Satellites, for *every* source. There was one exception. If any source system had the same key value for a customer (for example Customer Number 123 should be Alex Anderson in both systems), then the two source system Satellites shared one common Hub, as shown for sources "C" and "D". This is known as "passive integration", and it's a good thing. The rest of the design was straight "source system Data Vault".

- One *enterprise* level Customer Hub, and its conformed Satellite, was vaguely recognized as needing to exist, but most certainly was not designed. The enterprise-level objects are portrayed in dotted lines to communicate that they had a nominal place-holder, but little more. The whole idea of the business consuming the Data Vault's content was left to another day.

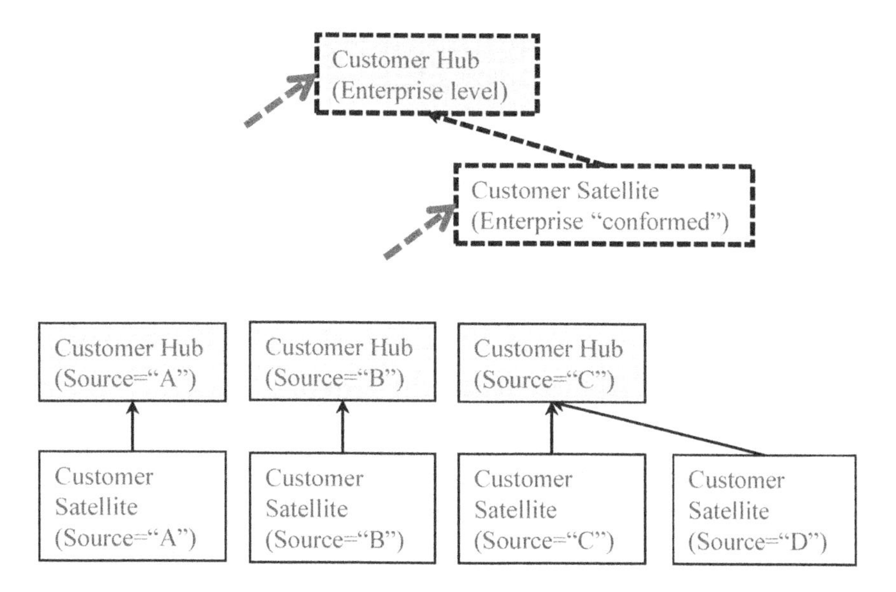

Figure 21: Customer Hub design, iteration #2

The argument for this approach was that it was really easy to load the source-centric Data Vault structures and that we didn't need to be held up by debates on what source systems would map to a common business Hub later. For now, just get the data in. It was arguable that even the business keys weren't necessarily *business* keys as some of them had names that suggested they were possibly little more than *source* system identifiers.

Further, the solution had lots of Customer Hubs, but the business wanted just one. Was this necessarily a problem? Possibly not, it was argued, as the multiple source-centric Data Vault Hubs *could* be consolidated into one enterprise-level Customer Hub later. But was it the best way?

The design was challenged as being too close to "source system Data Vault". The lead designer sought to rename source-specific Customer Hubs by removing the source system name and replacing it with something more generic. For example, if one source system was known by the acronym "CMS" for Customer Management System, instead of calling the Hub "CMS Customer Hub", he called it something like the "Managed Customer Hub".

Many in the business saw this renaming as little more than a thin veneer. There was still one Hub and one Satellite mapping to one source system. Worse, people looked at the new names and had to scratch their heads to work out what on earth this Hub represented. At least if they unashamedly had source system names, there was one less area of confusion. Many were not convinced it wasn't source system Data Vault behind a smoke-&-mirrors veil. If something walks like a duck, swims like a duck, and quacks like a duck, then it probably is a duck. If something looks like a source system Data Vault solution …

The business was persistent. They wanted one Customer Hub, and they wanted it now, not as some vague, promised feature for some distant future delivery. There were other Data Vault projects happening in parallel that also wanted to share a single Customer Hub. But some of the leading decision makers in this specific Data Vault project didn't want to wait for enterprise-wide consensus, especially as they had observed the difficulty in getting agreement between Iteration #1 and Iteration #2 within just one project team. How hard would it be to herd all of the cats across multiple teams?

Frankly, with the right approach, I contend it's actually not too difficult, and we will get to that. But let's see this story to its bitter end.

A compromise was made. This project team had an appetite for what approximated the source system Data Vault style, and they were allowed to retain that. What would be added, though, was an immediate inclusion of a partial, *project*-centric integration layer. Not quite the *enterprise*-wide Customer Hub everyone wanted, but a step in that direction. There would be one project-centric Customer Hub, not one enterprise-centric Hub – that would have to wait to some date in the distant future. Iteration #3 was about to appear!

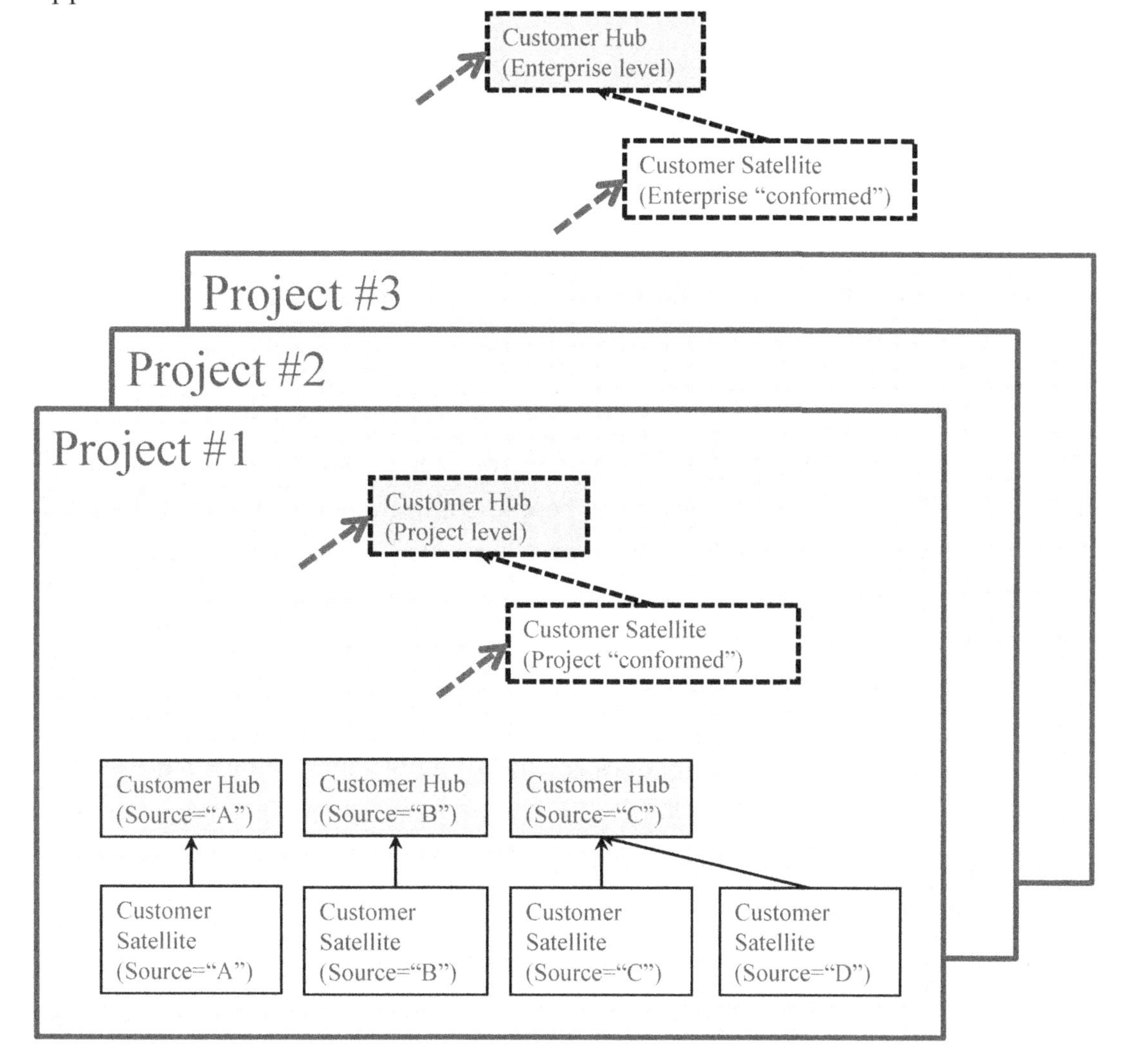

Figure 22: Customer Hub design, iteration #3

This iteration was basically a repeat of Iteration #2, but with the insertion of yet another layer between the source-system Hubs and the desired enterprise-level Hub:

- There were still the same multiple source-driven Hubs and Satellites.
- There were now multiple project-based Customer Hubs, with one per project. Each of these was intended to consolidate the multiple source feeds from one project, just like an enterprise-level Hub would, but it was seen as "insulating" each Data Vault project from the other projects. These multiple consolidation Hubs were to be later consolidated to populate the enterprise level Customer Hub.
- There was still one enterprise level Customer Hub, and its conformed Satellite, but put in the too-hard basket, to be resolved (much) later.

Getting ugly?

Yet another consultancy now comes on board, and challenges the underlying Hub-&-Satellite raw data that looks amazingly close to source system Data Vault. They want the source-system Hubs consolidated. Sounded good to me – at first.

But yet another compromise appeared. The business had consistently been asking for one Customer Hub, but now the technical people got in the way. Though not explicitly declared as a compromise on what the business wanted, the new team argued that if consolidation around business keys was too hard for *technical* reasons, *business*-centered consolidation would be avoided. Customer Hub design was now driven by technical aspects of customer business keys.

In the later section "Not only Semantics & Grain – now there's Key Values" we will look at different types of business keys, and how they can be handled elegantly, but for now it's enough to say the proposal was for each project to have one Customer Hub for *each* of the data structures for business keys. So now we've got Iteration #4 (Figure 23).

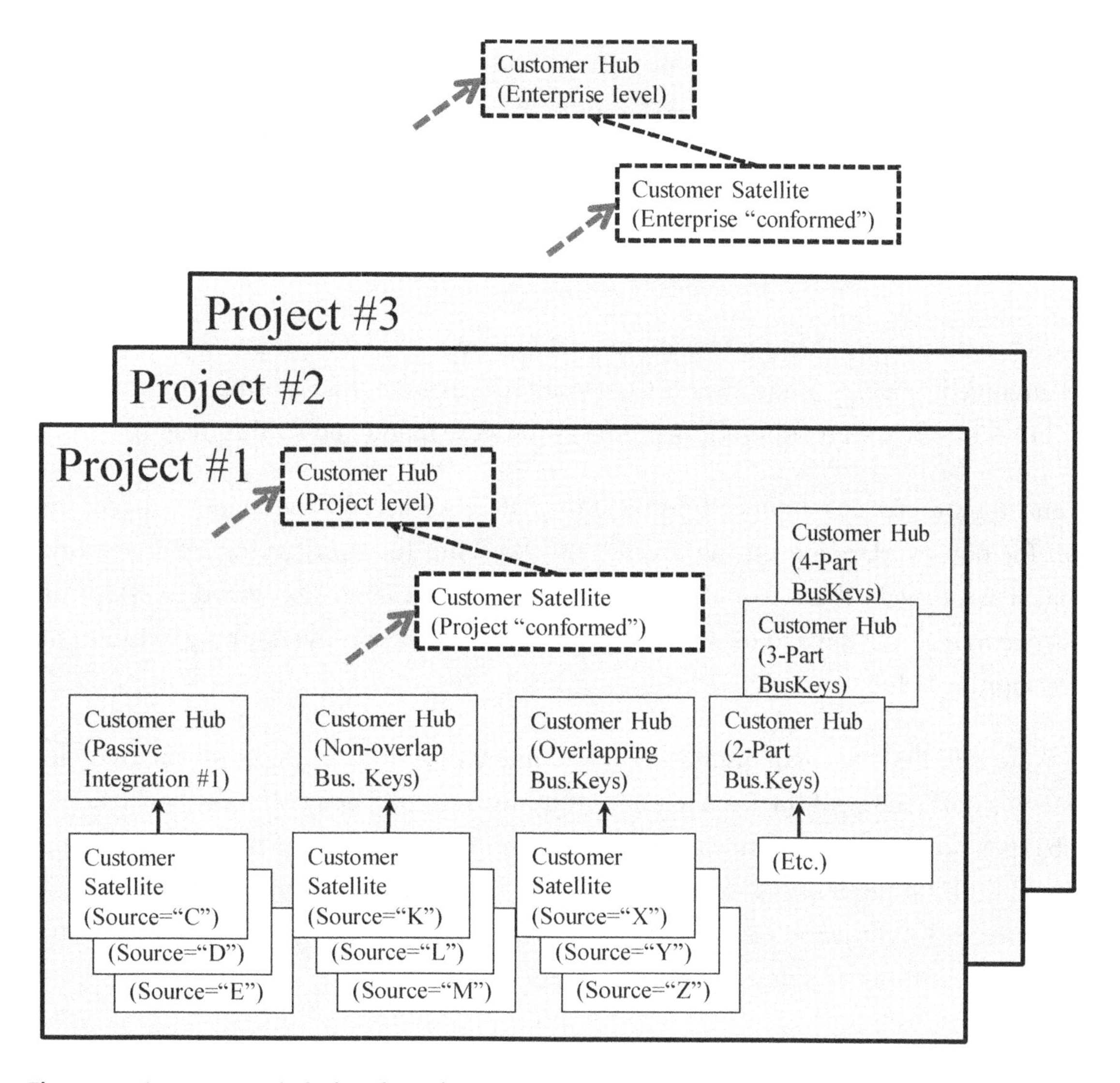

Figure 23: Customer Hub design, iteration #4

The bullet points below note focus of this design. For each project, it incorporated:

- One Hub as the "master" Hub for passive integration, based on the customer business key set seen as being the most widely recognized "master" keys.
- One Hub for all non-master sources where their Customer Number was a single attribute, and where the *values* used in each system *never overlapped*.
- One Hub for all non-master sources where their Customer Number was a single attribute, but where the *values* used in each system did (or might) *overlap*.

- One Hub for all source systems that had two attributes combining to form a business key. For example, if the unique business key required a Country Code plus a Customer ID attribute, this could go in the 2-part Hub.
- Another Hub for source systems with a 3-part business key, and another for source systems with a 4-part business key, and so on.

It was actually worse than that for multi-part business key Hubs. If one 2-part business key involved Country Code plus a Customer ID attribute, and another involved two attributes but they were different, separate Hubs were mandated by this design.

… and then there was another complication. There's a certain brittleness between the Hub for non-overlapping business keys, and the Hub for overlapping business keys. What if we *thought* there would never be overlaps, but later discovered overlaps are now occurring? We have to move the mapping from the "non-overlapping" Hub to the "overlapping" Hub.

We were told that the client organization had many dozens of source systems involving customer data, so to get the Data Vault design down to perhaps half a dozen Customer Hubs (per project!) was an improvement. But the main concern was that the Data Vault "integration" solution was being driven by *technical* considerations around key structures, not by *business* considerations as reflected in the enterprise data model that presented Customer as a unifying concept.

Are you still with me? It may be painful to read, but believe me, it was even more painful to be there. But we've got one more design, Iteration #5 (Figure 24).

This was a massive improvement on Iteration #4:

- Instead of several Customer Hubs for each project (each one being based around business key structures), the proposal was for one Customer Hub per project, accommodating all types of business keys.
- … but it still required the consolidation Hub at the enterprise level.

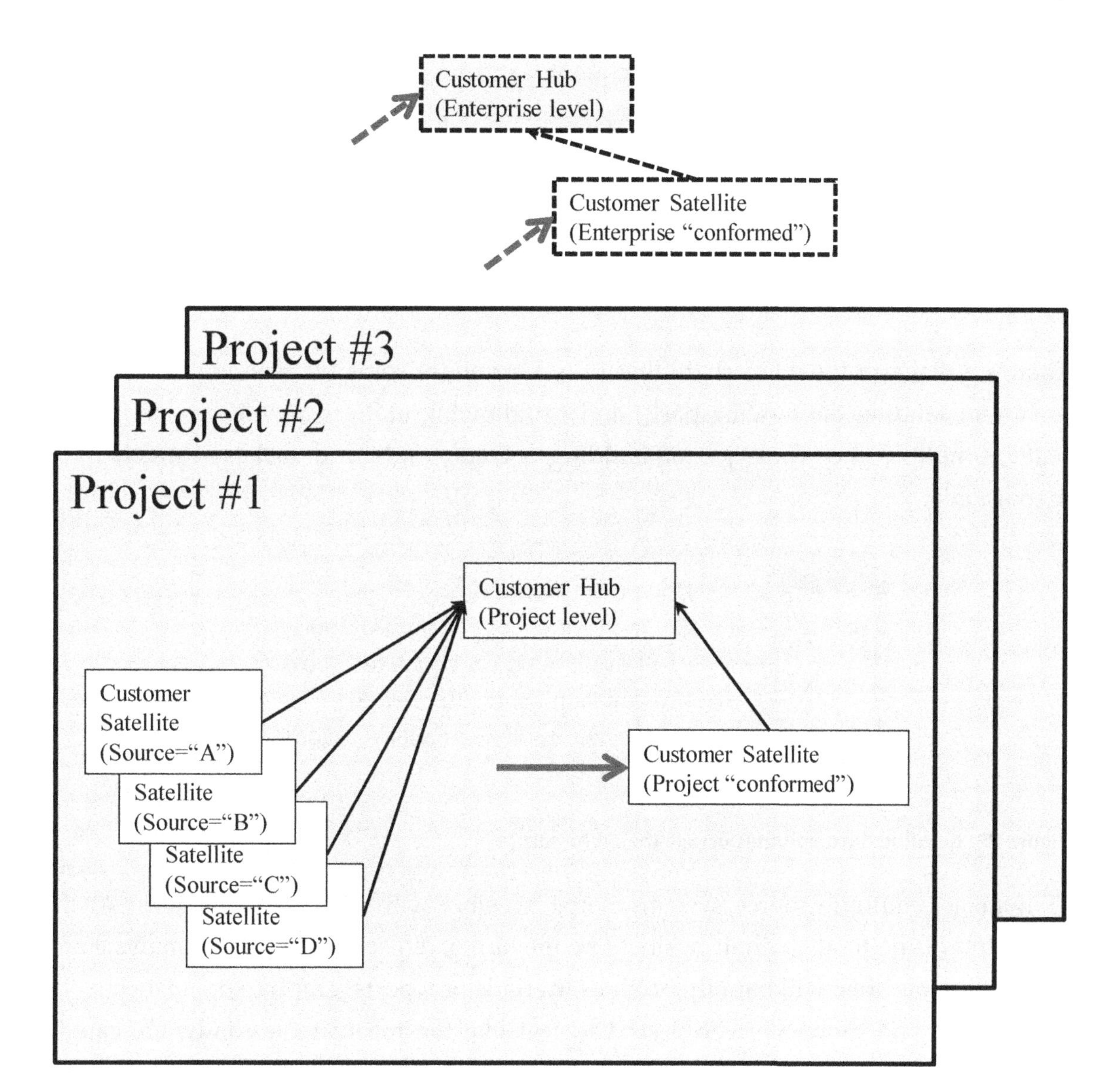

Figure 24: Customer Hub design, iteration #5

To me, the really sad thing was that after much time and money being spent, the project-level solution was technically the same as the enterprise-level design presented in the first iteration, just replicated by project. If the decision makers had simply applied the mantra of using an enterprise data model to shape the Data Vault design, and not let technical issues relating to business key structures get in the way of what the business said they wanted, Iteration #1 could have been the final, and successful, solution. Instead, those who wanted the simple elegance of a business-centric view were moved off the project. The subsequent word on the street was that not only was the project a failure, some without deep knowledge also unjustly classified Data Vault itself as being a failure.

I saw the whole saga as a missed opportunity. The project should have succeeded.

Please let's focus on the bit that gives the most leverage, and leads to success

There's a diagram I want to share that I think provides some hints about a framework for understanding the moving parts, and for allowing us to focus on the one bit that really simplifies the whole job of building a Data Vault, and makes it much more manageable:

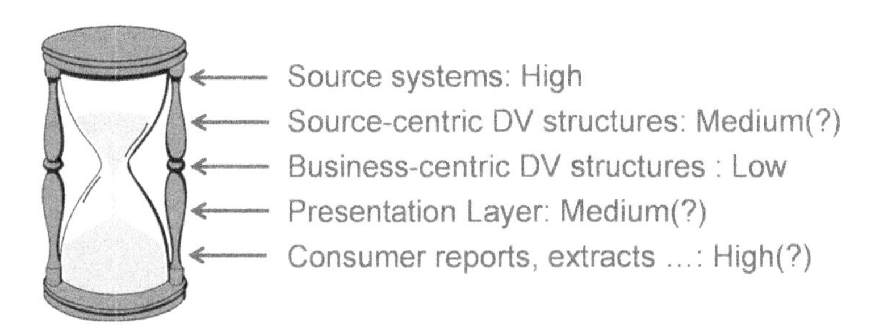

Figure 25: Relative data volumes across the architecture

IT manages multiple source systems, some possibly with hundreds of tables. At the other end of the food chain, if business people are given self-service data analysis and reporting tools, they will happily produce myriads of reports, graphs, spreadsheets, flat file extracts and more. We could start to feel like the meat in the sandwich, caught between a potentially massive palette of data sources, and massive demands and expectations from the business.

There's a way to reduce the complexity. And it involves the elegance of the Data Vault architecture, combined with the sharp, business-centric focus of an enterprise ontology. Sorry, I used that "ontology" word again. I really meant we want to focus on the "enterprise data model"! Let's look again at the egg-timer in the diagram above.

We've noted that the amount of data held in source systems is relatively high. The source-centric Data Vault structures can be typically expected to hold less data as not all source data sets are nominated for loading to the Data Vault. (I do concede that the volumes can creep up again if the source systems only hold current values but the source-centric Data Vault structures hold full history.)

The business-centric Data Vault structures ideally will have relatively little data – for example, multiple conflicting source-centric Satellites for a common parent may be resolved into a single, conformed business-centric Satellite.

Then the data volumes are likely to start increasing if the presentation layer is physically stored rather than being a virtual layer. Data Vault practitioners seem to be moving towards virtual layers, but sometimes performance considerations may require physical persistence.

And finally, the number of reports or extracts produced by consumers could potentially be huge.

The business-centric Data Vault structures are the heart of a Data Vault. They are the core because they represent the desired business information, and are founded on the business data model. Yes, you can expect some source-centric Data Vault structures such as Satellites from multiple sources, but even they should hang off Hubs (or Links) that are business-centric.

An investment in a well-considered design of business-centric Data Vault objects can pay huge dividends. That's where the data volumes (and data structures) are less, and where the business value is derived. All we need now is a well-formed enterprise data model.

Before we go any further, what is an 'enterprise data model'?

Terminology

In the heading for this part of the book I have referred to an enterprise view, implying an "enterprise data model". That's one of many common phrases, and you may see it in the DMBOK (Data Management Body of Knowledge) book. I like the phrase, but over the years, there have been many classifications of types of layers in data models. Some may remember talk coming out of the 1970s about a three-schema model, comprising an External Schema, a Conceptual Schema, and an Internal (or Physical) Schema.

Then there's John Zachman's six layers for the data area.

Another common classification scheme is to label a data model as Conceptual, Logical, or Physical. Seeing a Data Vault design is meant to be centered on business concepts, a Conceptual model looks like it might meet our requirements. OK, so we might just focus on Conceptual models.

But then there's debate about what constitutes a "Conceptual" model.

Steve Hoberman, Donna Burbank, and Chris Bradley in *Data Modeling for the Business*[8] have two levels above the Logical and Physical models – Very High-level data models, and High-level data models. I actually like these classifications as they make sense to the business.

Then along comes David Hay in his solidly founded and well-researched book "*Achieving Buzzword Compliance*"[9] which tackles head-on the whole topic of buzzwords in our industry, including terms such as a "Conceptual" model. Steve and his friends had two types of what some may call Conceptual models. David breaks Conceptual models into three types. I can't do his book justice in a few bullet points, but my simplification of his three Conceptual models goes something like this:

1. At the top (the most broad-brush view), he has Overview Models. They're great in giving the big picture to non-technical audiences, and helping us understand the scope of the following, more detailed, models.

2. Next come Semantic Models. While an enterprise may have one Overview Model, it may have multiple Semantic Models, each one describing a view of the enterprise from within one work group, using their language. David labels these

---

[8] Hoberman S., Burbank D., & Bradley C. (2009) "*Data Modeling for the Business*".

[9] Hay D. (2018) "*Achieving Buzzword Compliance*".

as "divergent" models – each view may diverge from the apparently simple, single, united Overview Model.

3. Finally we've got an Essential Model. Yes, just one of them. It is "convergent" because it pulls together the diverse views from the Semantic Models to create a new single, unified view.

I suggest that it is this single "Essential" enterprise view that should contribute to the design of the business-centric Data Vault objects. But didn't Dan say what we need for that purpose is an "enterprise ontology"? Here comes Wikipedia to the rescue. (OK, I know some treat Wikipedia as providing less than the ultimate, authoritative word on matters, but let's accept that it is a great resource if used with a touch of caution.) Under the topic of data models, Wikipedia suggests (emphasis mine):

"In the 1970s entity relationship modeling emerged as a new type of conceptual data modeling … This technique can describe any ontology, i.e., an overview and classification of concepts and their relationships, for a certain area of interest."[10]

So at last we've got it. We can do a Conceptual data model for the enterprise, call it an ontology if we like, and we've got the foundation for a business-centric Data Vault solution. [*As a side note, the Wikipedia quotation above seems to imply that a data model will use one of the forms of an Entity-Relationship Diagram (ERD) notation, but I suggest that use of the Unified Modeling Language (UML) notation may also serve you well as an alternative.*]

But what does one of these things really look like?

Sample snippets from enterprise data models

Given that there are so many definitions of what an enterprise (Conceptual) data model might look like, I will share a few examples that might give you a feel for their shape. Of course, others may provide other examples that are quite different, and their samples may well fit the definition, too.

---

[10] https://en.wikipedia.org/wiki/Data_model, August 2018.

Schematic

David Hay's definition of types of Conceptual models starts with an Overview Model. I often work with the business people to assemble a single-page schematic. I have created a pictorial overview which many have found helpful. An example of it follows, showing people involved with the buying and selling of houses and land, placing mortgages, and the like.

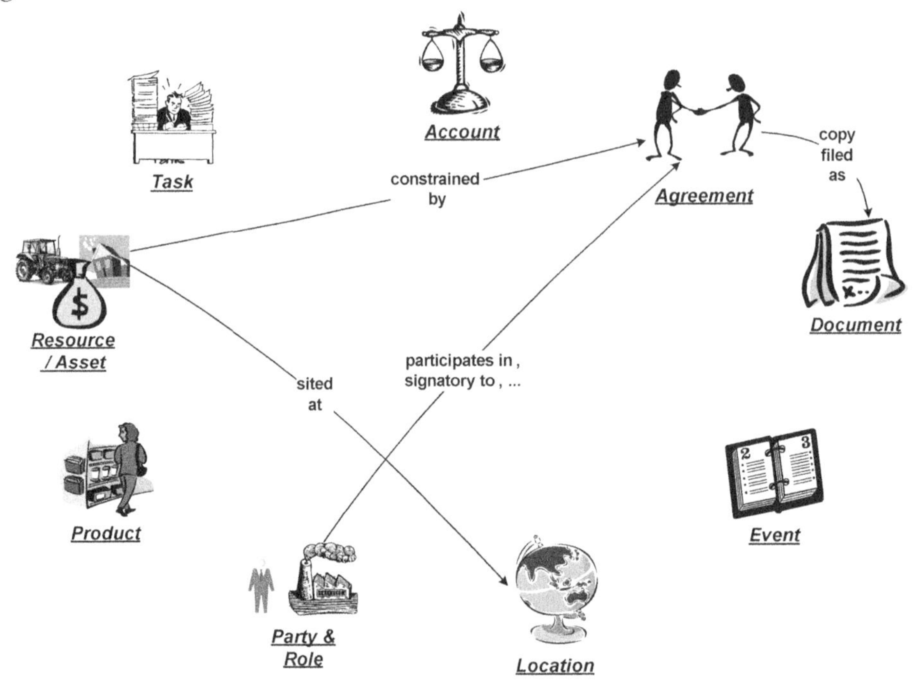

Figure 26: Schematic (overview model) for the land transaction scenario

We will go into the details behind each icon in the Appendix when we look at the technical details behind the patterns they represent, but for now, in this setting:

- Parties and their roles could include vendors (the sellers of houses and land), the buyers, their solicitors, involved real estate agents, banks and more.

- Agreements could include the most obvious one – a contract between the buyer(s) and seller(s) – but also the contract to engage a real estate agent, the bank loan contract, and maybe a guarantee agreement provided by loving parents to a young couple who can't quite borrow enough money in their own right.

- Important Agreements such as the loan contract typically require documentary evidence, managed by the Document icon. Note that sometimes an agreement is nothing more than a handshake and has no documentary evidence, or conversely, some of the documents such as photographs of the property are not tied directly to an Agreement.

- Resources (also known as Assets), are likely to include houses and land but also money.

- Some of the Resources such as land have a Location (a position on a map), while other Resources (such as money) don't have a Location.

Just to demonstrate the flexibility of these simple icons, let's look at one more enterprise-level schematic. This time, it's for an organization that is responsible for the registration of health practitioners (doctors, nurses, chemists ...), and for oversight of their on-going work.

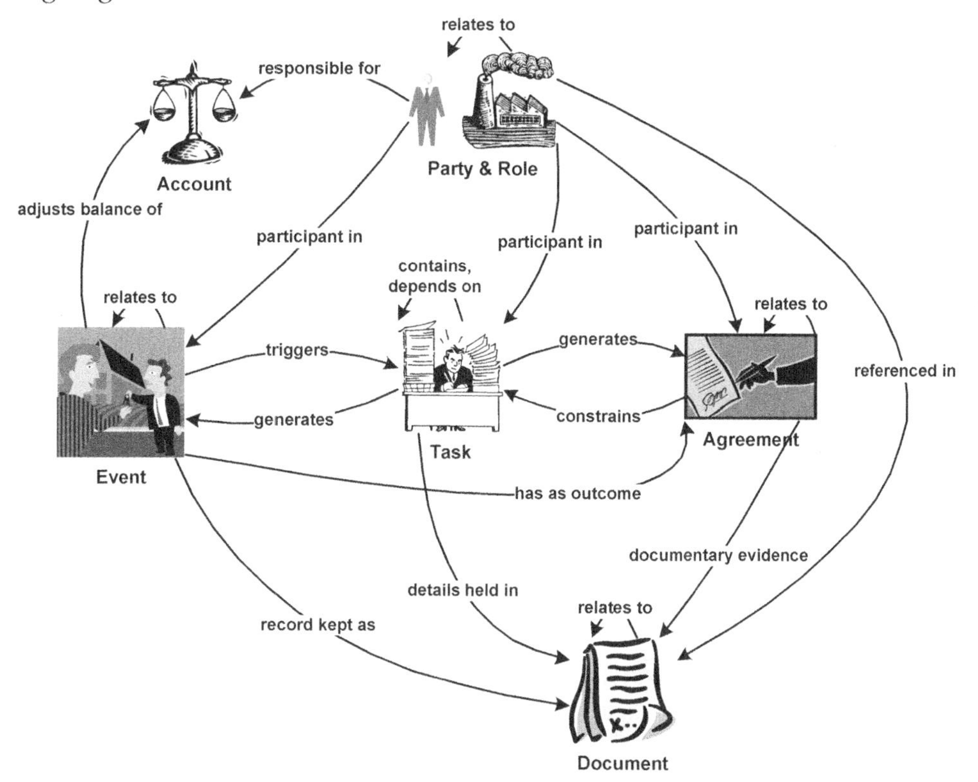

Figure 27: Schematic (overview model) for the health practitioner regulation scenario

If, for example, a practitioner has been found to have a personal problem with drugs or alcohol, the oversight might include managing an agreement between the parties to perform random testing as a condition for permission to continue practice. Some of the pictures for the icons are a little different (chosen by my client), but the themes are the same.

Let's quickly look at the details behind the icons:

- Parties and their roles this time include health practitioners, members of boards (the dentist board, the chiropractor board ...), students, hospitals, assessors, and so on.

- Agreements could include the foundational registration permit to allow the practitioner to work, but could, for example, include an agreement by a practitioner to allow random blood and urine testing for drugs. As for the previous scenario, some Agreements will have their details recorded in Documents.

- Events include calendar-based events such as annual renewals and reviews, or incident-based events such as the receipt of a complaint from a patient.

- Tasks represent work done by or on behalf of the regulation agency, such as the processing of a new application for registration, or the processing of a complaint.

- We can see a lovely "triggers / generates" synergy between Events and Tasks. An example follows:
    - A patient-initiated complaint (Event) occurs over apparent drug-impaired behavior by the health practitioner.
    - The complaint Event triggers initiation of whole series of Tasks to evaluate the complaint.
    - The outcome of the evaluation is another Event – the noting of an abuse of prescription drugs by the practitioner.
    - This Event of recording an adverse finding in the investigation triggers further Tasks, including the establishment of an Agreement for random testing.

  - One of the random test results (themselves further Events) indicate a breach of conditions, which in turn triggers more Tasks to bar the practitioner from further practice.

- Finally, Accounts are involved in managing finances, for example the recording of payment of annual fees.

Notice that the use of these building blocks (Agreement, Party & Role, or whatever) vary massively between enterprises, but the concepts behind each of them are remarkably similar. David Hay and Len Silverston have published profound insights in their books on data model patterns. I love the fact that Len calls the patterns "universal" data model patterns, because they are so often easily applied to a huge variety of situations.

Drill down

These one-page schematics provide what David Hay rightly calls an "Overview" model, but we need more. Let's look at how we can drill down into greater detail.

Each of the icons in the schematic has standard pattern details. For example, the Party and Party Role icon has lots of entity types, and many authors present many variations on the theme.

Some people love the Party and Party Role pattern, some don't, but before you write it off, I really do recommend you first read the book co-authored by Len Silverston and Paul Agnew[11] on the different levels for each pattern. Some levels are great for communicating with non-technical people, other levels are more aimed at technical implementation. David Hay[12] has a similar number of levels. Len and Paul refer to their levels as spanning from specialized through to generalized, while David talks of his levels as spanning from concrete through to abstract. I think there is much in common.

---

[11] Silverston L. & Agnew P. (2009) "*The Data Model Resource Book, Volume 3: Universal Patterns for Data Modeling*".

[12] Hay D. (2011) "*Enterprise Model Patterns: Describing the World*".

The full Party pattern defines entities for things such as name, address, phone number and so on.

A Party can play multiple roles. For example, an Employee of a company may also be a Customer of the same company.

We have just looked at the health practitioner regulation scenario, presented above as an overview schematic. Let's now look at it in a bit more detail.

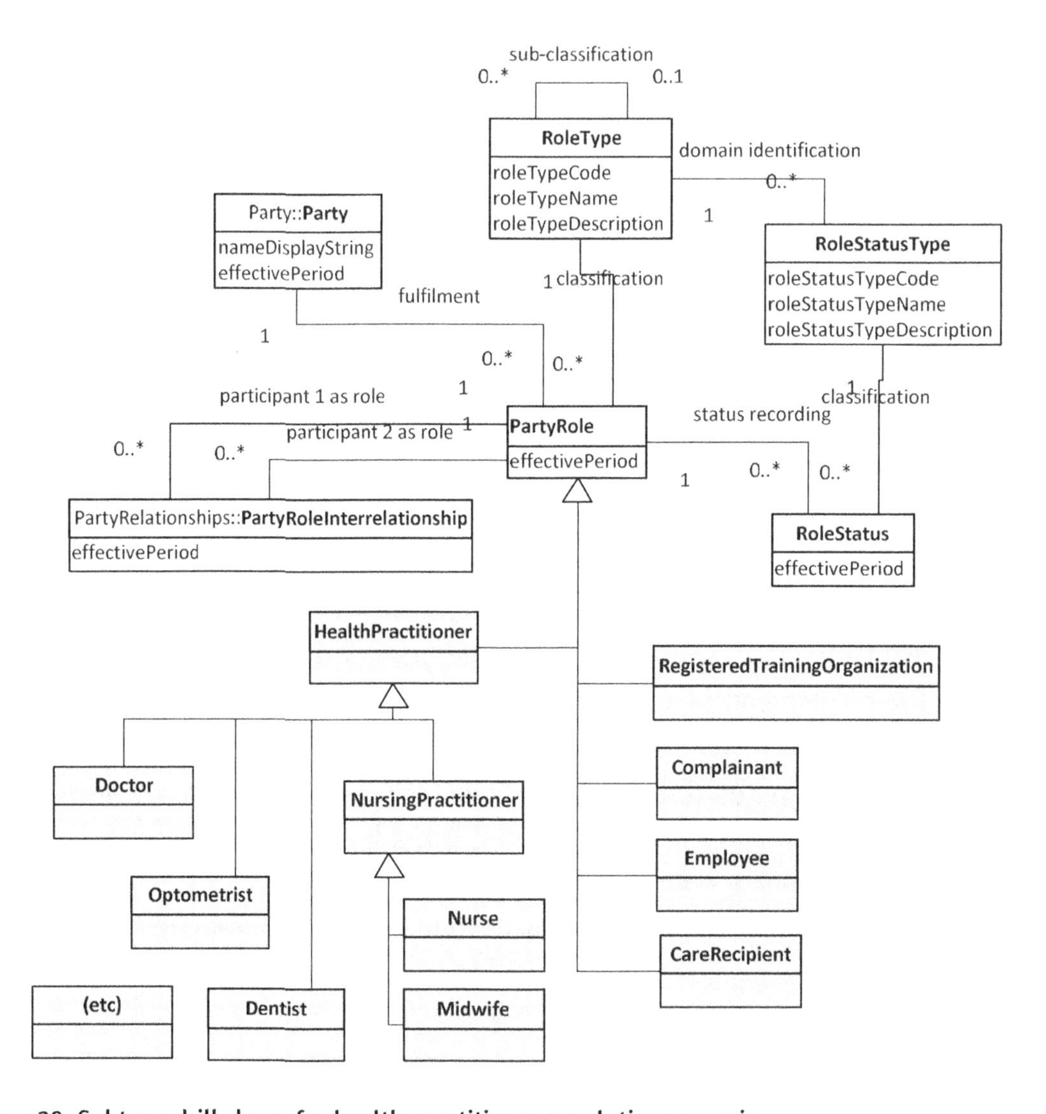

Figure 28: Subtype drill-down for health practitioner regulation scenario

The clear boxes at the top of the diagram represent a tiny fragment of a somewhat standard pattern for Party and Party Role pattern. The shaded boxes represent a few sample subtypes of "Party Role" in the health practitioner scenario, and show how we can do some simple drill-down into subtypes, and their subtypes, as deep as is helpful.

I strongly encourage not only doing pretty pictures of the subtype hierarchy, but also describing each subtype. In text, let's define what a thing such as "Dentist" means. Let's also describe what it doesn't mean. Is the full definition for a dentist a "dental surgeon"? Are "prosthodontists" included, or are they a separate category?

I also recommend the documentation of at least the major attributes expected in an entity. Add them, and document them, too.

I remember working with one individual who argued strongly that a conceptual model should have entity names only, and nothing else. In one of his models, he had "Product" as an entity, and strongly resisted supplying a description let alone indicative attributes. I suggested that if I saw attributes such as Recommended Retail Price, and Stock On Hand Quantity, each instance in a "Product" table was likely to represent one item in the company's product catalogue. On the other hand, if I saw attributes such as Serial Number and Date Purchased, each instance in a "Product" table was likely to represent one specific real-world instance that might be purchased by a specific customer on a specific date. That's a massive difference in meaning. Which leads me to the next point.

You may ask why do all this documentation of some enterprise model when what we're really after is a Data Vault model? One of many reasons is that Dan Linstedt, when we get to finding Hubs for the Data Vault, encourages all data feeds that load to a common Hub to have the same "semantics and grain". If we have clear definitions for what each entity in the enterprise data model means, we've got the "semantics" (meaning) bit covered. And I suggest we can use the supertype / subtype hierarchy to guide in our thinking about "grain". In the diagram above, a Nursing Practitioner has a courser grain than a midwife, and a finer grain than a Health Practitioner.

That's a bit on drill-down into subtypes of entities, but what about drilling down into finding more specific relationships? The following diagram depicts some of the many subtypes of Resource that may be used in an emergency response to Events such as Fires and Floods. Please don't get overwhelmed by the number of subtypes shown (and believe me, that's a tiny sliver of reality), but instead note the three heavy-lined "assignment" relationships.

At the top of the diagram there is an assignment between the Resource supertype and the Event supertype. It is a generalized relationship, saying that one or many of any type of Resource can be assigned to one or many of any type of Event. This is the sort of relationship the business might identify when it is assembling the top-down enterprise data model schematic.

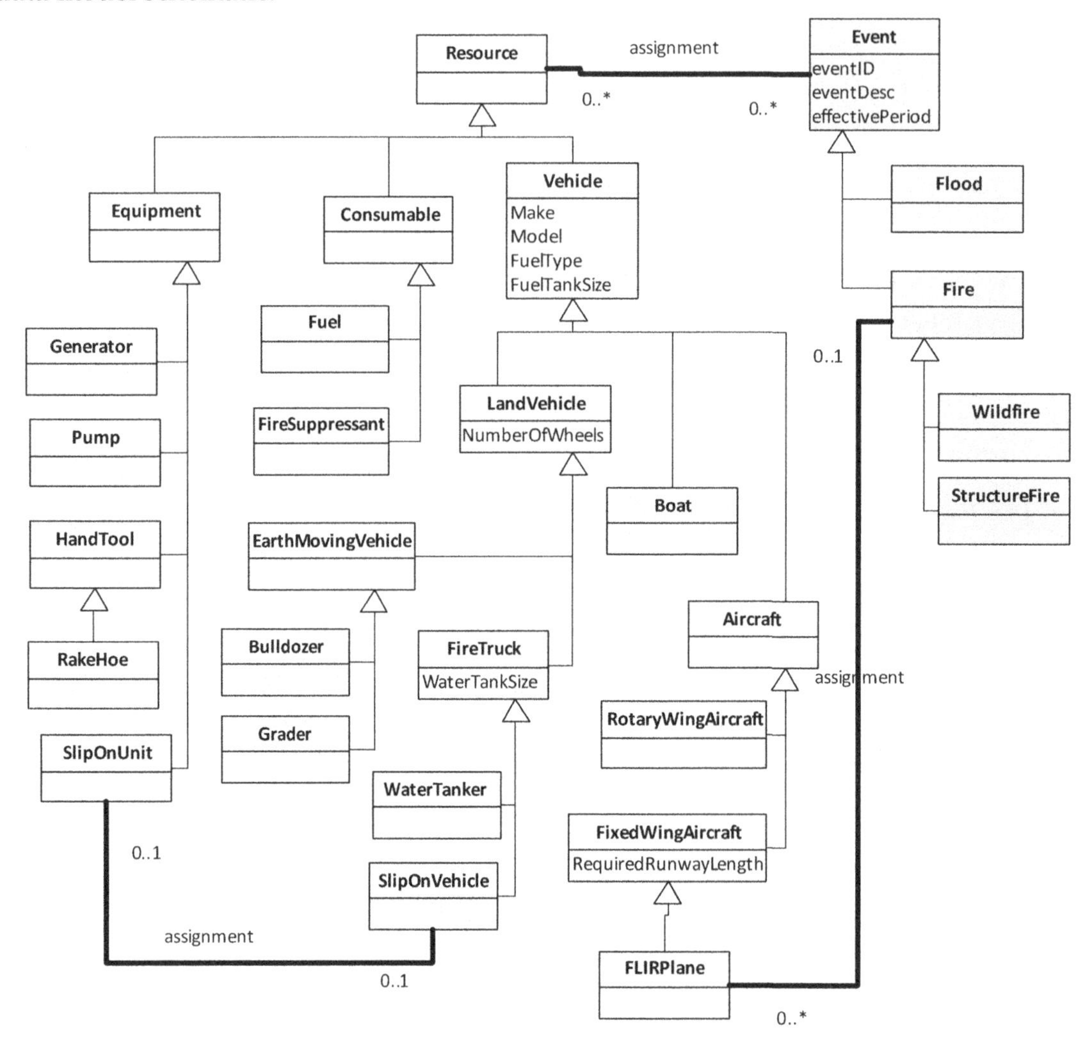

Figure 29: Resource and Event subtypes and relationships

At the bottom-left there is a very specific assignment relationship between a Slip On Unit (an assembly consisting of a relatively small water tank and a water pump) and a Slip On Vehicle (a cab-chassis tray Four-Wheel-Drive that is used during the year for general work, but during the fire season is paired with the Slip On Unit to create a light-weight fire truck). This relationship is between a pair of subtypes of the Resource superclass.

At the bottom right there is another very specific assignment relationship, this time between a FLIR Plane (a Forward Looking Infra-Red plane used to spot heat that is otherwise hidden from human sight by smoke) and a Fire. We don't look for heat in a Flood, and there's not much smoke to get in the way even if a flood caught on fire! This relationship is between a pair of subtypes across different superclasses. It is a specialization of the first, generalized relationship described.

One model, many views?

David Hay talks of three types of conceptual models – the Overview Models, the Semantic Models, and the Essential Models. But for a given enterprise, are the three model types just views of one underlying model, or do they require separate models?

A very good friend of mine, Rob Barnard, is of the opinion that we should aim for managing just one model where possible. That's the target. I believe he would argue that instead of having multiple separately maintained sets of enterprise models, why not have just one, albeit with different views. Similarly, if I was designing a Data Vault, I expect he would encourage me to try to have one model capturing all aspects, from logical through to the physical models.

Having less models, and therefore avoiding issues with keeping them aligned, seems an obvious goal, but is it possible? The answer is one of the favorite responses from a consultant – "It depends." I am not trying to avoid a direct response, but at least in part it can depend on the tooling at our disposal. I will share two quick examples.

At one of my client sites, I used a UML Class modeling tool. They wanted the three types of conceptual models David Hay encourages, and I was easily able to deliver all views via one tool, with one underlying model. I had one diagram providing the overall contextual view – the "Overview" model. It selectively presented the superclasses (supertype entities if we prefer), and the generalized relationships between them.

Then I had a series of views that reflected the scope of various diverse groups within the organization. Each group got to see "their" view of the world. Typically these views included carefully targeted subtypes and specific relationships. The subtypes didn't even need to declare what their supertypes were. I believe that these views at least in part reflected in what David Hay calls "Semantic" models.

Finally, I had a set of views of the one "Essential", consolidated model. It worked well, and it was just one model.

I did something similar at another client site, but they wanted the top-level overview model to be presented with lovely graphics that just weren't available in the modeling tool. Solution? Two model files, one using a graphics tool, and one using a serious modeling tool. Yes, it required manual synchronization, but seeing there were less than a dozen high-level concepts shared between one model's icons and another model's supertypes, and at that level there was massive stability, synchronization wasn't onerous.

Where can we find an enterprise data model?

Maybe you're saying, "OK, John. I'm hearing you. The folks at my place should base their Data Vault design on the model for our enterprise. But where do we look for one if it's not staring us in the face? And if we can't easily find such a beast, do we put everything on hold until one is delivered? Mightn't that take months or years?" Yes, it could take ages – if we do it the hard way – but that's not what I am proposing.

Commercially available industry models

One apparently obvious solution is just to fork out a wad of money and buy a so-called industry model. If that works for you, well done, but I do want to offer a caution. At a few sites where I have worked, industry models have been seen as unwieldy, complicated, abstract, and basically a poor fit for use, at least as a driver for a Data Vault design. In fact, sometimes the Data Vault team has been explicitly banned from using the industry model. If you've got an industry model, it's prudent to consider its usefulness, but please don't just assume it's going to suit without some modification.

Industry models by their very nature are pretty generalized, and for some purposes, that's a real strength. For Data Vault, not always.

Existing, home-grown models

Another option might be to see if your organization has already built its own enterprise model, tailored for their precise view of the world. Ideally, they might deliver what David Hay calls the "Essential" model – a single, consistent view. But I've come across too many organizations which have multiple, conflicting, inconsistent versions of what each claims to represent – the single, harmonized, consistent view. Spot the problem?

These home-grown enterprise models are built for a purpose (hopefully more than just because someone said we should have one). If we're half lucky, the model built for someone else may also suit our needs. Just check that the reason for the original construction wasn't part of ancient history, with the model never being maintained since. We want a model that reflects the current organization, and better, even takes into account likely future directions.

Is "agile evolution" an option?

There are some in the "agile" world who reject any idea of having architectural ideas forced upon them from outsiders. They want to be totally free to come up with any architecture they like. I do understand their point of view. Sometimes the lack of "head office" constraints can be a fertile ground for innovation. Over a few iterations, they may come up with a better architecture than those who do "big design up front" could ever imagine. That view has some merit.

Conversely, I take serious note of the messages in the book beautifully named "Balancing Agility and Discipline" by Boehm & Turner. I can't do justice to an entire book in a few words, but one of the messages is that the theory that:

"*... constant refactoring yields constant improvement* [is a] *fragile proposition* [and that sometimes] *architectural breakers ... cause breakage in the design beyond the ability of refactoring to handle.*"[13]

I got to know a great "agile" practitioner. He told the confronting story of one of his projects that kept slowing down. He would track the team's "velocity" (the metric to gauge progress), and one could expect and hope that as the team worked together more and more, the velocity would increase. But on this project, in each iteration things got worse.

The observation was that rather than minor refactoring of the underlying database, changes were more like a total rebuild, impacting the majority of the code that had already been delivered. He made a brave call. He approached the product owner, and requested one entire iteration be set aside to getting the data architecture sorted out. The aim was to have a bit of a look ahead, and see if they were able to sketch out a data model that could reasonably be expected to hold good for the longer term. They lost one iteration, but the actual, measured velocity after that one "lost" iteration increased 12-fold!

So what might that mean for a Data Vault project? Put simply, by assembling the business view at the outset, we are less likely to be doing costly rework. Instead of using the Data Vault project to iteratively generate the enterprise view, my suggestion is that we start with an enterprise view first that can then guide the Data Vault project.

---

[13] Boehm B. & Turner T. (2003) "*Balancing Agility and Discipline*", page 40.

Patterns to the rescue?

If we can't find a suitable existing enterprise data model, and if we agree that it's risky to try growing the enterprise model bottom-up almost as an incidental outcome of building a Data Vault, what options might we have left?

The first option I would encourage is to look at the pattern-based industry-specific models of David Hay and Len Silverston. These pattern-based models aren't "industry" models as we may expect. I see them as being more like a high-level framework to guide us. With a little shaping to suit the specifics of our organization, we just might find them to be the affordable kick-start we need.

In David's book, Enterprise Model Patterns,[14] he has a chapter for each of the following – criminal justice, microbiology, banking, oil field production and highway maintenance. Then we've got Len who has dedicated an entire book, the second volume of his 3-volume series, to models for specific industries, covering manufacturing, telecommunications, health care, insurance, financial services, professional services, travel and e-commerce.[15]

And if our organization isn't in the list, all is not lost. Firstly, Len notes that by grabbing bits and pieces of the models, we may be able to adapt appropriate components to our situation. And secondly, if that isn't going to work for us, don't despair. Their patterns are, as Len calls them, "universal". It is pleasantly surprising to discover how quickly we can use their patterns to assemble a "sufficient" framework to successfully drive our Data Vault project forward.

---

[14] Hay D. (2011) *"Enterprise Model Patterns: Describing the World"*.

[15] Silverston L. (2001) *"The Data Model Resource Book, Volume 2: A Library of Universal Data Models by Industry Types"*.

How to build a "sufficient" enterprise data model yourself

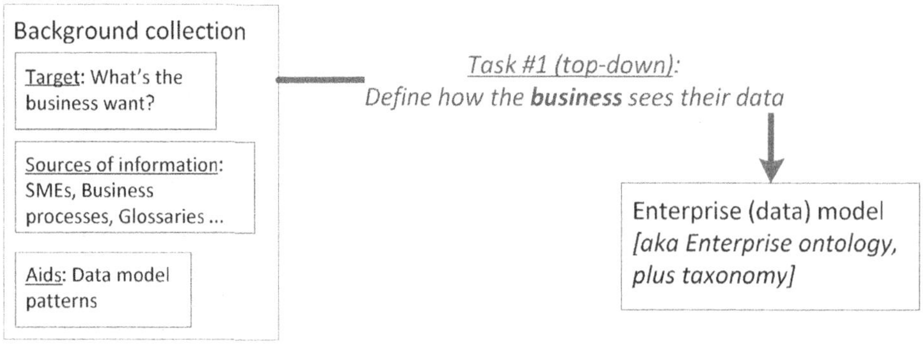

Background collection

Target: What's the business want?

Sources of information: SMEs, Business processes, Glossaries ...

Aids: Data model patterns

Task #1 (top-down):
*Define how the **business** sees their data*

Enterprise (data) model
[aka Enterprise ontology, plus taxonomy]

Figure 30: Building the "enterprise ontology"

Dan and others are clearly saying that it is an ill-advised strategy to race ahead and build a Data Vault that reflects source system thinking. Many may hear the call to start their Data Vault design based on an enterprise view. However, if they can't find an existing one, some may also fear that the building of one *before* they start their Data Vault project may introduce an unworkable delay.

I can empathize with such sentiments; I understand those who feel that their job is hard enough without introducing the requirement to align their Data Vault initiative with an enterprise data model, let alone first build one from scratch!

When the idea of "instant cakes, just add water" was first introduced, my mum gave a black-&-white set of two choices. I could either have good, or I could have fast. Good meant fresh eggs, fresh milk, and fresh butter. But good wasn't fast. Cake lovers had a binary "good *or* fast" choice. Now here's where we get some really good news. We can have "good" (in this context, a Data Vault designed on a solid enterprise view), and it can be surprisingly "fast", even if we have to build the enterprise data model from scratch. In the foreword to Len's second volume,[16] John Zachman says, "*By starting with an enterprise-wide universal model, you will save yourself one heck of a lot of work–that is, time and money–trying to create the model yourself. What's more, you're more likely to produce a*

[16] Silverston L. (2001) "*The Data Model Resource Book, Volume 2: A Library of Universal Data Models by Industry Types*", pages xiii to xiv.

higher quality model than if you started from scratch, since you can be assured that you won't overlook key components of the model."

There are a few caveats, though:

- John Zachman, while applauding Len's work, also suggests that "*Starting with a universal model does not absolve anyone of the responsibility of knowing his or her own enterprise intimately … Nor does it absolve anyone from the responsibility of learning how to build data models! What you have to do is start with the universal model and then, understanding data modeling and understanding your own enterprise, make the necessary modifications to make the universal model your own.*"

- Build for a purpose, not just because some data management guru said we should have one. Yes, these models can be used for many purposes, but have at least one use in mind! In the context of this book, designing a Data Vault is an excellent reason.

- Having identified our goal, we shouldn't feel we have to construct the entire enterprise model before we can start using it.

I am suggesting that a "sufficient" enterprise view can be assembled that is fast-&-good, but we may ask, "How fast?" If, as John Zachman noted, we understand the patterns, and if we have an understanding of the enterprise (or at least have access to people who do), we've got the foundation for constructing an excellent framework of the enterprise. My experience has shown that this can be accomplished in weeks, with the highest level assembled in just days. This book, including its supplementary material in patterns, shows how. And the approach works!

The heart of success is assembly of a team involving technical *and* non-technical people. In spite of what some may say about never presenting a data model to business people, if the engagement is done using light-weight data modeling concepts with a few pictures and a few gently introduced data model diagrams, business people "get it". After a 2-day workshop at one client site where I introduced business people to modeling concepts and got them to do some light-weight enterprise data modeling, I remember walking into a conversation in a kitchen where a very senior executive was sharing enthusiastically with a colleague about the enterprise data model *he'd* help develop the previous week. How's that for ownership from the business and the data folk!

The biggest benefit I've observed for these high-level conceptual schematics (in addition to ownership) is the way a common information model facilitates communication, between (1) business people from different siloes in the organization, and (2) between business people and data people. That's quite an outcome, and assuming the facilitator has read and absorbed the patterns from Hay and Silverston, all that can be achieved in a few weeks, if not days. Not a bad investment.

Step #0: Challenge anyone who says "Follow Step #1, Step #2 ..."!

I hope this first step has made you smile. It's taking a cheeky swipe at my own following suggestions. But behind the joke is a more serious message: Use the steps as an outline, but don't be rigid.

Sure, try a first pass through the steps, but don't be surprised if you don't hit perfection first time. Be comfortable iterating a few more times. I encourage "T-model" thinking, and I am not referring to the Ford motor company's famous early model. Rather, think of the letter "T". It's got width at the top, then it's narrow underneath. Start constructing your enterprise model as a mile-wide, inch-deep skeleton, then drill down to flesh out the detail, and apply it progressively. Build "sufficient" detail to keep momentum. And even on any one pass through, don't feel bad at returning a few steps. You picked the team (Step #1), and started defining the enterprise (Step#2), and with hindsight you want to change the team a little. That's OK.

Step #1: Pick the team

Here's a foundational message. Downstream, we want a Data Vault that delivers value to the business, and that reflects business thinking. So if the Data Vault is going to be business-centric, and if it's based on the view of the business that's been encapsulated in an enterprise data model, I suggest we'd be well advised to engage business people in shaping the enterprise model. Sure, we need the technical people too, but I'll be a little blunt here. If the attitude of the techos is that the business people should be grateful that they've been invited as passive observers who are there to be wowed by the geeky skills of the techo-nurds, something's wrong. Instead, the business people are front and center.

Now I'll perhaps surprise you with another suggestion. I was recently interacting with a dozen or so other "data" folk, and one asked me how I select the team. You might think we want a collection of people who share a common vision, but instead I told my friend that I often seek a widely divergent bunch of people. The main thing they have in common is passion and vision, not necessarily lock-step uniformity of opinion.

I don't care too much about job titles or seniority. If one of the team is a front-line worker who is seen by some as a trouble-maker for his open challenging of management decisions, and another is one of the management team he criticizes, that's OK. Surprised? Let me tell you a story.

The brother of one of my good friends formed a circle of five. If we're going to classify him, he was a Christian of the Protestant variety, and one of the other four was also a Christian, but was a Catholic Priest. In some situations, even that might be enough for a bit of tension.

Now add to the mix two more people with a "faith" – one Jewish Rabbi, and one a Muslim Imam. And to round it out, not just an atheist, but one of Australia's most vocal left-winger people. We've got one political party that's a bit left of center, but he was active in the Communist Party of Australia when it existed. The communists were more than a little left of the lefties!

And they were close friends, able to openly discuss widely divergent views, but to do so with respect for each other. As Jonathan Sacks, a Jewish Rabbi, puts it in the title of one of his books, it's all about "The Dignity of Difference".

Surely a little diversity within the teams you and I form to construct an enterprise data model can accommodate, and even encourage, differences? I think so, and I believe we are the richer for the experience, as long as the participants are guided to express their views with respect for others.

Be realistic. Sometimes this just isn't going to work – there's too much "history" to ignore - but let's at least consider forming a team with a variety of perspectives.

The bottom line I would like you to consider is forming a team with representation from the technology ranks, and the business ranks. And even within the technology group, it's OK to have some tensions sometimes between the "data" people and "process" people. Let's use this as an opportunity to lessen the gaps.

Once the team is nominated, there's one more task. I encourage all of the team members to prepare for the rest of the journey together by collecting and collating "Pain Points" from their corner of the enterprise. OK, not *all* pain points. If the cheap coffee tastes lousy, that's not something the data people are likely to be able to fix. But if there are pain points relating to data (integration challenges, quality, accessibility, or whatever), they are prime candidates for triggering discussion. Also I want to hear about "process" pain points, not just the "data" ones. Any data people reading this might be surprised how often some creative minds applied to solving "process" problems can identify ways we "data" people can assist.

Step #2: Define the "enterprise"

As addressed earlier, Dan suggests we start our Data Vault journey with an "enterprise ontology". We've already looked at what the "ontology" bit of his phrase might mean, but you might be surprised that I question the "enterprise" bit. Let me share a story.

A government department in my corner of the world is jokingly referred to as the Department of Changing Names. It can't seem to settle on a name that will stick. When I first did work for them, they were known as the Department of Natural Resources and Environment. In the setting of the story I am about to share, it was the Department of Sustainability and Environment. As I write this, it's currently the Department of Environment, Land, Water and Planning. And the word on the street is that in the next few weeks it's going to change again. I've got a theory that the name changes have a hidden agenda – to stimulate the local economy by keeping printers in business with new letterheads! (Just joking.)

Within the department, there was a group responsible for responding to the serious wildfires we get most years in our state parks and the like. Sure, this department is officially the lead agency for fires that start on government land, but it is heartening to see the massive response from others in the community. There's the police force and ambulance folk, the State Emergency Services team, and many more. I saw a list of 31 organizations that join in, and one of them in particular deserves mention. It's the Country Fire Authority, a volunteer-based organization with tens of thousands of members who risk their lives, and sometimes lose their lives, to protect the rest of us. In my opinion, the word "hero" can be overused and hence devalued, but firefighters are true heroes.

So here's the question. I was asked to assemble an enterprise model for this wildfire response scenario, but what's the scope of the "enterprise"? Was it the entire Department of Sustainability and Environment? Probably not – they were too big, too diverse (handling lots more than fires), and too changeable. I was being paid by the fire group within the department, so maybe the "enterprise" was just this focused group? That seemed a better answer. But the third option was the collection of enterprises that came together as needed to form a virtual, single emergency response "enterprise"? All 31 of them!

Another client of mine was a church-based organization with a massive social welfare arm. Were the church bits and the welfare bits separate "enterprises"? To their credit, when it came to money, they most certainly were. Anyone donating to their welfare work could rest assured that their donations simply would never fund church-related expenses. So some might say the welfare ministry was its own enterprise, but should the scope be stretched to include other welfare groups and government departments that worked cooperatively to assist the less fortunate members of our society?

I could share many more such stories, but the real point is to encourage you to question your colleagues. Someone may have told you that they want a Data Vault to integrate that data of the enterprise, but has anyone *consciously* challenged the boundaries of the so-called enterprise? It may be obvious, with everyone in agreement. If so, that's great. If not, please consider taking a moment to check expectations.

You might also choose to consider the possibility that the answer may change over time. For me in the wildfire emergency response situation, the initial enterprise model was for the department's fire group. A later iteration was for a larger group of fire-related organizations. And the last iteration was for the collective of "emergency response" organizations involved in not just fires, but other natural (and man-made) emergencies.

For you, the scope of the "enterprise" changing over time may not necessarily really be a problem. However, I do suggest that not knowing your scope expectations at any given point in time may be a problem. Worth checking?

Step #3: Get a feel for the enterprise

I'm often called in to help organizations that, before the engagement, I know very little about other than what I might find on the Internet. I recall being asked to assemble an enterprise data model for a sizable bank. They wanted an overall model as a framework, with drill down into details on a thing called "securitization".

There were two challenges.

First, there's a reason my wife looks after the accounts – I am pretty careful with money, but keeping records is simply not an area I have an interest in, nor would I go close to claiming a good understanding of the world of accounts. I empathize with a country bloke I knew years ago. He had been told by his accountant about there being two sides to the ledger. His response? "Listen, mate. I've got cattle, and if they're on my side of the fence, they're mine, and if their on the other side, they're not. That's what I know. I don't get this thing about two sides to the ledger."

The next problem for me was that I had never heard of "securitization". Not only had I never heard of it, I wasn't even sure how to spell it. In my line of work, I have to learn fast. But for constructing an enterprise data model, it's not just the lead consultant who has to get an understanding of the organization. The whole team, especially any IT members who may be a bit insulated, have to come up to speed.

But how do we gather the required perspective?

There's the low-hanging fruit. Company organization charts, statements of vision, marketing brochures, websites, and more. Gather what we can, and act like a sponge. Ask questions. Talk to people.

... and "ride the truck". What do I mean by that? Get out of the office and watch how the front-line workers operate. It's great to gather head knowledge second-hand, but first hand observation can be very informative.

I remember one time when I was at a telco. My colleague, Bill, told me to wear old clothes to work the next day. He wanted us to "ride the truck". We'd heard how telephone exchanges work, but he'd arranged for us to go and literally crawl around amongst the wires and cables. What Bill and I found by front-line observation, there and at other places, was invaluable.

Having encouraged you to get close to the action, I will confess I don't always go all of the way. I recently started working with forensic people who deal with autopsies of the deceased. I am sure you'd understand why I choose to draw a line at getting up too close to the front-line workers!

Then there's learning from the "process" people. Sadly, there are some who can't see how "process" people and "data" people can get along. Sure, we may have a different perspective and focus, but I really encourage data practitioners (including myself!) to be open to learning from those who have studied, mapped, and documented business processes. As Dan Linstedt explains, there can be a gap between how the business *thinks* its processes work, and the reality. Down the track, after we've built a Data Vault, it can shed some light on these gaps. But for now, let's absorb the theory of how things should work, supplemented by "riding the truck" and seeing the processes in action.

Another tack to get an idea where to focus our learning is to explicitly ask participants to collect what I call "pain points". I ask them, "Where are things broken right now, and if you had the money, resources and backing, what would the replacement future look like?"

I don't get stressed if the information I am gathering is sometimes inconsistent. For example, I have recently heard people from the same organization say:

1. We want a work flow management system that directs workers what to do next. If they don't have to think about the overall set of tasks and tomorrow's problems, they can put their energy and focus into doing the current task.

2. We don't want a work flow management system that tells us what to do next. We've got experienced, creative individuals. They know what to do, so let them work out the order they want to do things in.

Do I have a problem here? Not really. I call it creative tension. My friend, Roelant Vos, likewise refers to "embracing the ambiguity". The divergent views are a reality. Let's not hide them, because if we suppress one group of workers, there's a really good chance the underlying issues will fester rather than going away. I remember a time when I had identified 27 topics where there was clear disagreement. A well intentioned employee had organized a series of one-on-one interviews over a number of days. The opinions simply didn't stack up to create a nice, enterprise-wide, holistic view.

At the end of these formal fact gathering meetings, I asked if I could have all of the stakeholders in a room at the same time. One by one, I asked my 27 questions. At the end, one burly engineer came up to me and said he'd worked for the company for years, and didn't even realize some people saw things differently from the way he viewed the world. All parted with a new respect and appreciation for the larger team of which they were part, and always had been, though they didn't know it!

Finally, as I go through these exercises, I informally map what I am hearing to the data model patterns in my kit-bag. I can do that on the fly because I have already encountered so many of these patterns again and again. But for you, now might be a good time to get at least a high-level understanding of patterns.

Step #4: Facilitator learns the pattern basics

If we're going to build an enterprise data model using patterns, as John Zachman noted, we'd better learn about them!

Introducing data model patterns

There's plenty of praise for what data model patterns can do for us. Richard Barker, in his foreword to David Hay's first data model patterns book,[17] says "*... using simpler and more generic models, we will find they stand the test of time better, are cheaper to implement and maintain, and often cater to changes in the business not known about initially.*"

---

[17] Hay D. (1996) "*Data Model Patterns: Conventions of Thought*".

Then there's Martin Fowler in *Analysis Patterns*[18] who states, "*People often react to a simple model by saying 'Oh yes, that's obvious' and thinking 'So why did it take so long to come up with it?' But simple models are always worth the effort. Not only do they make things easier to build, but more importantly they make them easier to maintain and extend in the future. That's why it's worth replacing software that works with simpler software that also works.*"

Finally, I end with a quote from *Design Patterns*[19] that I feel carries the message that top-down modeling delivers greater flexibility for the future than the strict disciplines of bottom-up modeling of today's perceived realities. The authors proclaim that "*Strict modeling of the real world leads to a system that reflects today's realities but not necessarily tomorrow's. The abstractions that emerge during design are key to making a design flexible.*"

Ah, does this quotation ring warning bells for you? There is mention of "abstractions", and for some, this sounds potentially problematic. To put you at rest, I will mention again the books by David Hay,[20] and by Len Silverston and Paul Agnew[21] that skillfully demonstrate how one pattern can be presented in a number of ways, ranging from abstract/generalized through to more concrete/specialized. The sample provided below is at the more generalized / abstract level, but other more targeted levels exist for the exact same published patterns.

Could I see an example, please?

So what does one of these "pattern" things look like? In "Figure 28: Subtype drill-down for health practitioner regulation scenario", I briefly touched on one pattern, the Party pattern. It is one of the best known patterns. Some love it, and others not so much, but it's a good way to get an idea of what a pattern might look like. We will build up parts of the pattern, piece by piece. This introduction goes for several pages, but I'd

---

[18] Fowler M. (1997) "*Analysis Patterns: Reusable Object Models*", pages 2-3.

[19] Gamma E., Helm R., Johnson R. & Vlissides J. (1995) "Design Patterns: Elements of Reusable Object-Oriented Software", page11.

[20] Hay D. (2011) "*Enterprise Model Patterns: Describing the World*".

[21] Silverston L. & Agnew P. (2009) "*The Data Model Resource Book, Volume 3: Universal Patterns for Data Modeling*".

encourage you to make the investment. It's a great pattern for starting conversations with the business folk.

As an example of using this pattern, when people sell their home to others, the solicitors may talk of the "parties" involved in the transaction. The sellers (vendors) and buyers (purchasers) can be one or several individual people, or they can be "organizations" (limited liability companies, trusts, partnerships, and so on).

At its most basic, "Party" is a collective term for individual people and organizations. In data modeling terms, Party is the supertype, and Person and Organization are subtypes. Using the UML notation, the arrows point from the subtypes (the UML calls them subclasses) of person and organization, to the supertype (superclass) of Party.

One subtype attribute is noted for Person (gender). It is just an example, demonstrating that the subtype attribute applies to Person only, and not to the subtype Organization.

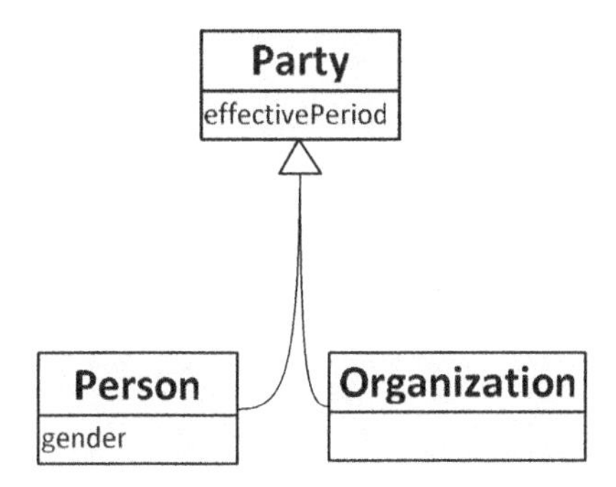

Figure 31: Party pattern core

The Party supertype has an attribute called effective period. Note:

- In the object-oriented world shown here using the UML, the data type of an attribute can be a user-defined extension to the base data types. For example, the data type of a "period" can be a pair of dates, such as the 'from' date and the 'to' date.

- This attribute on the supertype applies to all subtypes. For example, the start of the effective period for a Person might be their date of birth, and the start of the effective period for an Organization might be their date of incorporation.

The model below introduces a simple reference table to classify Parties. Most if not all of the types will relate to classification of Organizations rather than Persons. Types of Organization classifications may include government versus private, local versus overseas, or perhaps the type of industry (manufacturing, retail, hospitality, and so on) with their own hierarchy of subtypes. It's up to you and your needs.

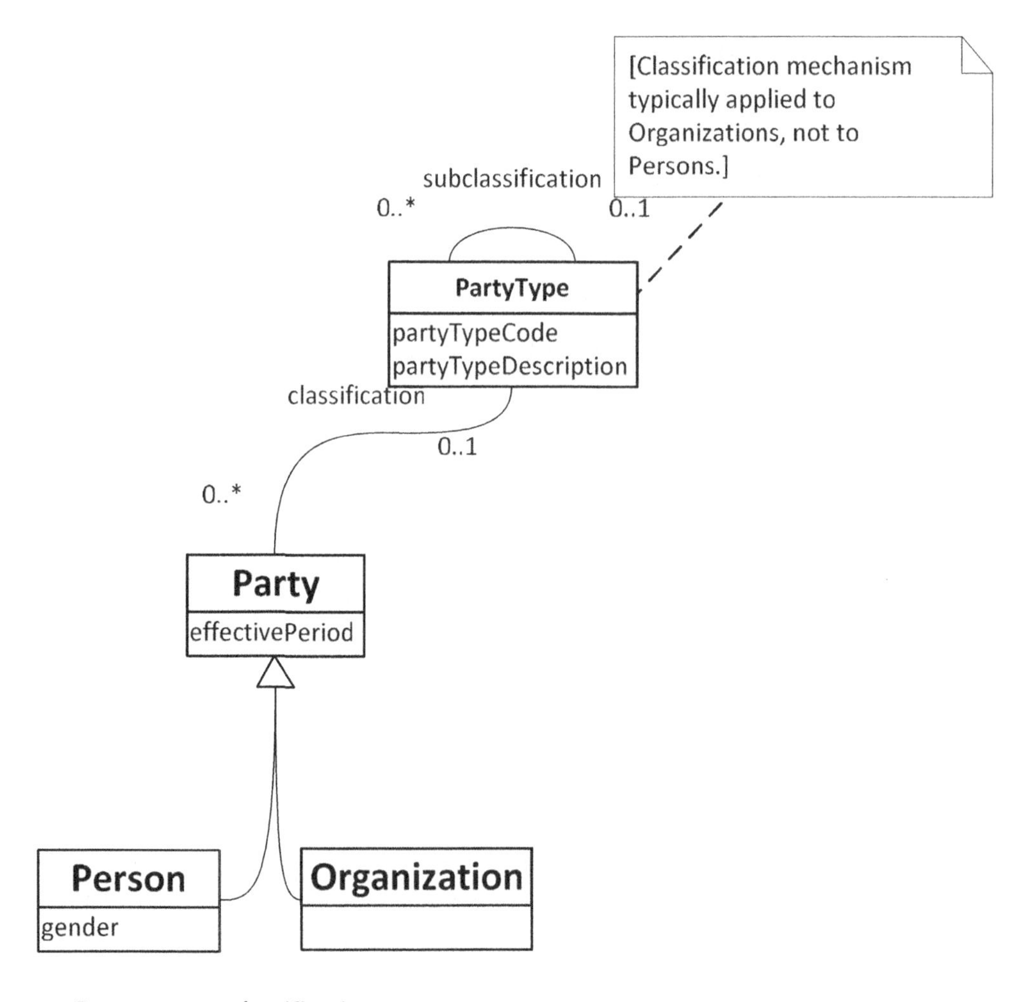

Figure 32: Party pattern classification

This first model is fine as an introduction, but it is insufficient. For example, it does not provide the expected structures for party names and addresses. Richer models follow.

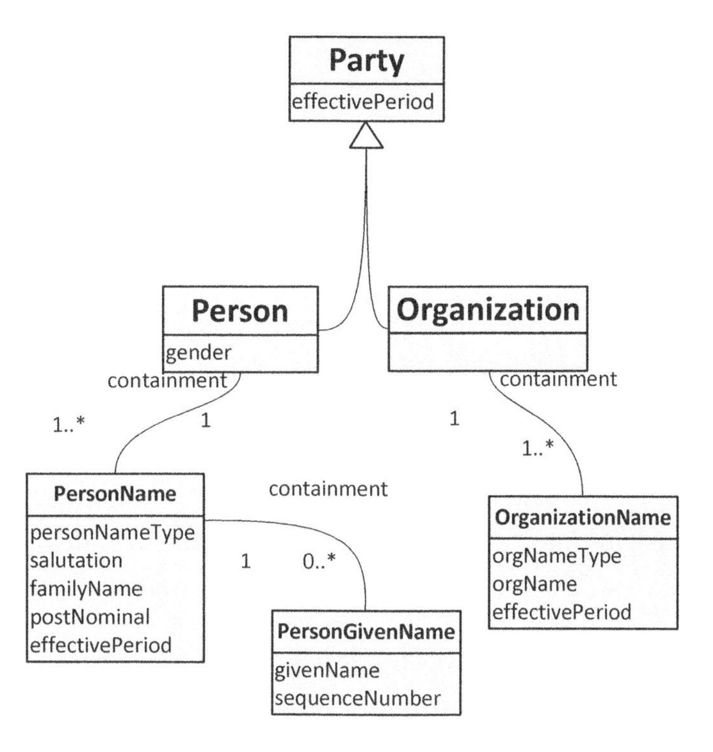

Figure 33: Party pattern names

A Party may have several names. For example, an Organization may have a registered name and a trading name, and a Person may have their birth name, a preferred name, and if they are an author, they may have a pen name, and so on.

This model accommodates each party having several names of different types, and for recording the period they during which they were effective.

An Organization Name is pretty straightforward, reflected here as a simple attribute. Person Names are a little more complicated, possibly including:

- Salutation, for example "Mr.", "Ms.", "Sir". This attribute can include concatenation of multiple salutations such as "Prof. Sir".
- Family Name (also known as Surname).
- Multiple Given Names (shown on the diagram via a separate Person Given Name class).

- Post Nominal, for example "FRACS" for Fellow of the Royal Australasian College of Surgeons. Like with Salutation, this attribute can include concatenation of multiple post nominal assignments.

This model's structure for person names can be seen as reflecting "western" thinking. Not all names across all cultures neatly fit such a model. For example, I encountered a scenario where names of a people group in northern Africa reflected a much richer construct. The "full name" formally included the job title, perhaps a bit like early English people had surnames such as Cook, Baker, Tailor, and Farmer. In this particular culture, the name also included such declarations as the name of the individual's father and grandfather, and sons and grandsons if applicable – a paternalistic view. It also added the form of Islam followed by the individual, and a statement as to whether the pilgrimage to Mecca had been performed or not. And on and on.

The conclusion? An Australian / western standard may not work for you! Use it if it fits, but adapt and extend it to meet your needs.

You thought names were complicated? Addresses can be much worse. Sorry.

Just like Parties can have multiple names, they can have multiple addresses. For example, an Organization can have its physical business address plus a postal address. A Person can have their home address, their work address, one or several email addresses, and one or several mobile phones (in this model, a phone number is a subtype of address, along with email address and other subtypes).

Not only can each Party have multiple addresses, but each Address can be shared by many parties. The address "1 Main Street" may be the home address for two or more people.

Now here's a point that needs to be considered. I have worked for several organizations where a physical street address is an entity in its own right. That's true for our state's land titles register. It's also true of water utilities that record addresses where water meters are installed even if the property has nobody living there. Each address has its own identifier, and can be created without any need to be associated with its residents or owners. It is its own primary thing.

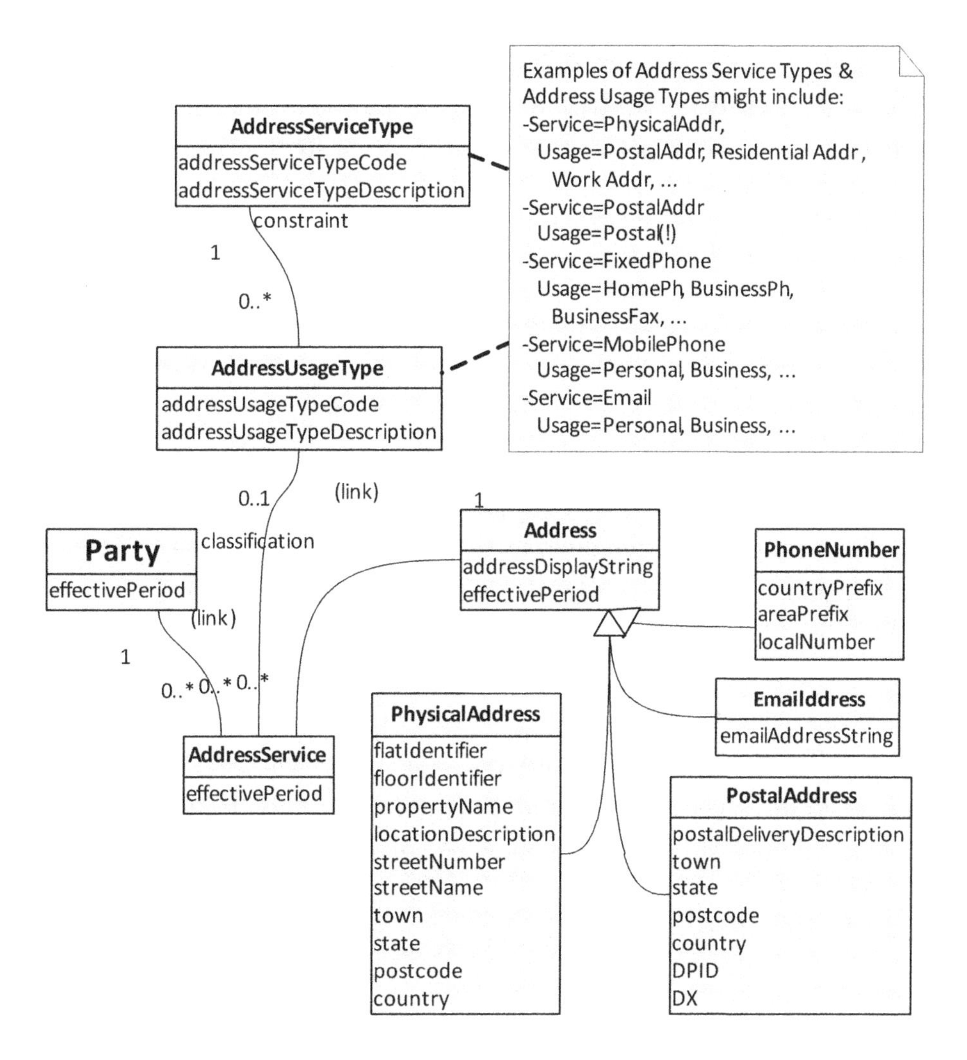

Figure 34: Party pattern addresses

Conversely, I have consulted to organizations where addresses are just attributes in a customer record or an employee record. If two employees (or customers) live at the same address, the text string is simply replicated in each employee (or customer) record. There is no desire to match addresses. In such cases, the Party model shown above is unnecessarily complicated and can be pruned back, moving the address details directly under Party, or maybe to the relevant subtypes of the Party Role pattern including Employee and Customer. But just in case we want to use some of the richness of this model, let's look a bit deeper.

- The Address class is a generic superclass, representing physical addresses, postal addresses, email addresses, and yes, phone numbers! In this pattern, any point of contact with a person or organization is an "address". This is extensible – if we want to add Twitter or Facebook addresses, they're just another form of contact.

- The Address Service is a many-to-many resolution entity between Parties and their Addresses. The usage by one party of one Address is typed – perhaps Alex, who works from home, uses 1 Main Street as both a residential address and a work address. The model presents two reference entities. The Address Service Type approximates the subtyping structure of the Address class (though potentially with finer grain such as distinguishing between a fixed phone and a mobile phone), and the Address Usage Type classifies the way the address is used by the related Party (for home use, for business use, as a fax ...).

- As noted, I have refined this pattern to in part reflect an Australian standard. For you, "Postcode" may be known as Zip Code, the "DPID" is the Australian "Deliver Point Identifier" for addresses, and "DX" is the Document eXchange number. Apologies for any confusion caused for my international friends.

Now let's look at identifiers for a Party.

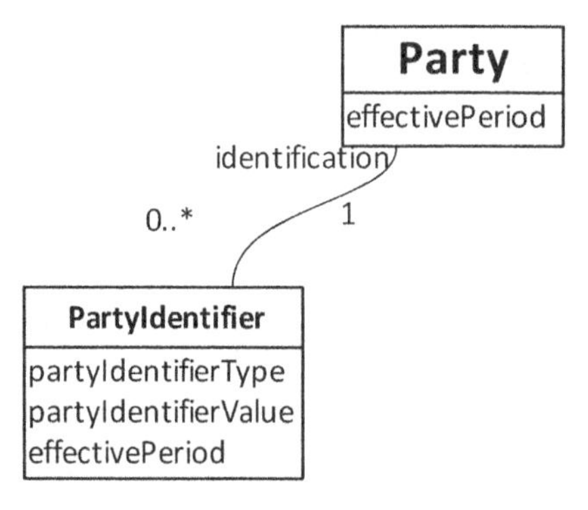

Figure 35: Party pattern identifiers

In Australia, two of the common identifiers for a company are an Australian Company Number (ACN), and a Tax File Number (TFN). The candidate identifiers for people are even more diverse – Tax File Numbers again, but also passport numbers, drivers' license numbers, plus role-based identifiers such as employee numbers or customer numbers.

Now here's where the model may surprise you, especially if you have a relational modeling background. As traditional data modelers, we're used to scenarios where the initial design for an entity might start with multiple *candidate* identifiers. We subsequently pick one as the primary key (assuming we don't use surrogates). However, the model above simply records that a Party can have multiple identifiers, and doesn't go out of its way to nominate the "primary" identifier. If we're assembling a big-picture view of the data to drive conversations amongst non-technical people at the enterprise level, and if we're not even sure how it's going to be implemented (maybe as an operational system in a relational database, maybe as a Data Vault, or ...), that really shouldn't be a problem for a conceptual/logical model. Of course, the physical implementation can vary from the platform independent view. That's fine.

So far, the Party pattern looks a little bit like the address book in our phone or computer. I wish my "smart" phone also included the ability to record rich interrelationships between address book entries.

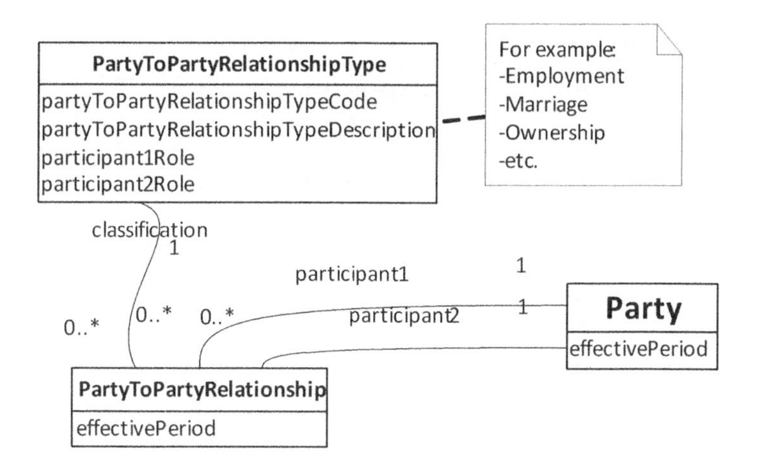

Figure 36: Party pattern inter-relationships

We can have Organization-to-Organization relationships such as one company owning another (the Participant 1 Role in the Party To Party Relationships Type class might be "Holding Company", and Participant 2 Role might be "Subsidiary"). We can have Organization-to-Person relationships such as an organization employing an individual.

And we can have Person-to-Person relationships. Two people can marry (well, at least in Australia, marriage involves only two people – polygamy is illegal here). The model above accommodates all of these, and more.

The preceding Party model holds data for a Party (an Organization or a Person) such as their name and address details. These Parties can also play one or several roles. For example, an individual named Alex might be an employee of Acme, but might also be a customer of Acme, and we might want to record the multiple roles played by Alex.

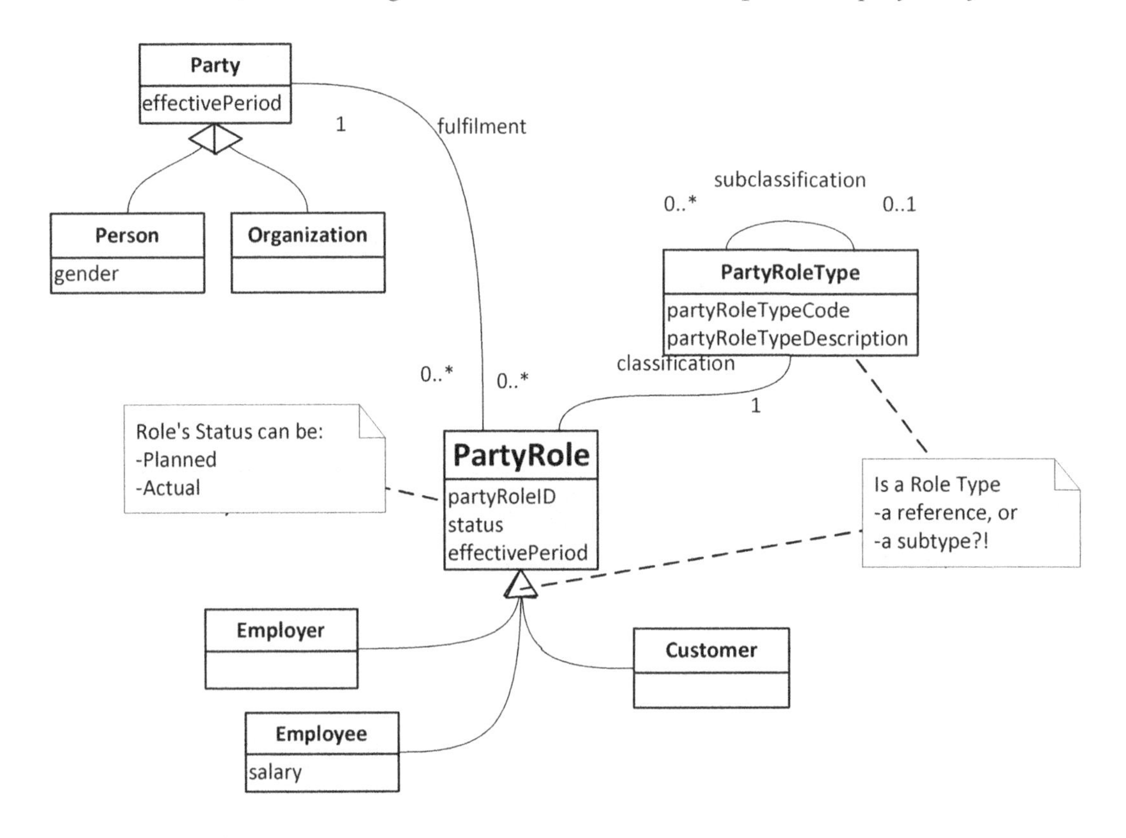

Figure 37: Party Role pattern

The Party / Party Role pattern is described in many information modeling "patterns" books – Hay's *"Data Model Patterns"*,[22] Silverston & Agnew's *"The Data Model Resource Book, Volume 3"*,[23] and Fowler's *"Analysis Patterns"*[24] to mention just a few. The core

---

22 Hay D. (1996) *"Data Model Patterns: Conventions of Thought"*.

23 Silverston L. & Agnew P. (2009) *"The Data Model Resource Book, Volume 3: Universal Patterns for Data Modeling"*.

concept is to separate a Party from its Party Role(s), and to allow specialization of the data structure of the Party Role class. For example, employees have a salary, but that attribute is not applicable to customers.

There's one interesting twist to the Party Role scenario. Len Silverston's book differentiates between "declarative" roles and "contextual" roles. Someone declares Alex to be an employee, or a customer, or whatever. They are "declarative" roles, and the above pattern caters for this.

However, some roles are more transient. If we think back to the scenario presented at the start of this introduction to the Party pattern, we spoke of the types of roles played by Parties involved in a transfer of land transaction. These included the vendor, the purchaser, real estate agents, lenders, and so on.

Perhaps roles such as real estate agent and lender are "declarative" roles – the signs outside their offices "declare" them to be a real estate agent or a bank. But perhaps the roles of vendor and purchaser are transactional roles, in the context of the sale. These can be handled by a simple classification attribute on an appropriate resolution entity, for example, the Contextual Role Type attribute on the Agreement Participation class as shown later in "Figure 115: Agreements pattern and associated Parties".

A palette of patterns

We've just looked at the Party (and Party Role) pattern. It's just one of the more common patterns that gets talked about. The diagram below portrays the suite of "9 pillars" I often use.

---

[24] Fowler M. (1997) "*Analysis Patterns: Reusable Object Models*".

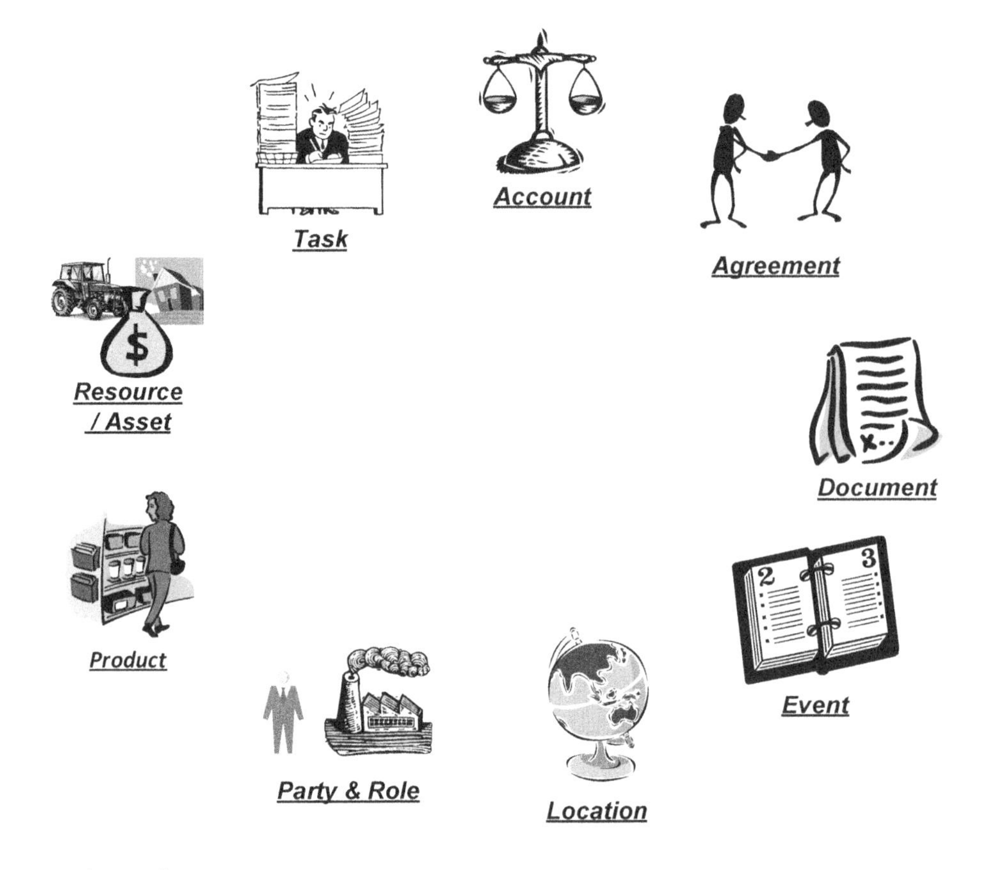

Figure 38: Palette of patterns

The Party / Party Role pattern has already been described in some detail, but here's a summary of the set of patterns.

Account	A simplified representation of records for financial accounting for bank accounts, creditor / debtor accounts …
Agreement	A formal or informal arrangement between parties such as a binding mortgage contract with a financial institute. Formal agreements such as contracts typically *also* involve the Document pattern to provide documentary evidence of the agreement – see the 'Document' pattern below.
Document	Either a hard copy document, or a soft copy (electronic) document. Examples may include a hard copy of a purchase-of-land contract, a scanned image of a loan guarantee agreement, or a smart phone image or video.

Event	A noteworthy event such as an accident at work or the outbreak of a fire.
Location	A geospatial location as it appears on a map such as the point at which a fire started, a line representing the current fire front, or an area that has been burnt by a fire.
Party & Party Role	A party (a person or an organization). These parties may fulfil declarative roles - for example, in the sale & purchase of a house, types of declarative roles might include banks, solicitors, real estate agents, and more.
Product	A goods and/or services item offered for purchase.
Resource	An asset such as company car, a computer, or a building.
Task	A planned or actual item of work such as the work involved in fighting a fire.

Table 1: 9-Pillar descriptions

That's a very brief introduction to common patterns. A more detailed description of the patterns (other than Party, which has already been described above) is in the Appendix.

No pattern is an island

There is a phrase "no man is an island". Well, patterns don't reach their full potential in isolation either. They need to achieve a value-add by having inter-relationships.

Earlier we looked at some real-world examples of organizations stitching the patterns together to represent a pictorial view of their data. In Figure 26 we looked at a land titles office responsible for recording things like sales of land or registration of mortgages. In Figure 27 we looked at a totally different organization, this time a government agency responsible for oversight of health practitioners across an entire nation. And below, we take another organization, this time a centralized register of exploration and extraction of mineral licenses.

At first glance, it looks a little like the schematic for the land transaction scenario in Figure 26.

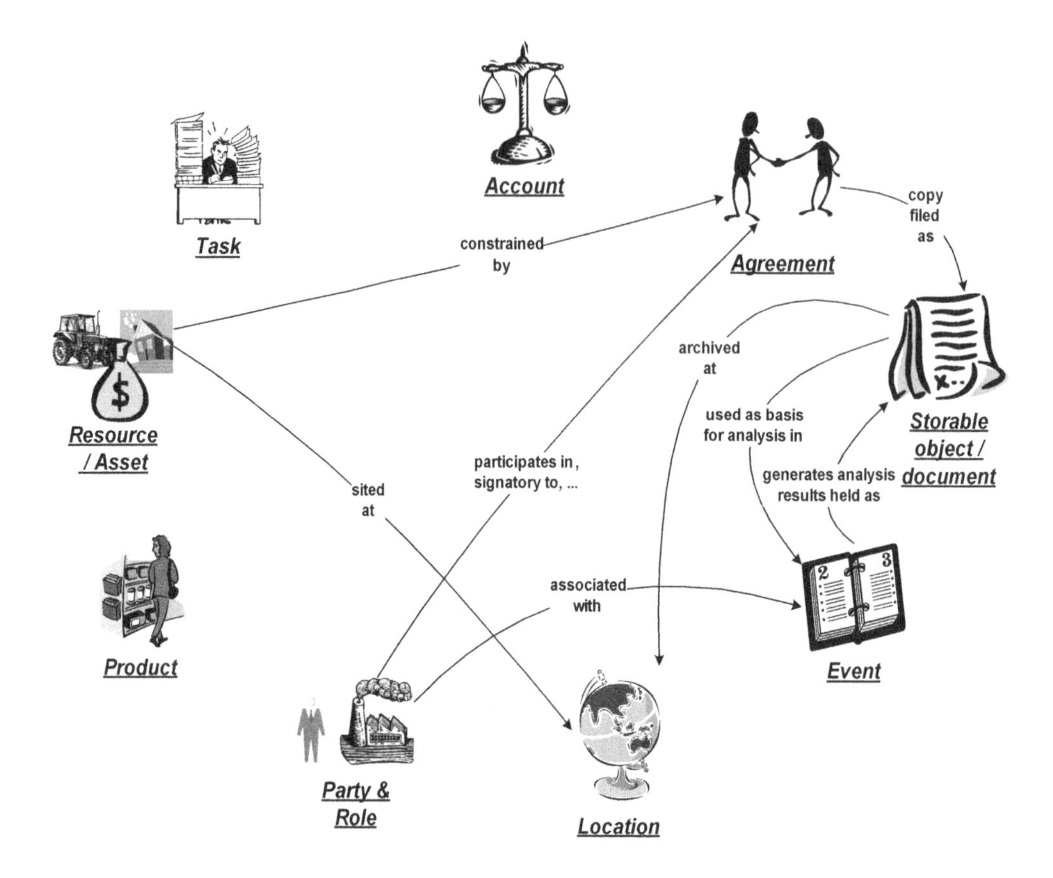

Figure 39: Schematic for the mineral resources scenario

They both have parties, but the roles for the land transaction involve roles such as the sellers, the buyers, their solicitors, involved real estate agents, banks and so on, whereas the roles for the mineral resources scenario involve roles for exploration and mining companies, the owners of the land, the government and more.

They both have agreements. The first scenario has mortgages, caveats, easements, and loans. The second scenario has exploration licenses and extraction licenses.

They both have resources, be it money and land in the first case and gold and oil in the second.

Not only are their similarities between the chosen patterns (Party, Agreement …), but there are some similarities between associations. Both have parties acting as signatories to agreements, and both have constraints on the use of resources defined in related agreements. Yes, there are differences, but there are also similarities.

Over the development of many such high-level frameworks, a few relationships begin to reappear. The following diagram captures some of the most common reusable relationships.

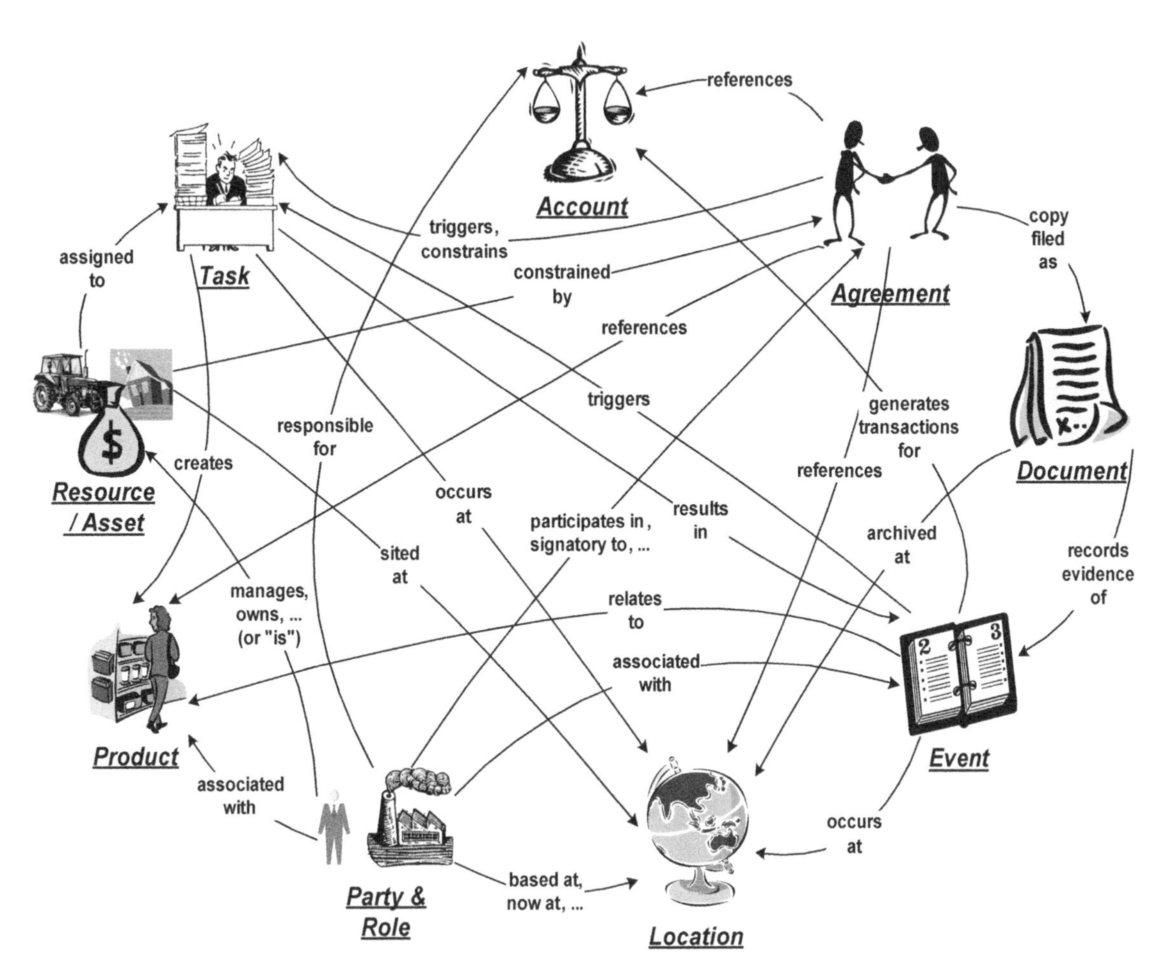

Figure 40: A pattern of patterns

There's a point to these comparisons. The same components get used again and again, though in different ways and different configurations. I see an analogy with a car. I've got a simple 2-wheel drive vehicle with one differential and one gearbox. I also used to own a 4-wheel-drive with two differentials, one for the front axle and the rear axle. And I currently own a 4-wheel-drive with three differentials, one at the front, one at the back, and one in the middle.

The role of a differential is the same in all cases. A single drive shaft comes in, and two drive shafts come out that can turn at slightly different speeds. It's just the way the differentials are placed in a vehicle that changes.

In a similar way, the land titles office and the centralized register of exploration and extraction of mineral licenses use a number of common components, and it won't surprise me if your organization might reuse some of these patterns and their interrelationships, though in a way that's unique to you.

Sharing the understanding

I've introduced data model patterns to you, and thanks for hanging in there with me. But if you're using the list of Steps as a guide to developing your own enterprise data model, please make sure the whole team (the business folk and the technical team members) all have a level of comfort with the ideas behind these patterns. I suggest you go through the material above, and gently introduce the ideas behind the patterns in the Appendix.

Step #5: Assemble a lightweight Enterprise Framework (in days)

We've seen some examples of what I call an enterprise model framework, to be used as a basis for our Data Vault. In its initial, formative stage, it can be as simple as a one-page diagram with icons for each pattern, labeled relationships between them, and supplementary notes on subtypes for involved patterns. Examples (though not showing the supplementary subtypes) have been presented earlier in Figure 26, Figure 27, and Figure 39.

So how do we go about getting the business people, and the technical people, to join together to produce one of these things?

A number of times, I have run two-day workshops. On the first day, I take the participants through a pre-packaged set of material and exercises, set in the scene of emergency response to wildfires. They get hands-on familiarity with the patterns, in a setting that deliberately takes them outside of their own organization so that they can get a perspective that's not cluttered by their own issues. Then on the second day, they revisit the patterns, this time applying them to their home turf.

Alternatively, I just jump straight into their world, introducing the patterns as we go.

Let's look at how this can work. I'm taking the essence from my one-day course on wildfire emergency response, and pretending that we're doing it for real with your home state's emergency services folk, as if we're looking over the shoulders of their workshop participants. This way you can get a feel for how you might run a similar session in your organization.

Preparation

I've picked the team (Step #1).

I've defined the "enterprise" (Step #2) as being the emergency response's own organization, plus the associated agencies that come together during a wildfire emergency.

I, and maybe a number of the team, have done some background research and looked at how the frontline workers do their job (Step #3). For some of the jobs I've done, I actually don't want to get *too* close to the action. I remember one time a fire team member took a carload of us IT people out into the country to meet the workers at a rural control center. During the trip, I pointed out a thin sliver of smoke rising from a nearby hill. The driver immediately swung into his professional role, radioed the control center, and sped to the location. Quite an impressive demonstration of emergency response in action, especially as it was anything but planned. But I was glad that it wasn't a full emergency.

And finally, the nominated workshop facilitator (me, in this case) made sure that they'd got a comfortable grasp of the foundational data model patterns (Step#4).

Now it's time to prepare for the actual workshop. The sorts of things I try to consider include:

- Checking availability of the participants on the proposed days, and booking a room with a projector and screen for showing the patterns, sample enterprise schematics, and the like.
- Acquiring a whiteboard for the facilitator plus another couple of whiteboards for workshop exercises.
- Photocopying the palette of patterns (please use a cropped and enlarged copy of Figure 38) and the pattern of patterns (from Figure 40). I'll tell you more about how these get used as we continue to work through this section.

Meet and greet

Like any workshop, there's always the kick-off bits such as pointing out the locations of kitchens, toilets, and safety exists. Importantly, it's now time for the participants to describe their role, and the particular perspective they bring to the table, including gripes about how things are today, and dreams of how they might be tomorrow.

Introduction to patterns

Perhaps half of the group doesn't have an IT background, and the idea of data models might sound frightening. And some of the other half (the IT professionals) might be comfortable with data models, but not have had much exposure to data model patterns.

I like to drill down into one pattern, usually starting with the Party / Party Role pattern as described earlier in "Could I see an example, please?" That gives an introduction to what a "pattern" looks like. For the Party / Party Role pattern, I liken it to an extension of the address book they've got in their phone – people and organizations, their names, addresses and contact details for phone numbers, and email addresses. Sure, the pattern offers some additional features, most notably the ability to record interrelationships, but that's not too hard to explain.

Already we've got comfort with one pattern.

Now I typically drill down into two more patterns, the Agreement pattern and the Document pattern. Both are relatively straightforward, and just as importantly, the Agreement patterns ties to the Party / Party Role pattern, and the Document pattern ties to the Agreement pattern.

The description of the Agreement pattern can be found in the section of the Appendix titled "Pattern: Agreement". "Figure 115: Agreements pattern and associated Parties" shows how the Party / Party Role pattern often Links to the Agreement pattern. Likewise, the section of the Appendix titled "Pattern: Document" describes the Document pattern and how it typically fits into the emerging landscape.

Now it's time to hand out the copies of the "Palette of Patterns" (see Figure 38, also repeated, for convenience, in Figure 41 below), and talk through the broad concepts of each of the remaining icons – it might be helpful to take a moment and refer back to Table 1 to see how I describe each of the nine foundational patterns.

To round out the introduction to patterns, I like to introduce how the patterns can join together in real-life situations. I present and explain a few enterprise data model schematics. The samples in Figure 26 and Figure 27, including the explanatory text, are great conversation starters.

Now they've drilled down into a few patterns, have been introduced to the larger palette, and seen some samples of enterprise schematics.

It's time to let them loose to have some fun and apply what they've learned.

Starting the model

I like to break the workshop participants up into at least a few groups so that we can get some differing views. Please note that each group is to be made up of some business people, and some IT people. Too often there is an unhelpful divide between the business folk and the IT folk. Both views are important, and we all need to hear conversations from the other side.

In the earlier section titled "Terminology", I mentioned that David Hay talks of three types of conceptual models. At the top of the stack is an Overview model that facilitates conversation between business people and IT. That's why I recommend the groups include technical and non-technical people – to get the conversation going. An overview is where we start, using patterns to represent the important objects in the enterprise.

Next David has multiple Semantic models, each representing the diverse views of different parts of the enterprise. That's why I suggest we break the workshop participants into groups, to actually encourage formation of different perspectives.

Finally David has one Essential model that brings the divergent views together. That's where we will end, grappling with consolidation of potentially conflicting views.

Everyone now gets a printed copy of the "Palette of patterns" for their own reference, plus an extra copy for each group to write on. You saw it earlier in Figure 38, but it is repeated below for your convenience.

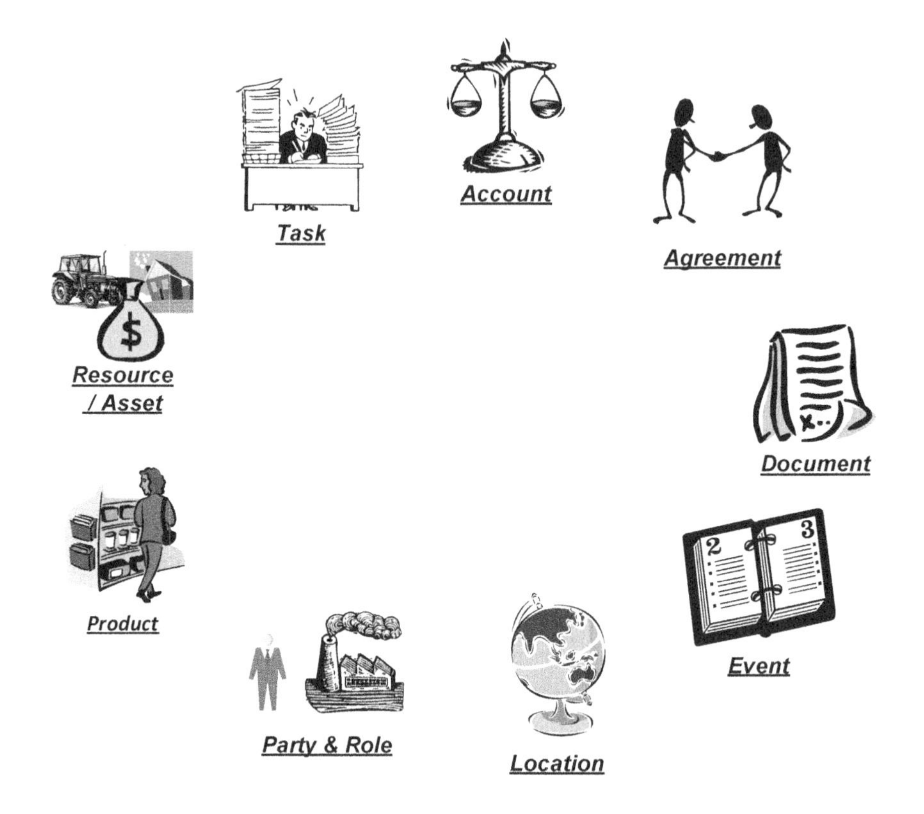

Figure 41: Palette of patterns

What happens now is really straightforward. I typically start with the Party / Party Role pattern. Its implementation, and the pattern details, might have some underlying complexity, but everyone can understand an address book of parties (people and organizations), and the types of roles some of them may play. I ask them to simply start writing some of the important roles beside the Party icon. For the fires scenario, the first cut might look something like this:

Figure 42: Fire Party and Roles

For this government organization, some of the full-time employees have what I call their "day job", but during the fire season, they are on call for fire duties.

In my home state, we've also got a community organization called the Country Fire Authority (CFA), with tens of thousands of volunteers. These people are highly respected by everyone.

Then we've got the front-line fire fighters, out there squirting water, and the back-room incident management team (incident controllers, logistics officers, planning officers, and more).

If you look critically at the role classifications, you might be able to poke holes in them. Aren't the CFA volunteers also the fire fighters? Should the incident management role be broken down into its specializations (incident controller, logistics officer, planning officer ...)? Isn't the list incomplete? The answer is that it may not be a perfect list, but we've made a start, and got the conversation going between the business and IT. Please don't underestimate the value of that.

OK, so we've drilled down into subtypes for one pattern. What's next?

This is when I hand out printed copies of the "Pattern of patterns" diagram. Again, you've seen it before (Figure 40) but another copy is shown below for your convenience.

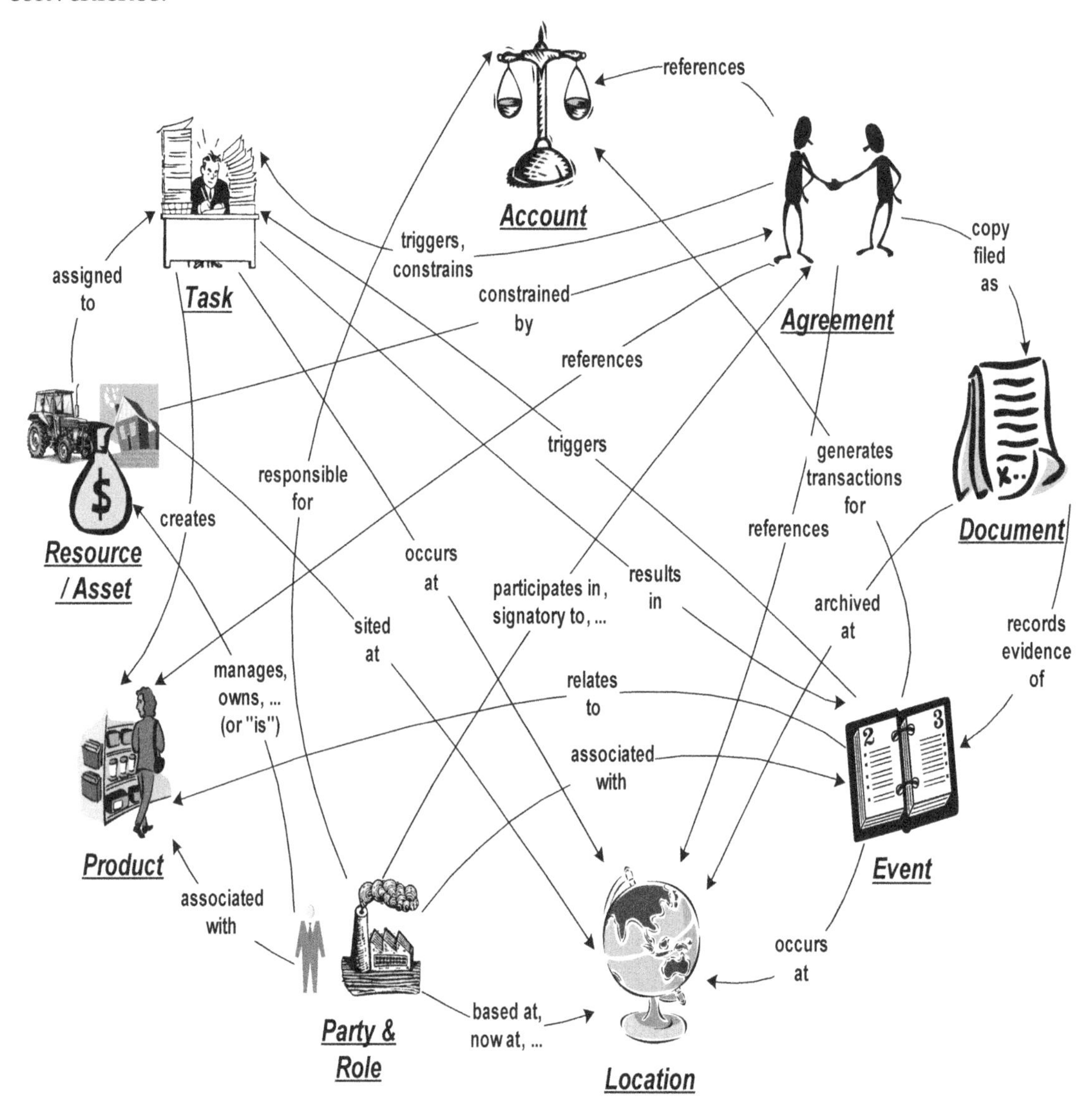

Figure 43: Pattern of patterns

This diagram displays some of the more common interrelationships between the patterns. The reason for introducing it at this point in the workshop is to use it as a checklist to see if some of these relationships might apply as we progressively introduce more patterns. After starting with the Party / Party Role pattern, I often go next to the Agreement pattern. It is very common for Parties to get involved in Agreements, and also to sign formal contracts. The business people can very easily understand this association between Parties and Agreements. It will probably come as no surprise that this relationship applies in the fires scenario. For example, an Agreement may be signed between some Aussie emergency response representatives and an American company that leases water bombing aircraft.

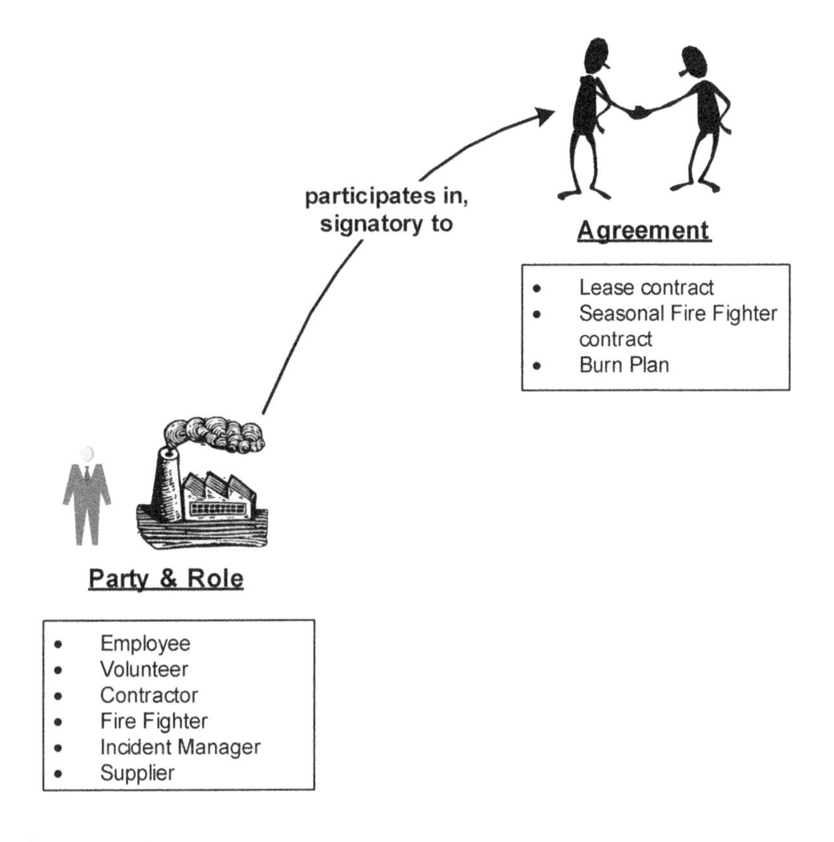

Figure 44: Fire Agreements

We not only recorded the relationship between parties and agreements, we also hand wrote some of the discovered agreement types on the diagram:

- In Australia, we often lease aircraft from the United States. The US is in the northern hemisphere, and we're in the southern hemisphere, so our fire seasons are generally six months offset. It works well for us to use their firefighting aircraft during our summer.

- While the government department responsible for fires on park land can redeploy some of its employees from their regular jobs, they also hire "seasonal firefighters" such as university students on summer vacation who want a bit of extra pocket money.
- Outside the peak fire season, we do "planned burns" to reduce vegetation in a safer way. Formal burn plans are prepared, documented, and signed off before they are acted on.

You might have spotted the additional role of "Supplier", added below the earlier list of Party roles. When we looked at types of agreements, we discovered that some parties played the role of supplier for the leased aircraft. Simple. In the actual workshop, it's all hand-written on the "Palette of patterns" sheet; we just change the working copy. The way I'm telling the story in this book, it sounds pretty straightforward. In reality, the changes can seem rather chaotic; as more and more patterns are introduced, there's more and more extension and reworking of what's come before. I call it "ordered chaos". Yes, the changes come thick and fast, but they are all bounded by the framework of proven patterns.

Not all agreements have related documents (or at least they may not have them available for central fling). Maybe the lease contracts have commercial-in-confidence elements, and the seasonal fire fighter contracts have personal privacy aspects, so are held safely in paper files somewhere. However, the burn plans are of vital interest to a wider audience, and we want their contents easily viewable. They will be filed electronically.

Not all documents relate to agreements. Sure, the burn plan agreement and its associated document are a matched pair, but evidence collected about suspected arson activity causing the fire might come in the form of smart phone photos and videos from the public. We want that filed, but there most certainly wasn't a formal agreement for some ratbag to set the forest alight.

The evolving schematic now looks like:

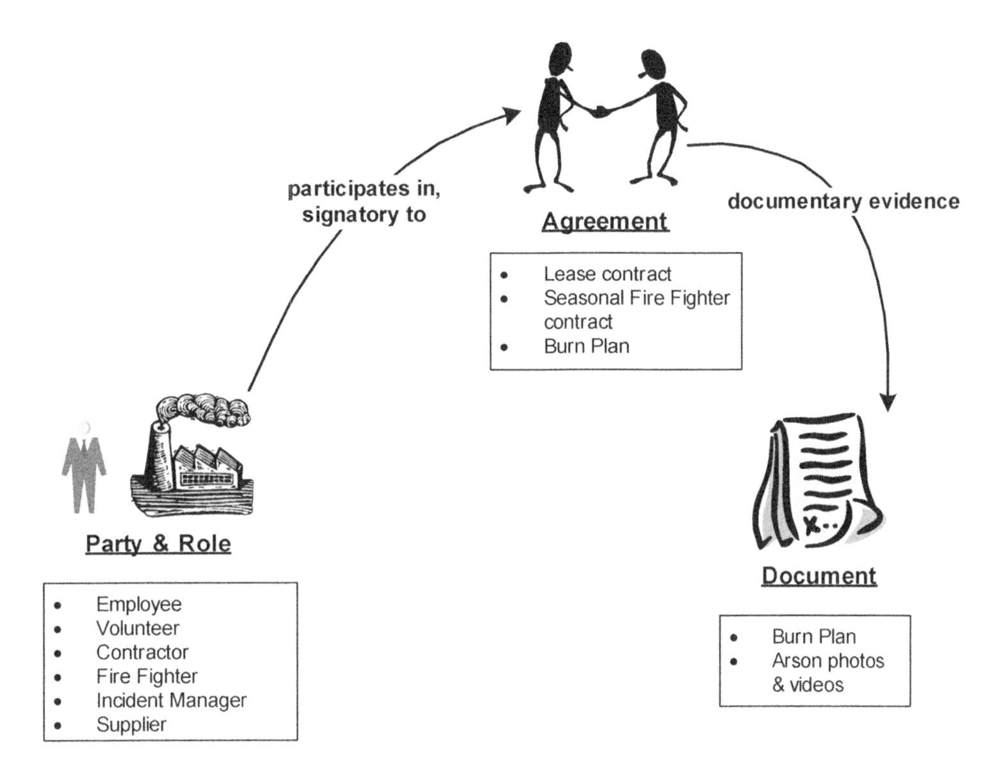

Figure 45: Fire Documents

Bit by bit we introduce the remaining patterns, and incorporate them into each group's diagram, adding (1) hand-written subtypes and (2) the interrelationships between the patterns. As we iterate to include new patterns, each group presents their work-in-progress model. The other groups should feel free to take on board any ideas they like, but at this stage the workshop is still encouraging diversity of opinion. Consolidation will come shortly.

Even though the emerging model can often fit on one sheet of paper or a whiteboard, it starts to get too big to fit easily on a page in this book, so let's look at the subtypes as a list, then we'll look at the discovered interrelationships between the patterns. We continue to use the fire scenario as we flesh out the enterprise view.

The Location pattern is typically implemented as a Geographic Information System (GIS). The subtypes can be thought of as "layers" that could be turned on or off from display, including:

- Roads, used to assist in finding the best route to the fire.

- Water points for collecting water.
- Airports for use by fire response aircraft.
- National and State Parks – these are important as in my part of the world, fires in parks are managed by government agencies but fires on private land are managed by volunteer agencies.
- Fire ignition points, fire line, and fire burn area.
- Conservation Zones within a park that have been set aside to study the ecology when it's not interrupted by man, including planned burns.

The Resource (also known as Asset) pattern has vast amounts of subtypes, arranged in a hierarchy. For example, Figure 117 in the Appendix shows a Fire Tanker as a type of Fire Truck which is a type of Land Vehicle which is a Vehicle which is a Resource! In reality, this pattern may have between 100 and 200 subtypes! They won't fit on a small diagram, but in the workshop the participants can include some representative types.

Next we look at the Event pattern. The workshop participants might identify types of events, including:

- Fire Detection, when a person in a fire tower, or a member of the public, notify the central team that a new fire has been spotted.
- Fire Cause Allegation event, where an individual reports reasons that suggest the fire might have been deliberately lit by an arsonist, lightning, a campfire, or whatever.
- Fire Status event, when a fire has its official status changed, for example from "Going" to "Contained" to "Out".
- Safety Incident, for example when a firefighter is hurt while performing their duties.
- Communication event, for example a public SMS message broadcast warning of a recommendation to evacuate.

As noted when the patterns were first introduced, there is a two-way relationship between Events and Tasks. For example, the Fire Detection event occurs, and Tasks are put in place to assemble and send a first-response team. The team arrives, and as one of their Tasks, they make a preliminary assessment of likely fire cause, and they suggest arson, hence creating an Event of type Fire Cause Allegation. This new Event then triggers tasks for forensic specialists to do a more detailed evaluation of the fire cause. Back and forth the Events and Tasks go. Within this context, the Tasks the workshop participants identify might include:

- First Response.
- Fire Cause Forensic Analysis.
- Fire Line Suppression.

These are some of the more obvious Tasks. But there are more, for example:

- Tasks such as Training and Fitness Assessment to prepare people for the upcoming season.

- For rostering purposes, not only is "work" on the front line treated as a type of Task, but "non-work" such as enforced Rest, Rostered Days Off, and Leave can be entered as types of "Tasks" in that they are entered into the calendar for consideration on availability.

There are two more of the nine common pattern pillars that have not been mentioned. The first is Product. In my interaction with the fire people, "Product" simply was not seen as being relevant. The one that might surprise you is that "Account" was also seen as being irrelevant! Sure, finances come into the larger picture, but the people I worked with to assemble the initial enterprise data model simply did not see money as being that important. Saving people's lives was.

That's the nine pillars, but the workshop participants added another pattern, especially suited to the recording of the analysis performed by the forensic team. David Hay calls it the Laboratory pattern,[25] as it commonly used for recording the analysis of diagnosis activities in laboratories. I recently worked in an organization performing forensics

---

[25] Hay D. (1996) "*Data Model Patterns: Conventions of Thought*".

analysis such as tests for alcohol or drugs in blood and saliva, and determining the DNA from skin samples. Their operational system used the Laboratory pattern.

The emergency response team also did analysis, for example to determine the cause of a fire. The business wanted to call it the Observation pattern, and that raises an important point. It's a business-centric model, and they can assign names to the patterns that make sense to them. In a similar manner, some businesses like the word "Task", and others like "Activity". Let's be sensitive to their perspective.

The teams have been writing their subtypes on the "Palette of Patterns" sheet, but they have also been adding the interrelationships between the patterns. The final result has subtypes *and* relationships. A cleaned up version of one team's hand-written schematic follows, showing relationships but suppressing the subtypes:

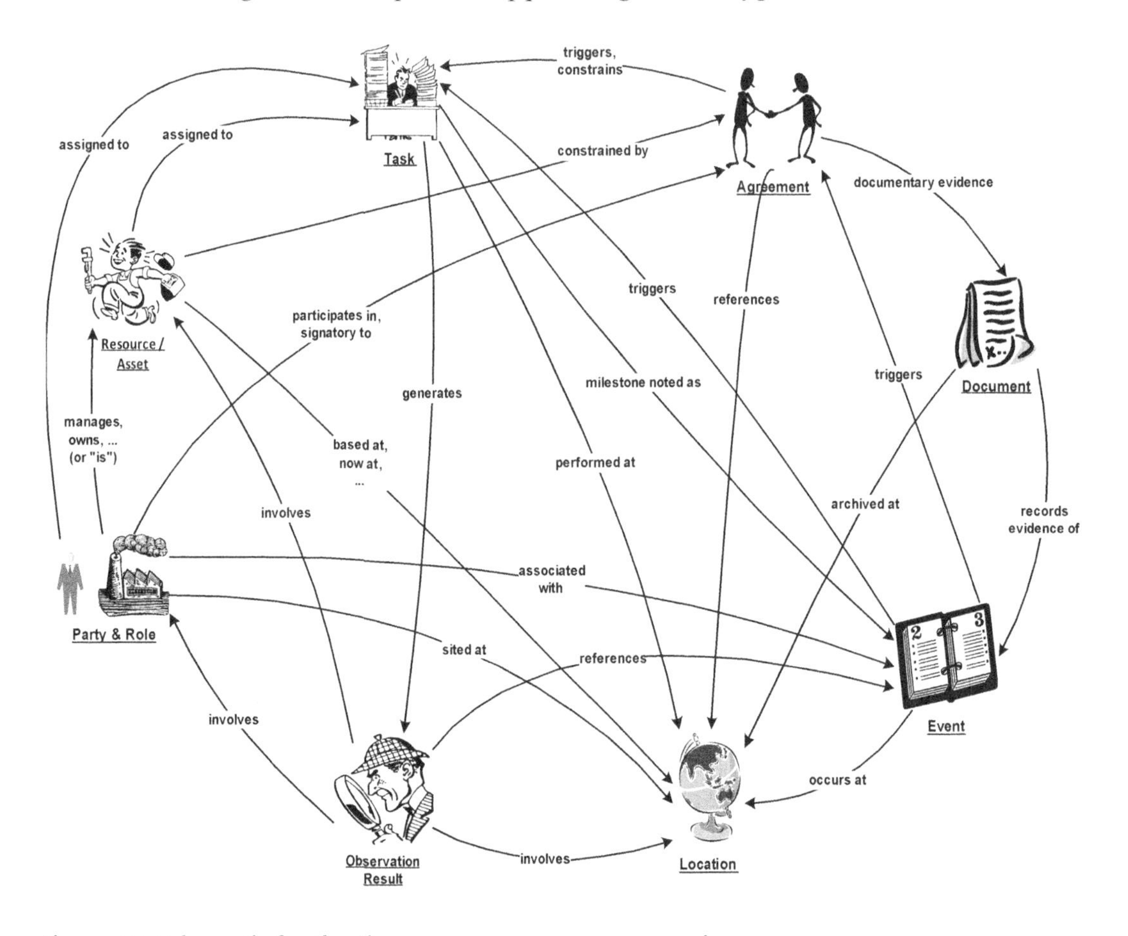

Figure 46: Schematic for the Fire emergency response scenario

That's the output from one team. The other team's models are likely to be a little bit different. Now we want a single enterprise model, somewhat aligned to David Hay's Essential model, but still at the high level of his Overview model.

A consolidated enterprise model

We've deliberately encouraged diversity across the models produced by each group. That's one way to discover subtle but important differences. But now it's time for each group to present their model, and for all participants to collectively work towards creating the one enterprise view.

If you've ever had to consolidate data from multiple sources, you will understand that merging models can be painful. Let me tell a story. It goes something like this.

During my home state's last major wildfire, a person seeking all available resources asked one organization how many fire trucks they had in the area. The answer was, "We don't have fire trucks, but we do have appliances – is that what you want?" This particular organization called their fire trucks "appliances" for years, and that's how they see the world. And they are completely entitled to that view.

The person asking the initial question then turned to the representative of another organization, and asked, "So how many fire trucks, or 'appliances' if you prefer, do you have?" The answer? "We don't have fire trucks, or appliances, but we do have Slip-ons and Tankers. Which do you mean?"

According to the way the story was told to me, the frustrated enquirer yelled, "I don't care what you call them, just tell me how many vehicles you have that can squirt water!"

I was subsequently engaged to create a Common Information Model (CIM) to facilitate data sharing amongst emergency response organizations. I suggested we model fire trucks as "Big Red Water-Squirting Vehicles". That got a few laughs, broke the tension, and we were able to reach consensus.

All jokes aside, I have found that having people work with the common patterns creates an environment where differences are lessened, and can often be relatively easily resolved. Often different people contribute different subtypes of the same pattern, and they can co-exist side-by-side. And if they actually represent the same thing, the participants can often agree on a name (other than Big Red Water-Squirting Vehicles), or simply use aliases. Too easy?

Unfortunately, there are times when the resolution can be a bit more challenging. It's time for another story.

We start with a fairly expectable snippet from the subtyping of Resource and Party.

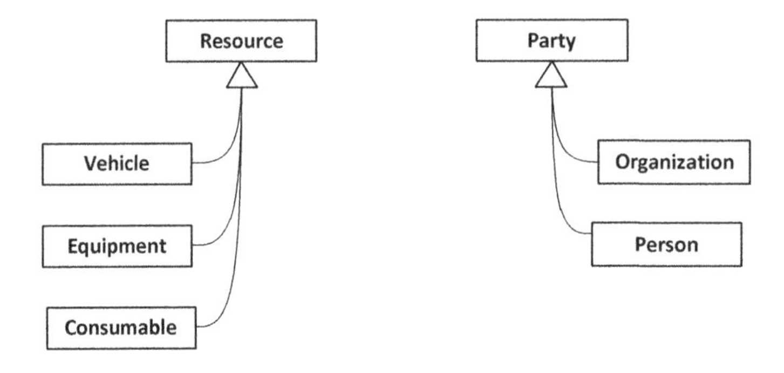

Figure 47: Common subtypes for Resource and Party

People have competencies (a license to drive a heavy vehicle, first aid training, ability to operate a chainsaw …). Resources have capacities. A water tank can hold up to 1,500 liters, a crane can lift five tons, a fire truck has a driving range of 500 kilometers, and a chain saw can cut up to 500 mm/20 inches depth in a single cut. We add a person's competencies, and a resource's capacities, to the model.

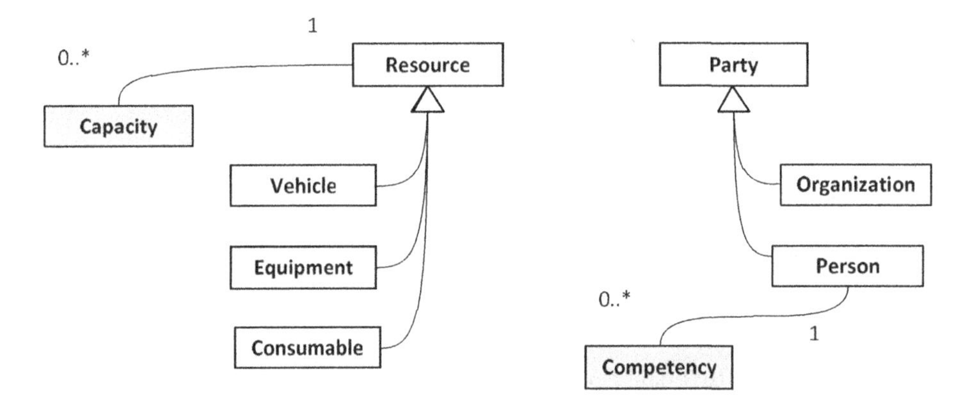

Figure 48: Capacity and Competency

Here's the twist. One of the groups suggested an alternative, based on one of their member's perspective as a Logistics Officer. To them, there's little difference between a person and a fire truck. Both need refueling (hamburgers in one case, diesel in another). Both need regular servicing (8 hours sleep for one, a grease and oil change for the other). Both can be requested to be sent to the fire. Both can be deployed to front line duties. He saw the similarities going further. He suggested that we could say that competencies and capacities can be generalized and called "capabilities". His model for Resources was interesting.

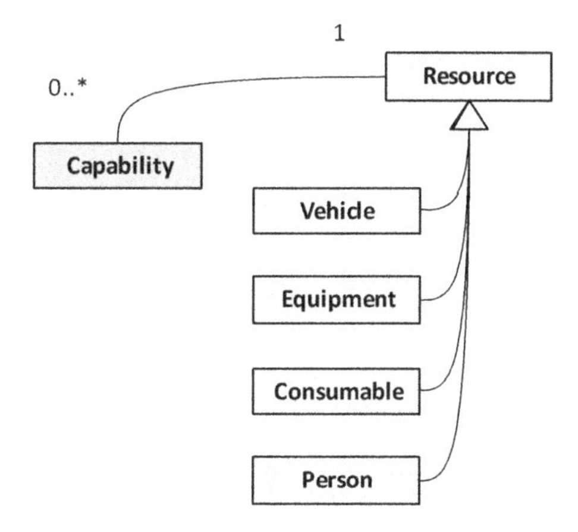

Figure 49: Person as a Resource

I called his model "interesting". The human resources (HR) people found it confronting. How dare someone liken a human being to a fire truck?!

We reached some sort of a compromise.

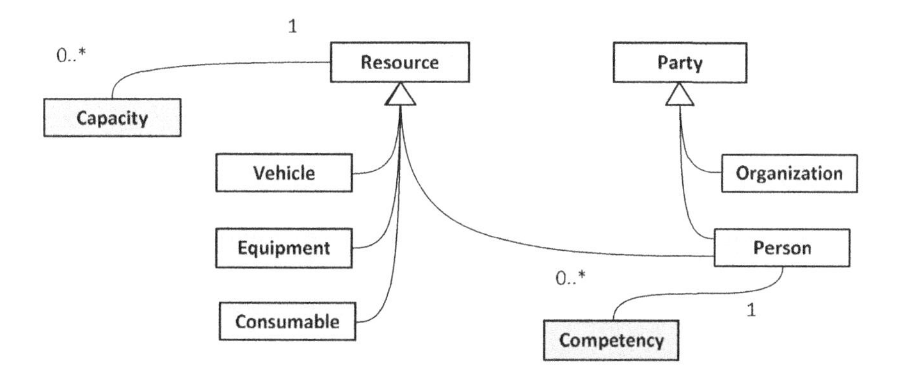

Figure 50: Person as a Resource and a Party

For those of you familiar with the UML, it's called multiple inheritance. A Person is a Resource, and a Person is also a Party. Would we directly implement something like this? Possibly not, especially as some object-oriented languages don't seem to be too comfortable with multiple inheritance.

But here's an important message. This is a model about business concepts, and at this level, some people see a person as a type of party, and others see them as a resource. The model captures both views, and if nothing else, will generate discussion when implementation has to be faced, be it for a Data Vault or something else that requires an enterprise view.

After a few twists and turns, we end up with a very high level schematic that looked a bit like the group model presented in Figure 46.

Next steps

Assuming prior familiarity with the patterns, and a good selection of creative participants, it is possible to assemble this framework in just days. It's helpful, it gives the business and the technical people a common vocabulary, it is pattern based and hence likely to be able to be extended as new aspects are discovered. That's all good news.

But it is only a schematic, and for many purposes, we are going to need a bit more detail, though not so much that we drown in a never ending search for the last attribute, so we want to target our drill-down efforts to where we will get the most value. Before I end the workshop, I seek feedback on "data" problems that have caused pain in the past. That can serve as a checklist for focus as we seek to flesh out the model where it can first deliver value.

Step #6: "Pain Point" & "Process" drill-down (in weeks)

We've got a great start. We've built a foundational framework that the business and IT folk are happy with, but it's little more than a skeleton. While it may be sufficient for some purposes, we probably want to go into a bit more detail before we launch into constructing our Data Vault. The good news, though, is it should take a few weeks, not months. And again, as for the construction of the lightweight enterprise framework, it doesn't have to be hard labor; it can be fun.

I've already suggested that looking at "Pain Points" – where data problems are hurting the business – can provide real focus. But can looking at business processes help, too? The answer is yes, sometimes! Let's look at both of these sources of insight.

Using "Pain Points" to drive the drill-down

If you recall, in Step #1 above, we encouraged team members to collect and collate their pain points. Now we use them to drive the drill-down. As a team, we look at the collection of pain points, and prioritize what we're going to tackle. Then we grab the first one, decide who is best to work on it (some members from the original team, plus others from across the business), and get to work.

The good news is that the technical and non-technical people now have a common language for grappling with the problem, based on the mutually agreed concepts from the high level enterprise data model schema.

The initial focus is to *understand* the pain rather than too quickly jumping into solution mode; solutions will come soon enough. It reminds me of a time my lovely wife was upset. Being the sort of bloke I am, I immediately tabled a perceived solution. The response? "I don't want a solution, I want to know you've heard me." There's a time for solutions, and there's a time for simply understanding the problems.

So what does a drill-down involve? It's not too hard, really.

We've already got the high level schematic, showing core concepts and their interrelationships. We've also identified a smattering of subtypes under the core building blocks. A sample of our starting point was presented in Figure 29, and is repeated here for your convenience.

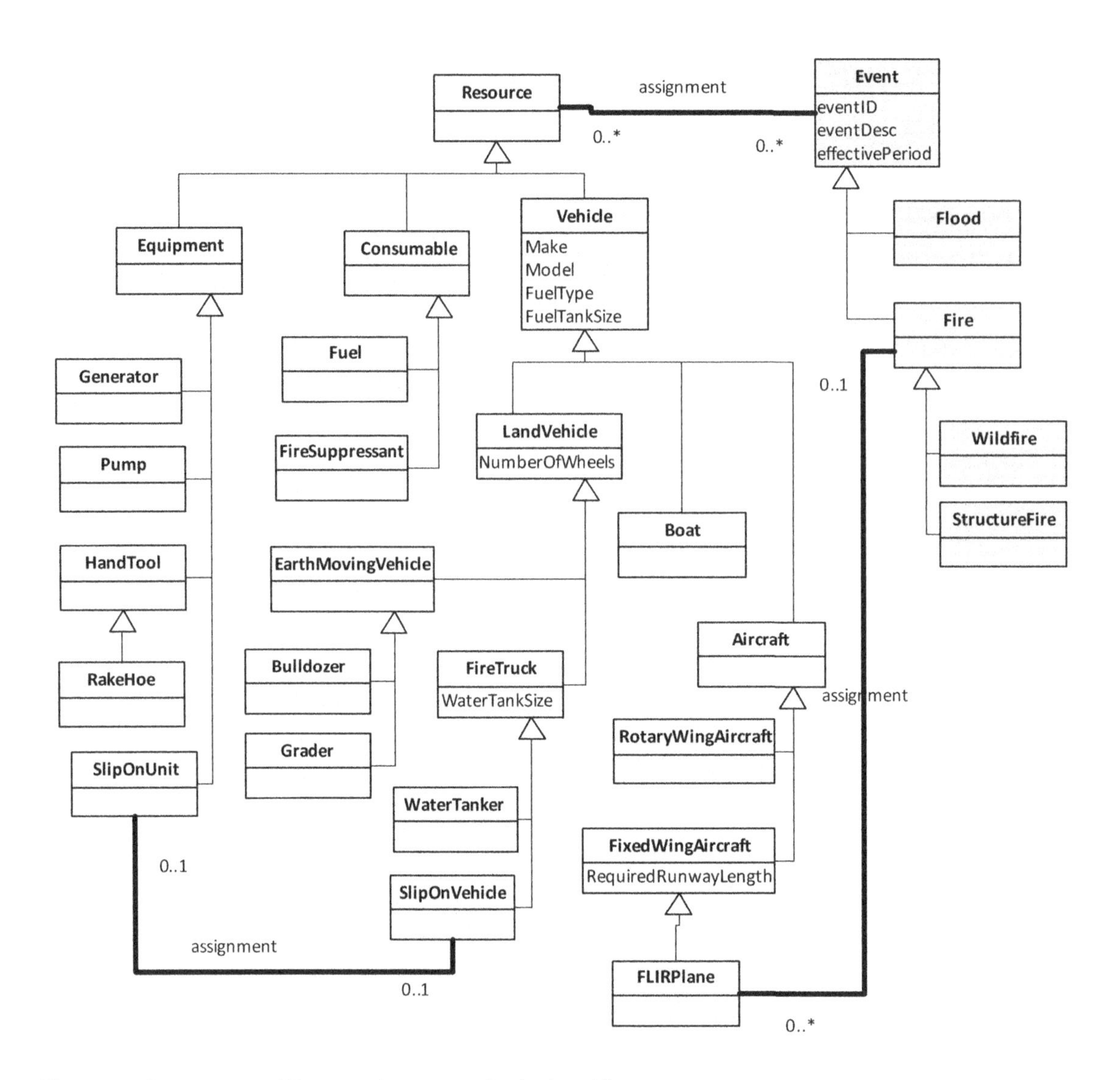

Figure 51: Resource and Event subtypes and relationships

Some of the subtypes may have been identified in the initial workshop to create the schematic. "Figure 47: Common subtypes for Resource and Party" shows some of the Resource pattern's high-level subtypes (Vehicle, Equipment, and Consumable). The diagram above drills down a lot deeper, showing some of the additional fine-grained subtypes that might be discovered progressively as pain points (and processes) are analyzed in detail.

It is important to note that the subtypes are represented in a multi-level hierarchy. When it comes to physical implementation, the hierarchies may be simplified / flattened

— for a relational implementation or for a Data Vault design. But for the business data model, multiple levels are fine if they aid in communication.

In addition to identifying the subtypes of the patterns, we also recorded our discovered specializations of inter-relationships. These could have been relationships between subtypes in one hierarchy, such as between a Slip On Unit and a Slip On Vehicle. They may also have been relationships across domains, such as between a Forward-Looking Infra-Red (FLIR) Plane as a subtype of Resource, and the Fire it is monitoring.

So in this Step, we discover and document new subtypes and new relationships. Additionally, as we go I encourage documentation of major attributes. And seeing we are intending to use the resultant model to help us shape our Data Vault design, I most certainly would like participants to identify which ones of those attributes represent business keys.

It's important to note that I don't try to boil the ocean. Only those pattern stubs that need further investigation to address the pain points prioritized by the business need to be worked through to discover more detail.

Can "Process" help, too?

I have encountered debates over the role of business processes when it comes to a Data Vault.

Two of the best-known spokespeople in the Data Vault world, while not agreeing on everything, both emphasize the centrality of "business concepts" to a Data Vault. In Dan's first Data Vault book,[26] he states "*Data Vault models are built based on the conceptual understanding of the business.*" Similarly, Hans' book[27] notes that the Hubs hold business keys for "*...the core business concept.*" These central business concepts appear in the enterprise data model, which in turn shapes the Data Vault design. But where does "process" fit in?

---

[26] Linstedt D. (2011) *"Super Charge your Data Warehouse: Invaluable Data Modeling Rules to Implement Your Data Vault", page 7.*

[27] Hultgren H (2012) *"Modeling the Agile Data Warehouse with Data Vault", page 60.*

Some have argued that a Data Vault is process-centric, even going so far as to claim that there is no such thing as a business concept in Data Vault, but instead claiming a Data Vault's reason for existence is to show how business processes relate to each other. Taken at face value, this claim suggests we should focus our Data Vault design on business processes, and ignore the business concepts we've worked so hard to capture in our emerging enterprise data model. Quotes earlier in this book, in "Is the enterprise view really that important?" demonstrate clearly that Dan and Hans place a foundational, primary emphasis on business concepts and business ontologies.

Others have argued it's all about the data. After all it's a *Data* Vault, intended amongst other things to integrate *data*, highlight *data* inconsistencies, and repackage *data* in the business-centric *Data* Vault structures ready for those people hungry to consume meaningful *data*. OK, in some of those places where I emphasized the word "data" I could have (should have?) spoken of "information", but you get the point that there seems to be a lot about data in their conversation. And not much about process.

I did say, in the previous paragraph, that a Data Vault was "… intended amongst other things …" to do some data stuff. That phrase was deliberate, because one of the things that Data Vault is known for is what Dan calls "gap analysis", which is all about using the Data Vault to get insight into gaps between the perception about how business processes work in theory versus the reality of what's actually happening. So Dan has been noted as saying the business concepts in the enterprise ontology (which I see as a data construct) are foundational, *and* he also says that a really valuable use of a Data Vault can be this process-centered gap analysis. Is there some data versus process confusion here? I think not. Here's my summary:

1. Initiate the design of the Data Vault model by first discovering or building our enterprise data model. That's what Steps #1 to #7 are all about.

2. Enrich, challenge, refine our enterprise data model by throwing scenarios at it, whether these scenarios are based on pain points, or business process analysis, or anything else of importance to our business. That's part of this Step #6.

3. Apply our enterprise data model to the job of assembling our Data Vault model. That's the focus of the next major part of this book.

4. ... and after we've built and deployed our shiny new Data Vault, don't forget that one of its valuable uses is "gap analysis" on the processes.

Instead of data versus process competition, there's a lovely synergy. Points 1 and 3 above happen to be a bit more about "data" than "process", and points 2 and 4 swing the emphasis around the other way. But they're intertwingled. That's another synergy – a combination of intertwined and intermingled!

With some of the misunderstanding I have observed hopefully cleared up for you, let's see if we can use a process view as an insightful way to discover fresh, new underlying data. The business people will be comfortable with analyzing processes, and later we can expect a feed-back loop from using our Data Vault to look for gaps between process theory and process reality. Just as we did for pain points, we start as a team to collectively identify some core processes, then we selectively revisit the growing enterprise data model to see if we can use some of the insights for data discovery.

For fire management, we had several processes articulated. Below I share an outline of just one of them to give you an idea of how we can look at processes as a means to refining the data model. The process is presented as a hypothetical scenario for initial response to a fire. It's a bit lengthy, but it serves a purpose – as you read through it, I would ask you to consider the work-in-progress schematic from Figure 46, and the preceding supplementary subtypes for each of the selected patterns, to see if you can spot some missing bits in the enterprise model one group has already drafted.

A member of the public reports the outbreak of a fire and, thanks to mobile phone technology, the position is also known. Details of the reported fire outbreak are recorded (who reported it, their contact details, the time of the reporting, comments, any sighting of suspicious activity, etc.).

Based on the fire location (state boundaries, public or private land, etc.), the authority responsible for managing the response is identified.

An estimate of the likely rate of spread of the fire is calculated. Variables to be considered include:

- *The current and forecast weather in the vicinity of the fire (temperature, humidity, wind strength and wind direction).*
- *Known vegetation type in the area (forest, wheat crops, ...).*

- *Contours. (Fires burn more quickly when going uphill, especially if pushed from behind by a hot, strong wind).*

Based on expected spread, threatened assets are identified, including:

- *Community assets (residences, schools, hospitals, farmland, etc.).*
- *Natural assets (conservation zones, threated species, etc.).*

Access options to the fire are determined (sealed roads, 4WD tracks, airstrips in the area, etc.).

The target profiles of suitable first-attack teams are chosen from a list of templates (for example a team in a 4WD fire truck, or a rappel team for delivery by helicopter in a remote location).

Candidate resources for formation of the first-attack team are identified based on:

People who:

- *Have suitable competencies to perform the roles identified in the templates.*
- *Are in the right location.*
- *Are available for deployment (for example not already assigned to another task).*

Equipment that:

- *Has suitable characteristics to perform the roles identified in the templates (adequate water-carrying capacity for water bombers, 4WD ability for fire trucks, etc.).*
- *Is in the right location.*
- *Is available for deployment.*

Based on the available information, a single crew (typically one crew leader and four general fire-fighters) and their resources are selected.

A request for assignment is made.

The request is confirmed as being authorized by the proposed crew leader's manager, and the person responsible for the required physical resources.

The assigned people are notified and dispatched.

Records are kept for each person involved, including hours worked and the role played, for payroll and experience tracking purposes.

Wow, these process scenarios can certainly be rich, and they can highlight missing bits in the data model! Here's just a handful of possible topics arising from just that one process scenario. As you read the scenario description, you probably identified others.

- Is a helicopter with a rappel crew on board a different type of aircraft?
- We've got subtypes of Party as people and organizations (and organization units such as departments and divisions), but is a "fire crew" a type of organization, even though it is formed on the fly and may disappear just as quickly?
- The workshop had identified the Observation pattern for use by the arson forensics specialists, so might the same pattern be useful for holding weather observations?
- It looks like we need to seriously consider rostering and timesheet recording. Where do these things fit in? Are they part of the existing patterns, or do we need more?

It's clear that a process perspective can really help us refine the enterprise data model. But here's a strong warning. Please don't try to analyze every possible business process and cross check it. That runs the risk of being a long project, with diminishing returns over time. You're doing this modeling for a purpose, and I encourage you to do enough to make good progress. Earlier I have referred to a "T-model" approach. The following diagram and subsequent discussion helps explain it.

	Account	Agreement	Document	Party/Role	(etc.)
High-level logical subject areas	☑	☑	☑	☑	☑
Standard logical assembly patterns		☑		☑	
Refined logical assembly patterns		☑			

Figure 52: T-model

Like the letter "T", we can use the lightweight patterns to represent the width of the enterprise, and then selectively consider business processes to discover areas of the data model where we want to perform drill down into detail to add value. The high level subject areas are likely to often align with our common patterns. For a given focus, we might have decided that the Party / Party Role need a bit more detail, and the Agreement needed a lot more. So what's my conclusion on the role of "process" in forming a Data Vault? That while the focus of the data model is on data (a self-evident fact?), considering business processes often adds value, but not always. My recommendation is pretty simple: drive the drill down into data model detail based on business "pain points", and supplement that discovery by process analysis when it is likely to add value.

Step #7: Cast the net wider

OK, we've finished the drill-down on prioritized pain points, and selectively applied a bit of a "process" perspective. The core team has been involved, along with hand-picked people from across the organization. That's great, but it's an *enterprise* data model, and there are others who are likely to be interested and who may give valuable feedback on areas for extension or refinement. It's time to share the model with a wider audience.

Some say that a data model can't be understood by non-technical people. I remember a particularly challenging model I had developed, and that absolutely needed sign-off from the most senior members of the organization. A challenge?

I roped in some business people to work with me to hone a few business scenarios that would grab the attention of the executives. I then created and printed two piles of paper. The first pile had one major supertype per page. Prior to the presentation in the board room, I posted the supertypes on the wall. The second set was much richer. For each business scenario I had multiple pages mapping hypothetical values to the supertypes. Let me explain by a massively simplified example.

- The scenario starts by declaring that "Customer Sam Samuels contacts our organization". I have one page that is headed "Sam Samuels", with a few details such as address and contact phone number. I attach this sheet to the wall, directly under the Customer subtype of Party Role.

- The scenario continues that "Sam enquires on our Acme Eco product". I attach my second sheet of paper headed "Contact Event" under the Event supertype, with details such as contact date. I also attach a third sheet, this time headed "Acme Eco", under the Product supertype, with details such as stock-on-hand quantity and recommended retail price.

- Sam places an Order, and up goes the Order sheet under the Agreement supertype, with details of delivery address, etc.

- And on and on …

Get the picture? These non-technical decision makers see the data model populated before their eyes. Well, actually they see their business stories unfold, and bits of paper attached to the wall. They don't even care that the emerging scenario maps to a data model, because they don't really care about data models.

The actual model was much more complicated than Customer, Product, and Order, but I am just telling my story. What's important is that I didn't call what I had on the wall a data model. I didn't call it a database. I just told some stories, in their language. They loved it, and signed it off.

As it turned out, there was no feedback warranting change to the data model, but if it had occurred, in the words of my agile friends, it is good to "fail fast". If there is need for change, let's hear about it early. In a few weeks, we've assembled a "sufficient" enterprise data model. Now it's time to apply it to designing our Data Vault.

… but before we leave this neat 7-step process, can I please remind you about "Step 0"? The steps are guidelines only, and it's OK to iterate, to go back and refine something you did earlier. You might finish the first pass in a few weeks, but the enterprise data model is better seen as a living document that can change over time.

CHAPTER 4

Task #2: Apply the Enterprise View to Design a Data Vault

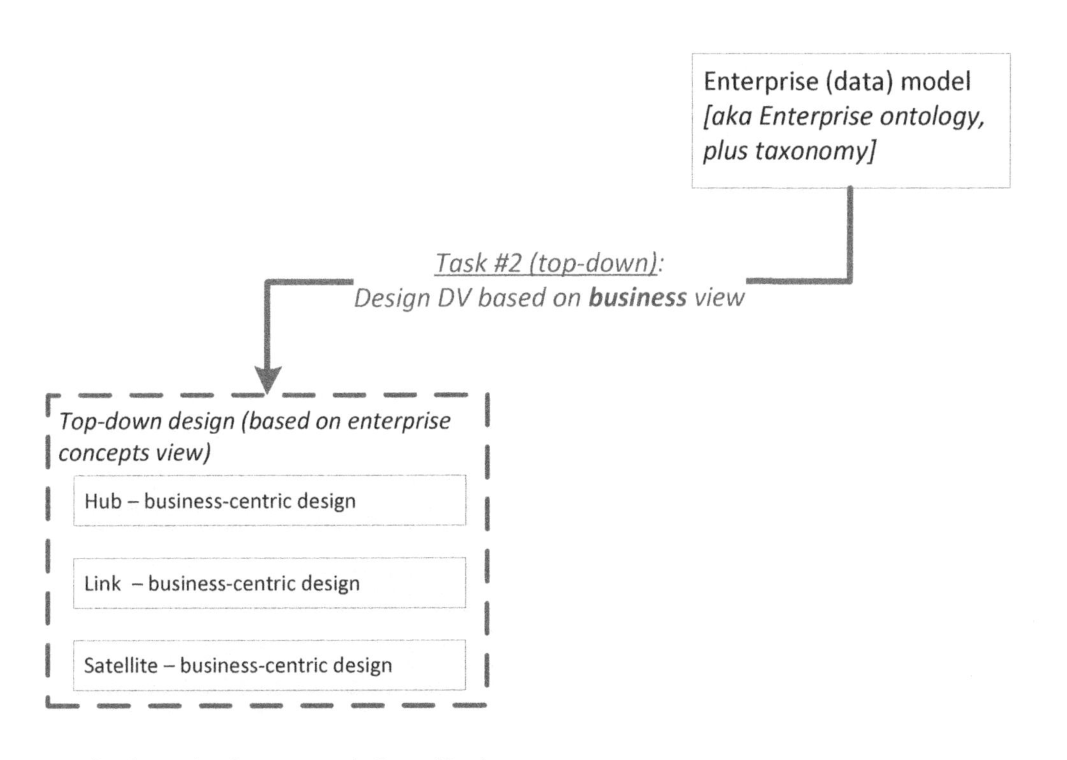

Figure 53: Design a business-centric Data Vault

The important bit: Getting business data out

At one of my client sites, the CEO wanted to know how many people worked for the organization. It took too long for IT to answer his question, and he wasn't happy. In part, the challenge for IT was that source systems didn't think in terms of people who were "workers". The payroll system understood about salaried staff. The contract management system knew about long term contractors / consultants. Another system knew about short term or casual contractors. And what about the person who mowed the lawns each fortnight and submitted an invoice – why shouldn't that individual be considered as a "worker"?

The underlying problem was that the business saw things one way, and many IT operational systems saw things differently. At the extreme, if we build our Data Vault to blindly follow the views of the source systems, we've missed the mark badly. Dan says, *"If you build a* **source system Data Vault Model,** *the value of the solution drops to one tenth of one percent overall."*[28]

The business wants access to their data, seen their way.

Well-formed Hubs: Getting the right foundations

Confusion over "Semantics & Grain"?

[or, "***We might look a bit different, but surely we belong together***"]

[28] https://danlinstedt.com/allposts/datavaultcat/datavault-models-business-purpose-data-as-an-asset/.

I've heard a number of long and sometimes unresolved discussions about what should be chosen as a Hub. One of the arguments put forward for setting a boundary around what constitutes a Hub is that all of the objects in one Hub should share the same "semantics and grain". I actually have no fundamental problem with that principle. It's just that the interpretation of that phrase seems at times to be imprecise and contradictory. I will share some of the views I have encountered in case you, too, come across them, and then propose what I think are some simple and very workable solutions to close the gap around unnecessary tensions and debates.

I've heard the claim that if two types of things are in a one-to-many relationship, they cannot have the same grain and therefore must be in separate Hubs. That may be true sometimes, but not always. In Dan and Michael's explanation of hierarchical Links,[29] they use the example of aircraft parts. An aircraft is made up of many parts (such as a tail rudder, two wings, one or several engines, landing gear ...), and each of those parts can be made up of many parts – for example, the engine is a complex thing, itself made up of parts that are made up of parts. And all of these things that have one-to-many relationships can happily be held in the one "Part" Hub.

Another scenario on this "one-to-many means different grain" topic can be seen when we look at customers. I've got customers A, B and C, all stored in a Customer Hub. Then Customer A acquires companies B and C, but B and C continue trading in their own names. So I've still got three customers, but A has a one-to-many relationship between the holding company and its subsidiaries. I most certainly don't want to create a Hub called "Subsidiary Customer" just because of the "one-to-many" rule.

So now let's look at how we might use the enterprise data model to defuse this "semantics and grain" discussion. First let's look at semantics, or the "meaning" of something. For example, does this source system's "client" mean the same thing (have the same semantics) as this second system's "customer"?

Why might I have observed lengthy debates on such matters? I suggest that doing Data Vault design bottom up, starting with source systems without the context provided by the enterprise data model, is at the heart of the problem. If we do bottom-up discovery,

---

[29] Linstedt D. & Olschimke O. (2016) *"Building a Scalable Data Warehouse with Data Vault 2.0"*.

we're going to be trying to derive enterprise meaning on the fly as we pick up one source system after another.

Conversely, if we've already built an enterprise data model, it turns out these "semantics" issues may be delightfully simple to resolve. We've already had many conversations with the business, including the difference (if any) between one system's "client" and another's "customer". Instead of arguing about it again, we can go to the enterprise data model. Every entity type in the model should be fully described as to what it is, what it is not, and have examples provided also in the documentation.

We know what each entity type means; now all we have to do is map source system data to the existing entity type that matches. Of course, this mapping may uncover some holes in the top-down model, but that's just part of proving any top-down model by cross-checking against bottom-up details.

Grain should be relatively simple, too. Taking the example shown earlier in "Figure 51: Resource and Event subtypes and relationships", Resource is a coarse-grained supertype, with Equipment, Consumable, and Vehicle as finer-grained subtypes, and under Consumable, Fuel and Fire Suppressant are even finer-grained.

The conclusion is simple – each entity type in the enterprise data model identifies one class of thing that has a consistent "semantics and grain".

Finding the sweet spot

A Hub is a collection of unique business keys, but it's not just any old collection. For example, it wouldn't make sense to have a collection of customer numbers, car registration numbers, and case file numbers all in one Hub. That might fit the "unique collection" expectation, but the business keys must all belong to one core business concept, such as a Customer.

It sounds easy to find a business concept, and its business key; but it's not always that straightforward. If we've successfully assembled an enterprise data model, with a nested level of supertypes and subtypes, should we have a Hub for just the supertype, or just the most atomic leaf nodes of the hierarchy, or all of them, or what? Let's return to a simplified version of the Event supertype hierarchy for fire emergency response.

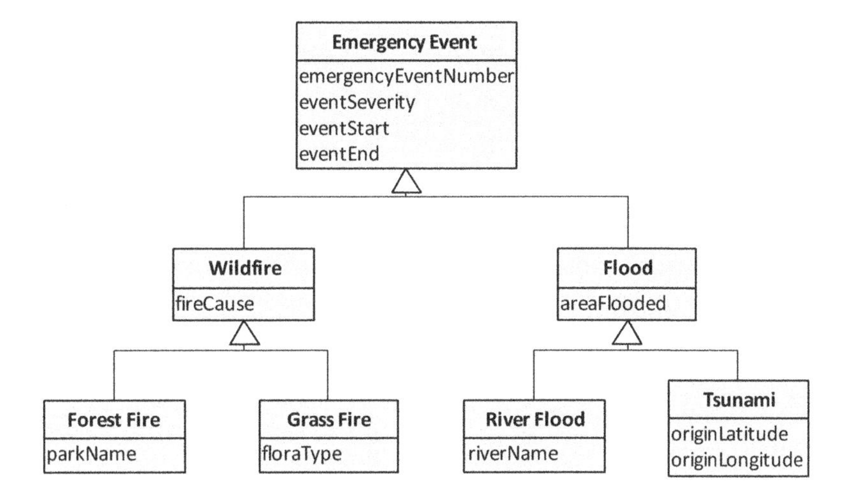

Figure 54: Event inheritance hierarchy

In this diagram, Emergency Events are a supertype (superclass) with attributes that are common to all subtypes (subclasses). The diagram is far from comprehensive – for example it doesn't include earthquakes and tornados – but it may be sufficient for our discussion here.

The business recognizes the hierarchy of types (we could call it a taxonomy if we like), and they have identified major attributes for each entity type. Now what they want is the Data Vault to reflect their view of the world.

One design option might be to define a Hub called Emergency Event, and implement at that level, but supertype Hubs are not generally recommended. At the other extreme, we could implement a Hub for atomic subtypes (forest fire, grass fire, river flood, and tsunami). Or, heaven help us, we could have a Hub for every entity type (class) across the entire hierarchy, with Data Vault "Same-As" Links (described later) between them.

So what do we do to resolve the best approach? We talk to the *business*. The example above has only three levels in the supertype/subtype hierarchy, but in our real world there may be more. If we listen to how people talk about the things in their business, we won't be surprised if they only sometimes talk about the highest levels of generalization or at the lowest levels of specialization, but more frequently chat about the middle layers. In our example, that translates to lots of folk chatting about fires and floods, but less frequently discussing emergency events at one extreme, or forest fires, grass fires, river floods, or tsunamis at the other extreme. Listen to the business, and try to find the "sweet spot" that seems to most commonly reflect their conversations,[30] then nominate that as the default level for the design of our business-centered Data Vault Hubs.

The next step is to check against business processes. If the subtypes of wildfire in the enterprise data model (forest fire and grass fire) follow the same or similar processes, and use the same or similar data, then a Wildfire Hub is looking good. Note that the *logical* subtypes of the Wildfire Hub may require a "Wildfire Type Code" attribute to distinguish between forest fire and grass fire instances in the common Hub. It is quite likely that this is really simple – source systems may well provide just what we need as a "type" attribute to be stored in their Satellite.

Conversely, when we look at floods and their subtypes, if we discover that river floods and tsunami's are processed in a totally different manner, we might decide to have a River Flood Hub and a Tsunami Hub. It may not be black-&-white, but use the enterprise data model to guide the conversation.

Not only Semantics & Grain – now there's Key Values

One of the goals for Data Vault is to achieve integration of data around business keys. We will often find multiple sources offer data feeds for what has been determined should belong to the same Hub – remember, a common "semantics and grain" – but the business key structures can be problematic. At the heart of the issue is a very simple question – what are the business key values for what is in reality one real-world entity? Assume that there's a real-world employee, Alex Anderson. (Please also note that where people's names are given such as Alex, Brook, Chris, Dan etc., I have sought to have gender neutral names – is "Chris" a Christopher or a Christine?) What Employee Numbers does he or she have in different IT systems? If they don't have the same value, should they?

---

[30] Hultgren H. (2012) *Modeling the Agile Data Warehouse with Data Vault.*

Let's take a simple hypothetical for employees from the fire emergency response scenario. It's quite a long and detailed analysis we're about to launch into, but believe me, unless this topic is neatly nailed down, it can cause massive pain. Please hang in with me.

Organization	State Government			
Source System	Human Resource (HR)	Payoll	Building Access Control	Contract Manage't
Business Key	Emp No	Emp Num	Card Holder ID	Contractor No
Alex	1	1	A	
Brook	2		B	1
Chris	3	3		
Dan	4		C	2

Figure 55: Business Key scenario – State government employees

Alex and Chris, are salaried employees, managed in the Payroll system. Brook and Dan are contractors, managed in the Contract Management system. All four employees are also recorded in the central Human Resource (HR) system. In addition, Alex, Brook, and Dan have been issued with cards to get access to the head office building (Chris doesn't need one for his/her line of work out in the field because he/she rarely if ever visits the head office).

In the diagram, we also have arrows. These denote one system's knowledge about the business keys of another system. The first row, for Alex, indicates that the Building Access Control system obviously knows about its own keys, but also knows the Payroll system's Employee Number for Alex.

In this hypothetical, the HR system generates its own employee numbers, which are the "business keys", used and known by each employee as their identifier. They enter it on timesheets, and quote it if they ever have to record other activities. Yes, it is internally generated by the HR system, and some may argue it's a surrogate, but it is externally visible, and it is used by the business as the identifier for employees.

The Payroll system also has employee numbers, but it doesn't generate its own. It simply reuses the employee number as generated by the HR system.

The Contract Management system is a little different. When someone is added as a new contractor, the Contract Management System generates its own key which is issued to the contractor – it's another business key! But what's more, the Contract Management System also records the HR system's employee number. Please note that while both systems use integer numbers for their keys, they are generated independently. As it turns out, the number "2" appears in both systems, but Employee Number 2 is for Brook (whose Contractor Number is 1), and Contractor Number 2 is for Dan (whose Employee Number is 4). Confused?

Finally, we've got the Building Access Control systems' Card Holder Numbers. Again, these can be used as "business keys", as they appear on the card itself, and can be recorded by people at the front office desk. Thankfully, these business keys are alphabetic, and cannot be confused with any of the other business keys for employees. Please note than when a card is issued (and its Card Holder ID generated), the system also records

- the Payroll system's employee number for salaried employees,

or

- the Contract Management system's Contractor Number for contract employees.

That's provided a baseline sample data set. Let's look at how the data might be stored if loaded into a Data Vault.

Passive Integration: Same "semantics-&-grain", same key value for the same real-world object

Let's just look at loading data from the HR system and the Payroll system. If (heaven help us) we chose to apply the dreaded "source system Data Vault" approach, we would have one Hub for the HR system, and one Hub for the Payroll system. We might try to improve things a little bit by creating a "Same-As" Link (shown as arrows in the following diagram) between the Hubs to explicitly record that Employee Number 1 in the HR Hub was the same as Employee Number 1 in the Payroll system, though the value of creating this Link is questionable seeing a simple relational join could achieve a simpler outcome.

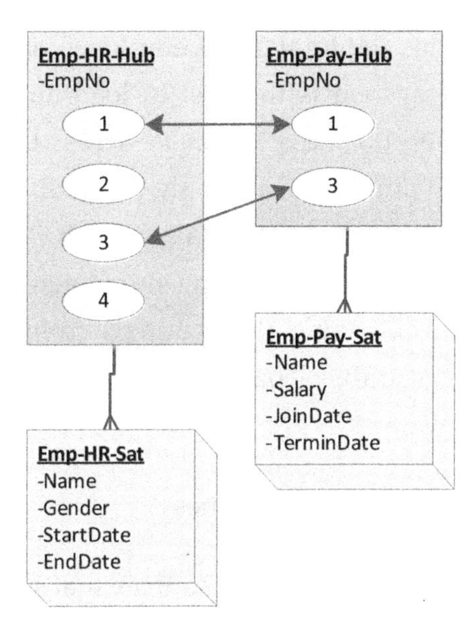

Figure 56: Source system DV for identical key values

Now let's look at how this might look if we applied "passive integration".

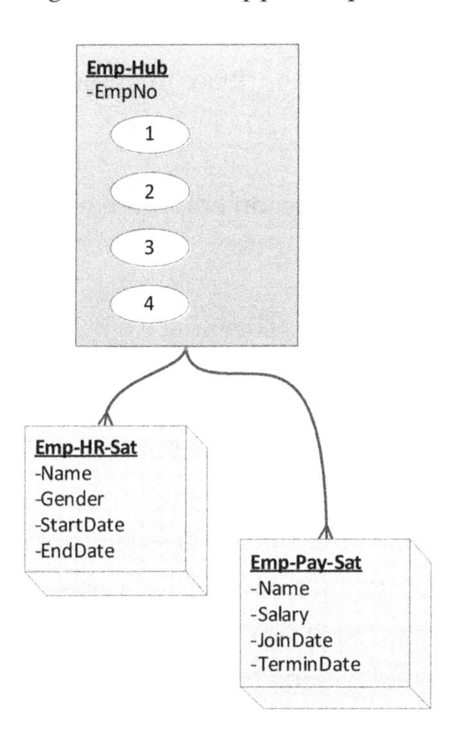

Figure 57: Passive integration for identical key values

Now we've got one Hub. It has the total set of employee numbers for both systems. It doesn't matter which source system is the first to load any given Hub instance. The important fact is that the same business key *value* across both systems is expected to represent the same real-world employee, and only one Hub instance is created for each real-world entity. Alex is employee number "1" in both systems, and the same Hub instance can be shared, with one Satellite being populated with the HR system as its source, and another Satellite managing data sourced from the Payroll system. Their values can be compared because they "passively" integrate by sharing the same Hub instance with the business key of "1".

Different, non-overlapping business key values

In the previous example, we clearly had two sources that fed data into the Data Vault where both:

- had the same semantics (they agreed on the meaning of an "employee"),
- had the same grain (both mapped to the same entry in our business-driven enterprise data model, rather than mapping to different subtypes or supertypes), and
- had the same business key value (an employee number of "1") for the same real-world entity (Alex).

Now we look at another source system. This time it's the system that records employees and the building access cards that were issued.

Let's look at "semantics". In our example shown in Figure 55, we have business keys A, B, and C. If the business key is a code for the employee, but identified by the card they have been issued, maybe A, B, and C are business keys for employees. Alternatively, if A, B, and C are really business keys for the physical cards themselves, then the meaning is very different. If "A" represents an access card, and Employee Number "1" represents a flesh-&-blood employee named Alex, the semantics are different and we could argue that they each deserve their own Hub. I look in more detail at this topic in the section titled "Hubs with more than one business key", but for now, for the sake of the example, I will ask you to cut me some slack and accept that business key "A" represents an employee identified by an access card rather than representing the card itself.

With that as a basis, we've now got a third feed, but it has totally different business keys for employees. If we lean a bit towards the source system Data Vault way of modeling, we might represent the Data Vault design as below.

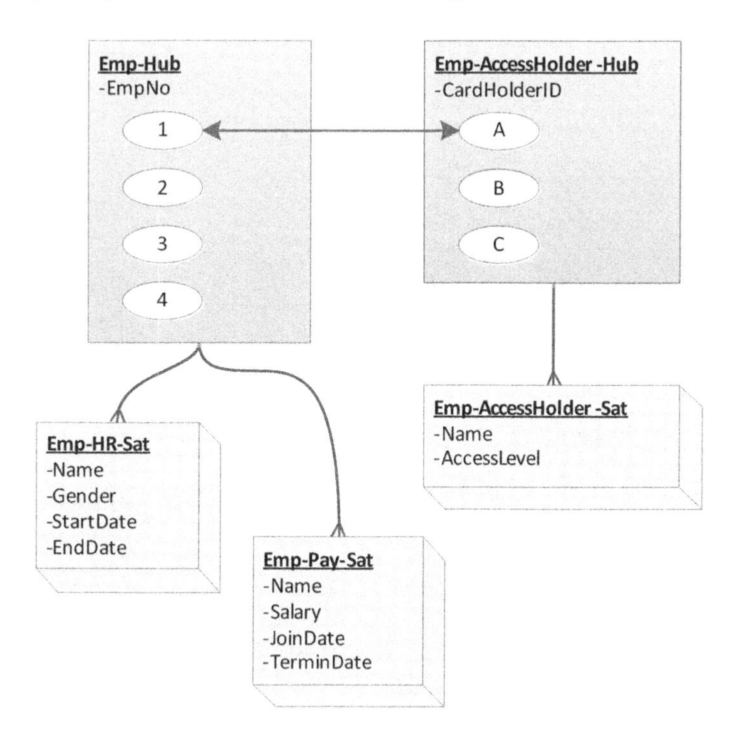

Figure 58: Source system DV for different but non-overlapping key values

If we refer back to the scenario presented in Figure 55 and the supporting text, we will see that the Access Card system knows its own card number but also knows the Payroll system's employee number. This explicit knowledge can be used to create a Same-As Link between employee Alex with Card Holder ID "A" and the same employee with employee number 1, as represented by the arrow on the diagram above.

We've still got the passively integrated Hub for HR and Payroll, but we can't use passive integration for the Access Holder system, because the real-world entity Alex has a business key of "A" instead of "1". Assuming the same semantics-&-grain, could we hold all source fees in the same "Employee" Hub? Most definitely.

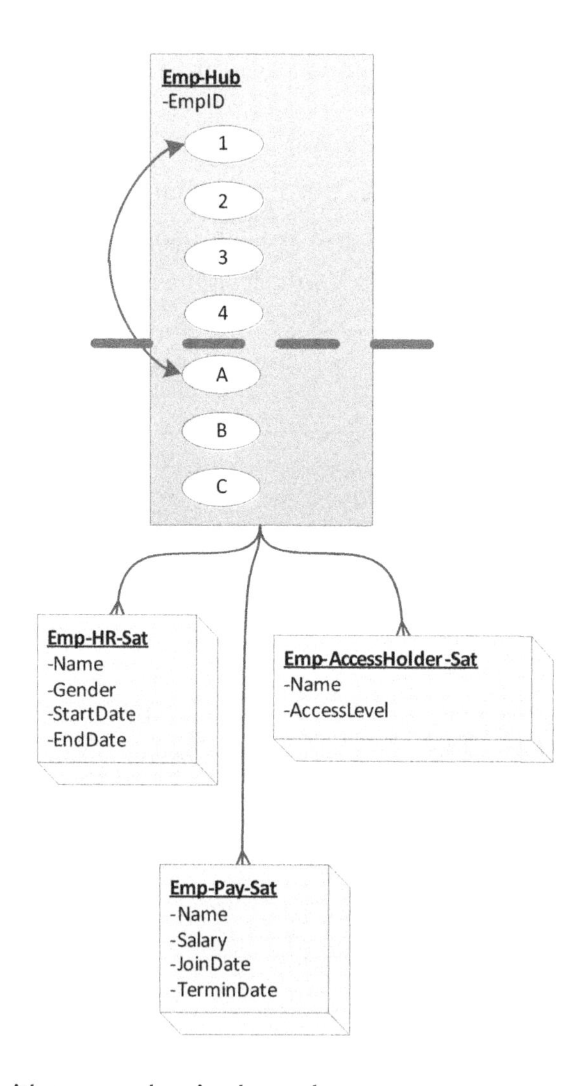

Figure 59: Shared Hub with non-overlapping key values

In this scenario, the business keys can never clash. One set are numbers, and the other set consists of alphabetic characters. We simply hold all of the employee business keys in the one Hub. (OK, the numbers are going to have to be recast as text strings so they can fit into the same column for the Employee ID business key, but we have to do that for hashing anyway.) Though not shown on the diagram, two of the Satellites will always relate to the Hub instances with numbers, and the other Satellite will always relate to the Hub instances with alphabetic business keys. The data contents between the two diagrams (Figure 58 and Figure 59) above are the same, but we've got all of the data for employees (remember, the same "semantics and grain") in the one Hub.

I know this example is about employees, but if we move the conversation to customers, an observation from a recent client site was that the business was most emphatic that it wanted all customer data in the same Hub, no matter what the key values or structures. At least then they would only have one place to go to as they worked towards untangling the mess that reflected the reality of their source systems.

Different, overlapping key values

In the previous example, we had the same real-world object (for example, Alex the employee) with different key values in different systems – employee number "1", or Card Hold ID "A". The business keys could happily coexist in the same Hub because they could never overlap. If we look back to the sample data set presented in Figure 55, and look at the Contract Management system, we see a new problem. The HR and Payroll systems use numbers 1, 2, and so on for their employee numbers, and the Contract Management system uses numbers 1, 2, and so on for their contractor numbers. If employee number 1 and contractor number 1 represented the same real-world instance, we could have passive integration, but we don't have this simplicity. Employee number 1 represents Alex, but contractor number 1 represents Brook (who has employee number 2, not to be confused with contractor number 2 for Dan)!

It's OK. Each system knows their own numbers, and thankfully the Contract Management system not only manages its contractor numbers but also records the associated HR system's employee numbers – the foundation for another Same-As Link. (And by the way, the Access Card system also knows about contractor IDs, too.) That's good news, but how do we store this data in our Data Vault?

If we use one Hub with a generic business key of "1", it's going to get ugly if we hang Alex's HR and Payroll Satellites off business key "1", and Brook's Contractor Satellite off the same Hub instance. Sure, all three sources that use numbers for their business keys may share the same "semantics and grain", but identical key values don't represent the same real-world entity, and that's not a good design. One horrible solution (that leans towards source system Data Vault) is to have a new Hub and Satellite just for the one source.

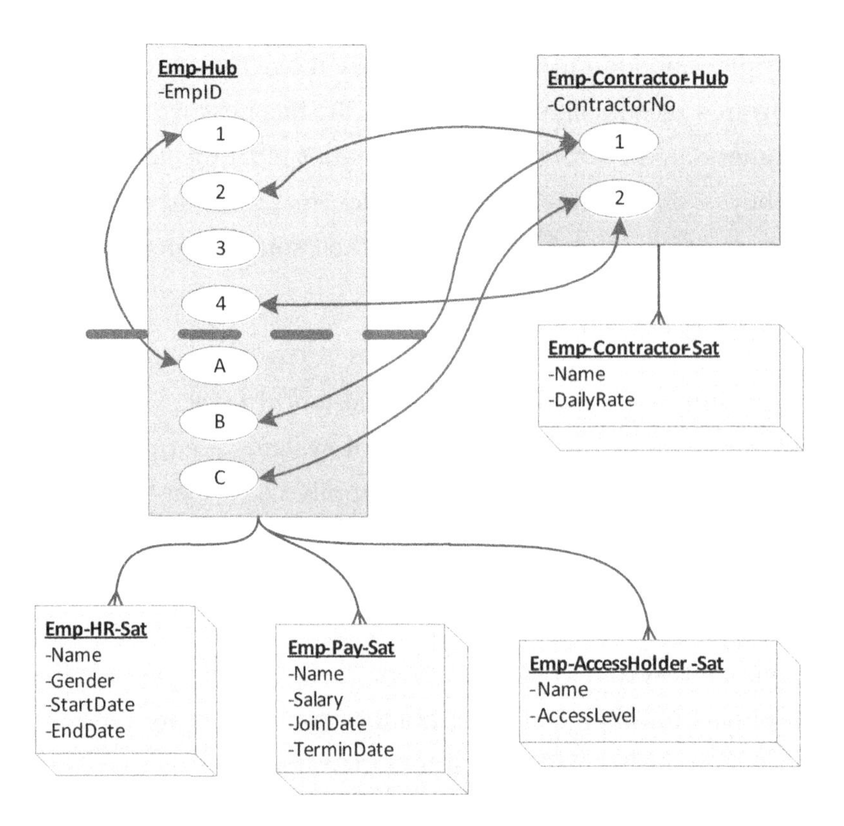

Figure 60: Source system DV for different but overlapping key values

We're progressively building on the emerging solution. We've still got one Hub for the passively integrated HR and Payroll employee numbers, and it also manages the non-overlapping alphabetic business key values for the Access Card system. But we want to keep the overlapping key values (for example, a business key of "1") separate so that we don't confuse employee number "1" with contractor ID "1". We've successfully avoided confusion over what business key "1" means, so that's good. But again assuming the business has agreed that contractors and salaried employees mean the same thing and have the same grain, the business still wants one employee Hub, so how might we deliver that?

The solution is pretty simple, really. We can add a new column to the business key to act as a discriminator to identify the source of the code set, and concatenate it with the raw business key value, using a separator such as the "|" character. Note that this new column can be a separate column in the Hub table, with the concatenation only occurring when we want to hash the business key.

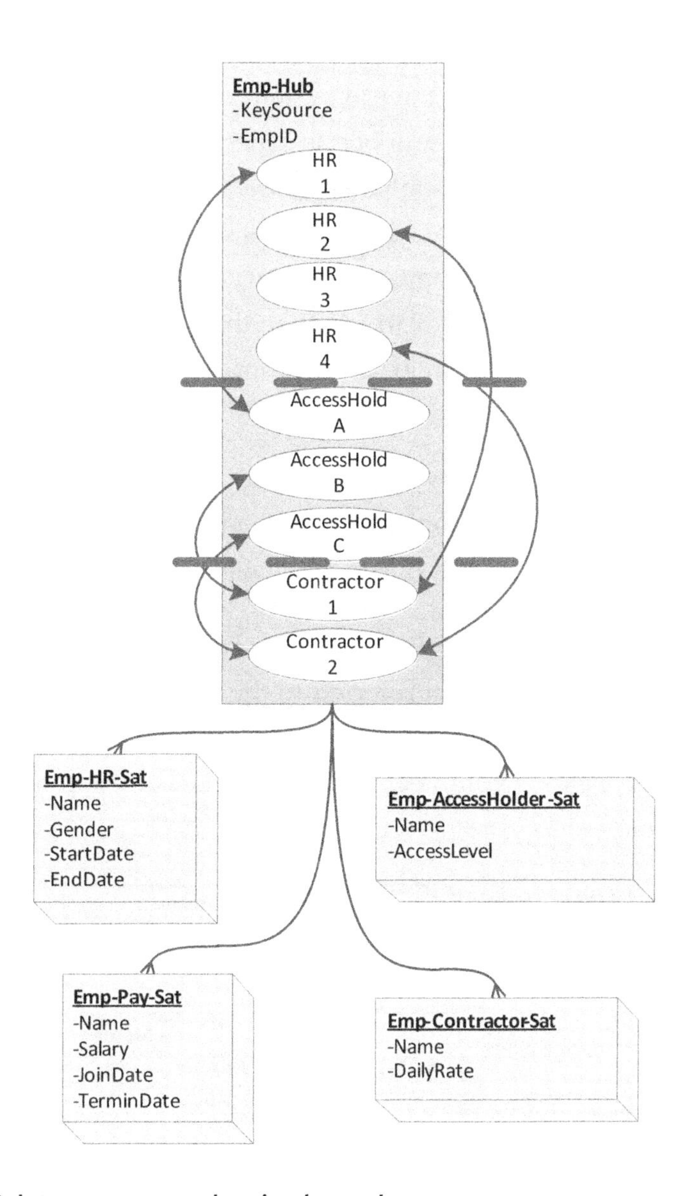

Figure 61: Shared Hub to manage overlapping key values

So now Alex has a business key in the Data Vault for an employee number of "HR|1" which won't have a clash of values with Brook's contractor ID of "Contractor|1", and Brook will also have an employee number of "HR|2", not to be confused with Dan's contractor ID of "Contractor|2". How easy is that!

Note that I mentioned this new column being the "key source". In the introduction to the sample data set, I noted that the HR system generates its own employee numbers, and that other systems such as the Payroll system don't generate their own business key, but simply reuse the employee number as generated by the HR system. So even if an instance in the Employee Hub is sourced by a data feed from the Payroll system, the Payroll system's *key* source is the HR system. If this sounds a bit confusing, let me take another example. If multiple IT systems use Country Code as a business key, if the key source for those codes is the United Nations, then that's the *key* source for the country codes, no matter which source system loaded countries to the Country Hub.

Multi-part keys

We're nearly there on getting a design to hold all objects of the same grain and semantics in a single Hub. But there's one more challenge.

In Figure 55, we introduced Alex, Brook, Chris and Dan as employees of a state government department. We've often referred to the fire emergency response scenario, so here we go again. The first four are more traditional "employees". But in my home state, we've also got a massive volunteer fire brigade. Let's look at another four people, this time as volunteers.

Organization	Volunteer Fire Brigade			
Source System	Human Resource (HR)			
Business Key	State	District	Brigade	Member No
Dan	VIC	EGIPPS	ABC	1
Ed	VIC	EGIPPS	ABC	2
Fran	VIC	EGIPPS	DEF	1
Glen	VIC	MALLEE	XYZ	1

Figure 62: Business Key scenario – Volunteer fire fighters

Sure, they're volunteers, but from the perspective of the overarching organization, they can be seen to be as much "employees" as people who get paid for the job. For the sake of this exercise, I am going to presume that they share the same "semantics and grain" criteria and should belong to the same Hub. But there's a problem. Their business key is a multi-part key, made up of four columns – each volunteer is identified by a Member

Number within their local Brigade, within a District, within a State (we have volunteer fire fighters across the borders – a wildfire doesn't politely stop and ask permission to jump state boundaries). So Dan is member number 1 in the ABC brigade of East Gippsland, Victoria.

If we build a new Hub for the volunteers (for the moment, separated from what we've already constructed because volunteers have a multi-part key), our Data Vault could look like this:

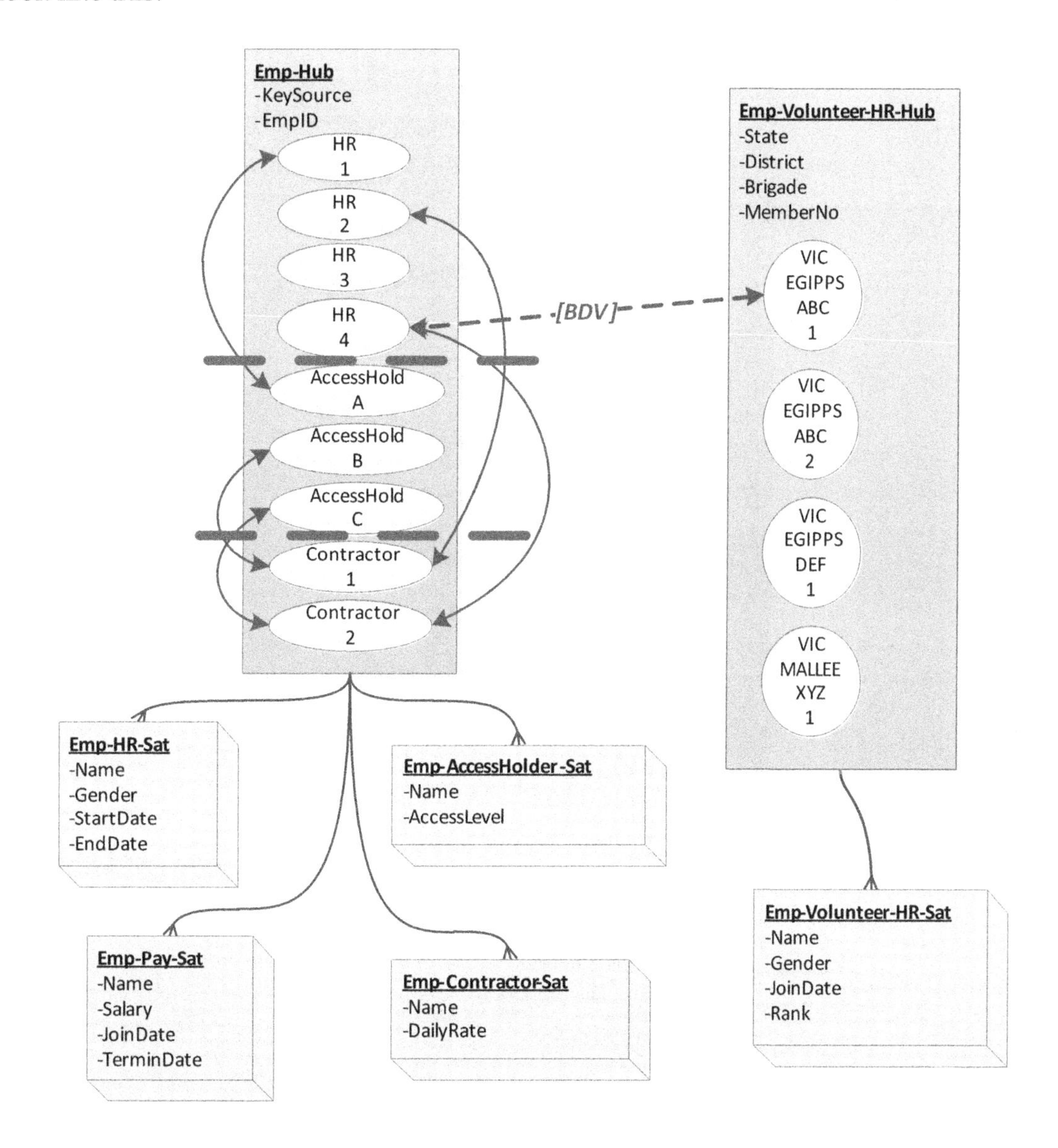

Figure 63: Source system DV for multi-part key values

There is another twist to this story. The person named Dan has a "day job" within the state government, but the same Dan is also a weekend volunteer. If we have some soft business rules to identify that match, we can have a business-rule-generated Same-As Link, shown here with a dotted line to reflect that it's not a hard Link created from raw source data. As in the other cases, the business wants all "employees" to be held together, so we restructure our Data Vault.

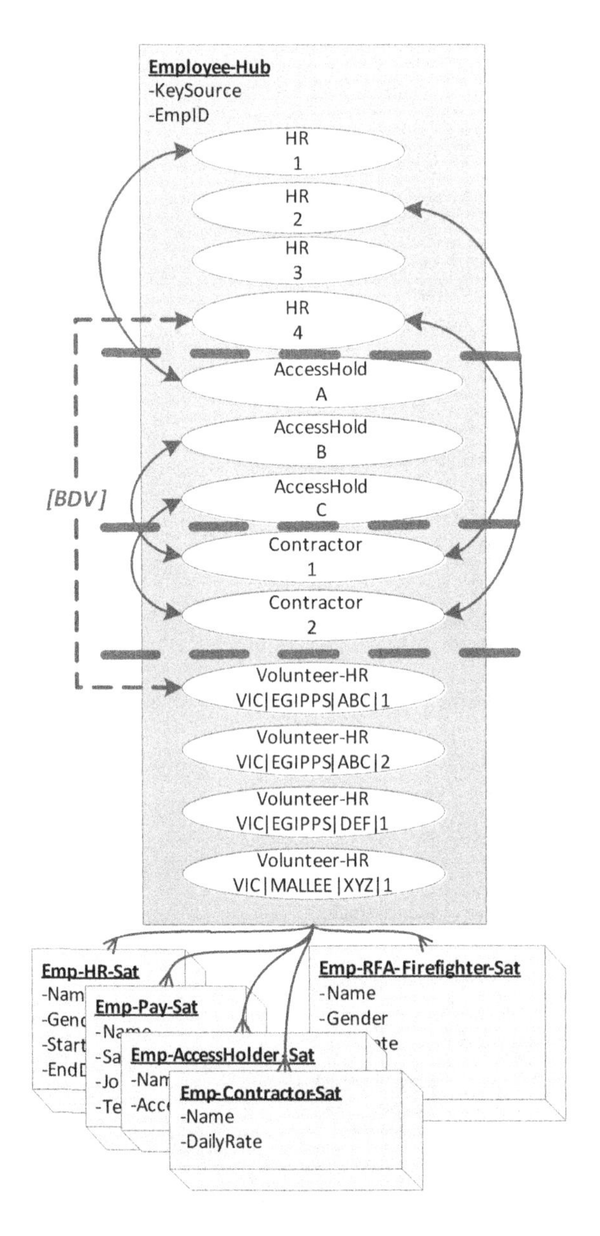

Figure 64: Shared Hub to manage multi-part key values

The Employee ID component of the business keys for the new Hub instances are a concatenation of the parts of the multi-part key. To fit in with what we did in the "Different, overlapping key values" section above, we've also still got a key source, nominally represented as "Volunteer-HR" to suggest the source is the volunteer organization's HR system.

Some people have quite valid hesitations about a business key that holds a concatenation of the parts that make it unique. The major concern I have heard is the requirement for downstream business consumers to be able to see each element, clearly and separately labeled. In the above example, let's say a query is required to select all volunteers from East Gippsland ("EGIPPS")? Sure, we can do substring stuff, but I agree that it's easier if each part of the business key is in its own, named column.

So where do we go from here? First, I like to recognize that in Data Vault 2.0 where the business key is hashed, there has to be a text string that concatenates the parts. We have to store the result of the hashing algorithm, and I feel comfortable also holding the concatenated text string as well. But that doesn't solve the issue of downstream data analysts wanting to see the component parts.

One option I saw proposed was to have the multi-part business keys held in separate Hubs, as shown in Figure 63, where the Employee Volunteer HR Hub held details of Volunteer Employees with their State, District, Brigade, and Member Number key as distinct columns. To reduce proliferation of Hubs, if another source system data feed for Employees was discovered to also have a 4-part key, the idea was that it could also load data into the same 4-part key Hub. To make it generalized, rather than calling it "Employee Volunteer HR Hub", it was suggested it could be named something like "Employee Hub for 4-Part Business Keys" (or something a bit more cryptic).

The benefit of this approach was that we had four explicitly named columns, being State, District, Brigade, and Member Number. But what if the state police force had a data feed from its Payroll system with employees identified by (say) Region, District, Station, and Police Member Number. The meaning of some of the four columns was different. The suggestion was that it would require its own Hub. Then we ended up with a Hub called:

- "Employee Hub for 4-Part Business Keys – sourced from Volunteer / HR"

… and a Hub called …

- "Employee Hub for 4-Part Business Keys – sourced from Police / Payroll"

Note that this is starting to look suspiciously like source system Data Vault for everything but single-part business keys.

And it got worse. So far we've got a core, single-part business key Hub, plus two 4-part business key Hubs (assuming that we don't find more 4-part business keys with different meaning for their columns). But we might also need one or several 2-part business key Hubs, one or several 3-part business key Hubs, and heaven help us if we find business keys with more than four parts.

Other options thankfully exist, based around having just one, central Hub with a concatenated business key, supplemented by mechanisms to facilitate presentation of their component parts. Some of the alternatives I have heard discussed include:

- Generalized key components in Hubs: This can be as simple as having columns called Part1, Part2, Part3 … in the Hub. It does mean queries can be run against the discrete elements of the business keys, but it doesn't overcome the problem of different *meaning* for each of the columns – for the volunteers, the first column is State, but for the police force members it is Region.

- Specific key components in Hubs: This is a variation on the above, with hard-coded names for every possible meaning. The benefit is that we can see exactly the column we need (State, Region, or whatever), but there is no end to the number of columns that might be required, with Nulls allowed for all of them.

- Key components in Satellites: If we consider a relational table, all data is held in columns whether it is part of the table's primary key or it's just changeable data. The data values for business keys could be held in source-specific Satellites. Sure, the business key values don't change over time like other Satellite values, but it's a place to store the data.

- Leave the business key in the foundational Employee Hub as a single column with concatenated values, but deconstruct the concatenated business key, using some business rules, and store the results in a business-centric Data Vault structure.

Whatever approach we choose (including options not listed above), I highly recommend that we don't let technical implementation issues budge us from the business-driven requirement of having one Hub for any given "semantics and grain" identification, no matter what the constructs of the business keys are, or what their values might be, or how many parts they have in a given business key. We may need some metadata defined to support our implementation, but that's OK. My recommendation, however, is that whatever approach we choose, we mustn't compromise the business fidelity and have multiple Hubs just to try to work around technical implementation issues. Stay true to the business!

Hubs with more than one business key

In traditional data modeling for a relational database, it's not uncommon to identify several candidate keys, where an entity can be uniquely identified by more than one key. For example, a person might get identified by their birth certificate number, their passport number, their tax file number, or possibly one of several other identifiers. Similarly, a car might be identified by its registration plate number, it Vehicle Identification Number (VIN), or the engine number on the engine block. A story challenges some easily made assumptions.

My wife and I were travelling in the Aussie outback. We were on a remote track when the engine died. We were carrying enough food and water to keep us alive for a very boring few weeks, and we also had an EPIRB – an Emergency Position Indicating Radio Beacon – so if we got close to the end of the food supplies and nobody had wandered down the track, we could press the button and wait for a rescue. Thankfully, it didn't take too long for Angelo, a worker from a nearby mine who was checking the water bores in the area, to discover us. He kindly arranged for our retrieval and transport to the nearest (!!!) mechanic. That's the rescue team below. Including the friendly police:

We had a few days in the mining town, and learned an interesting fact about their vehicles. The underground vehicles drove on wet-down surfaces and got caked in slush full of salt and other chemicals. Their bodies rusted out amazingly quickly – often in less than one year – but the engines were nearly new, having done very few kilometers. Vehicles such as Angelo's were the opposite. They drove amazingly long distances on the dry, desert tracks. There was little if any moisture to cause the body to rust in the dry desert air, but the engines were old before their time as the vehicles covered enormous distances. The solution? We grab good engines from the underground mine vehicles and good bodies from the surface vehicles, and we've got a new car.

But here's the catch. If we have a Data Vault Hub called Vehicle, what's the business key? We can't use the Registration Number, because many vehicles at the massive mine aren't registered for public road use. So we're left with Engine Number, or the body's VIN. But no matter which one we pick, what happens when engine/body swaps occur? If there are attributes such as number of cylinders and fuel type, they presumably belong to the engine, and body color and number of seats belong to the body.

There's a simple solution that works well for this scenario.

We can have a Hub for the body, with the VIN as the business key. Its Satellite (not shown here) can record body attributes such as color (which can change over time). Similarly we can have a Hub for the engine, and a Satellite for its attributes. We complete the design by having a Link that records the association of a body and an engine, and if the Link has a Satellite recording the effectivity dates for the association, we can record when an engine and a body were "amalgamated" to form a vehicle.

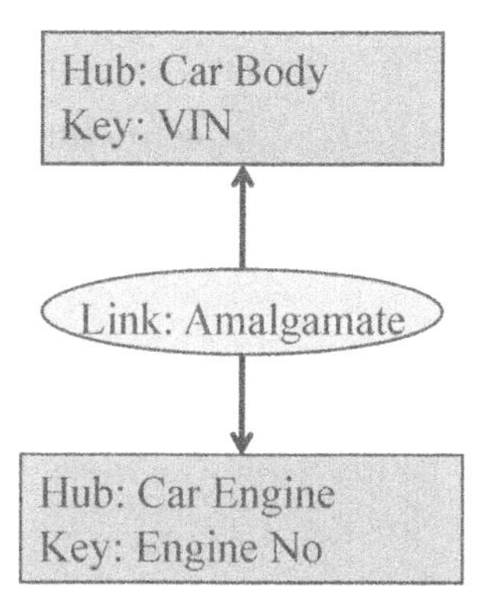

Figure 65: Hubs for a "Vehicle"

I encountered a similar situation when working on a Data Vault for a water utility. A water meter has a meter number stamped on it. Sometimes there are remote read devices attached to the meter to allow the meter reader to electronically get a reading without having to enter a property with a vicious dog guarding the meter! The remote read device also has a number, which it transits electronically along with the usage reading.

The one device (a physical meter with an attached remote read device) could be seen as having two business keys – the stamped meter number on the meter, and the electronically visible identifier for the remote read device. But like with the mine vehicles, the meter and the remote read device can be separated and paired up in new combinations. The physical meter can get old and worn out, and get replaced at the property, but the remote read device is still at the property. Or the vicious dog can get old and worn out and no longer be a threat, and the remote read device can be moved to another meter.

I did initially try to see if I could twist Data Vault a little to allow one Hub to have multiple business keys. With the help of a very friendly and very competent programmer visiting from Ireland, we actually forced Data Vault to accommodate multiple business keys (well done, Johnny). But the side effects of my suggested design were not good, and we returned to tried and true Data Vault standards. We had a separate Hub for the physical water meter, and another separate Hub for its associated remote read device, each with one business key, and associated by a Link.

The conclusion is straightforward. If we have a business entity with multiple business keys, and especially if the business keys represent changeable components of the whole, it can be simpler to have Hubs for each of the component parts. It's just a pattern for us to consider.

One final comment. We may encounter literature that is less than precise on differentiating between a Hub with multiple business keys, and a Hub where one of its business keys has multiple parts. Please take care when reading design comments to make sure which of the two situations the author is referring to.

Business-sourced Hub and Satellite instances

The distinction between Data Vault structures that are raw source-centric versus business-centric was introduced earlier, as was the distinction between instances in these Hubs, Links and Satellites that are sourced from loading of raw data versus being sourced from the execution of business rules. A few key reminders might be helpful, though:

- The so-called "raw Data Vault" and the "business Data Vault" are not separate databases, or even physically separate parts of one Data Vault. The distinction is simple. If the source of an object's data is raw data from an operational system, that instance has a "Record Source" attribute that references a raw source data feed. Conversely, if the source of an object's data is computation according to a business rule, that instance has a "Record Source" attribute that references a business rule.

  It is important to note that I said that a Data Vault *instance* can have its data come from a raw source or a business rule. I did ***not*** say that a Data Vault table (a Hub, a Link or a Satellite) will necessarily have all its instances come from just one source (raw or business). That is likely to be true for Satellites, but not always for Hubs (or Links). For example, some instances in the same Hub can come from raw source "A", others from raw source "B", and yes, some instances might be generated by a business rule. It is the individual instances (or rows if you like) that get classified as raw or business. Of course, if all of the instances can only ever come from one of these sources, you may choose to classify the whole Hub, Link or Satellite as raw or business, but that is a derived classification.

- Business-sourced instances can be physically stored (for example, as a table in a relational database), or they can be virtual (such as a view).
- By default, the design structure of Hubs in a Data Vault should be based on a business perceptions (from the enterprise data model, or an "enterprise ontology" if we prefer). This is true whether the instances in the Hub are created from raw source system data or from business rules.

Using business rules to populate instances in Satellites

Some of the most common business-centric structures in a Data Vault are "conformed" Satellites that hold values constructed selectively from several other Satellites from disparate sources and/or from derived values. We might remember the Data Vault Hub and Satellites we looked at earlier for Fire Trucks? Let's look at how we can use source-centric data to assemble some computed values better suited for downstream consumption.

On the left, we've got the source-centric Data Vault Satellites for Fire Trucks – one Satellite populated from the Fleet Management source system, and the other populated from the Shared Resource Pool system. Some people may classify them as being part of the "raw" Data Vault because (1) they are structured to reflect source-system attributes, and (2) they are populated from source system feeds, with the Record Source recording the precise source feed.

On the right, we've got a new Satellite that I have called the Fire Truck "Business" Satellite. Its structure is business-centric - the names of the attributes reflect what the business wants to call them, not necessarily what they were named in source systems. It also is populated based on business rules, and hence many might label it as being part of the "business" Data Vault. Again please note that it is not in a separate database – it is just another artefact in the Data Vault that just happens to be business-centric in its structure, and with the Record Source attribute holding something like "System Generated" (or even the specific Business Rule used to generate the values).

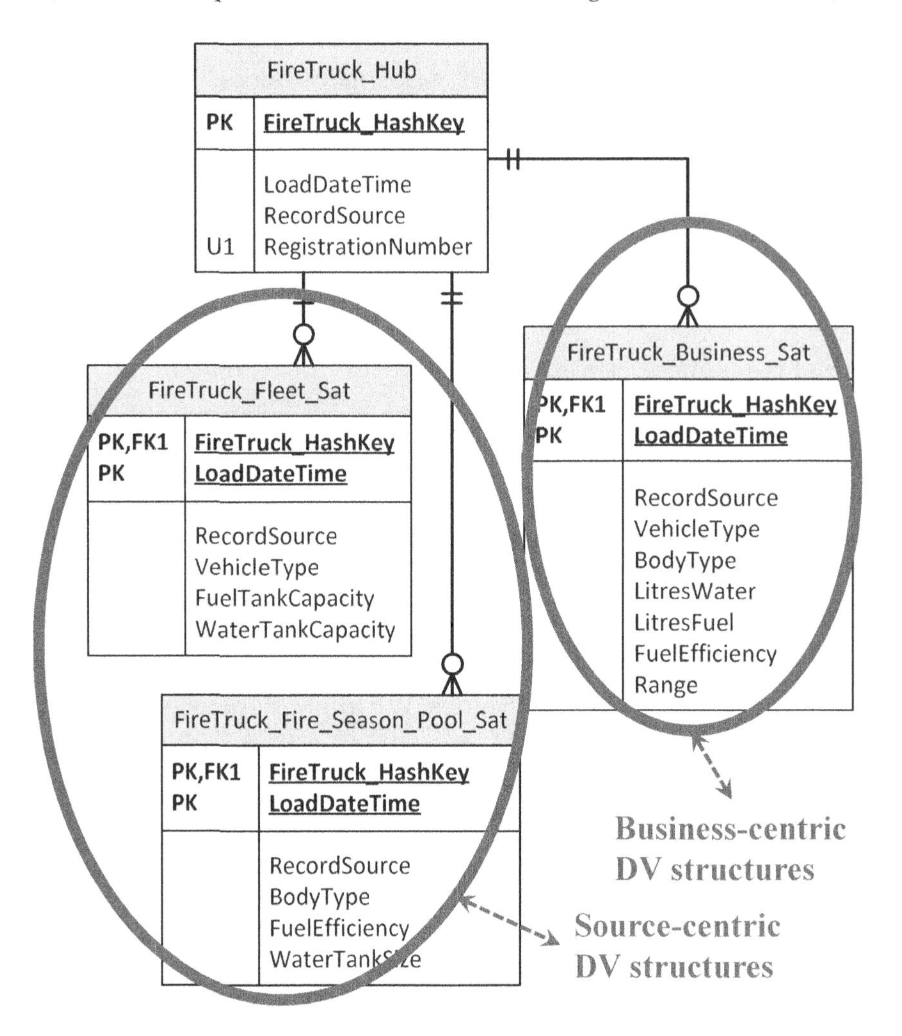

Figure 66: Business Satellite for the Fire Truck Hub

Remember that for any given Fire Truck in the Hub, there may be:

- values for that fire truck in only the Fleet Management Satellite, or
- values for that fire truck in only the Shared Resource Pool Satellite, or
- values for that fire truck presented by both source systems.

Let's look at some of the attributes in the "Business" Satellite above, and consider how we might populate those "business" attributes:

- Vehicle Type: There is a matching attribute in the Fleet Management system's Satellite. It can be used directly if the fire truck has values in the Fleet Management Satellite.

- Body Type: There is a matching attribute in the Shared Resource Pool system's Satellite. It can be used directly if the fire truck has values in the Shared Resource Pool Satellite. This is exactly the same logic as for the Vehicle Type attribute above, other than the values come from the other source-centric Satellite.

- Liters (of) Water: This one's a bit more interesting.

    - Firstly, there is no attribute of the same name in either source-centric Satellite, but the good news is that the business confirms that the Water Tank Capacity and Water Tank Size in the respective source-centric Satellites both carry values related to how much water the fire truck carries.
    - There's a minor issue, though. While the value from the Water Tank Capacity attribute can be used directly because its unit-of-measure is liters, the value from the Water Tank Size attribute is recorded in imperial (UK) gallons and must be converted by multiplying its value by the constant "4.55".
    - There's one more consideration. For any given fire truck, there might be values in both source-centric Satellites. If so, which one is to be used, especially if they disagree? Again, the business provides guidance, directing that they trust the Fleet Management system's values more, and they are to be used if there is a clash. If we look back to the sample data provided for Fire Truck CCC-333 in the tables earlier in this chapter, they appear to hold contradictory values. But as a light-hearted comment, perhaps they do mean the same thing - a measure of 450 Liters (roughly) equates to 100 imperial (UK) Gallons!

- Liters (of) Fuel: This is relatively simple. The values exist in the Fleet Management system's Fuel Tank Capacity attribute, even though it uses a different attribute name.

- Fuel Efficiency, in Liters per 100 kilometers: This is another simple mapping from the Shared Resource Pool system's attribute of the same name.

- Range: Ah, now, here's a challenge. We can't find any attributes, even with a different name, that look like what we want. Again the business comes to our rescue. From the Liters (of) Fuel attribute above *and* the Fuel Efficiency attribute above, we can compute the vehicle's theoretical driving range; the larger the tank size, and the better the fuel efficiency, the greater the vehicle's range.

Source-centric Satellite instances are created every time a source system feed presents different values to the Data Vault. The triggers for creation of business-centric Satellite instances may, for example, be based on either the creation of a relevant source-centric Data Vault Satellite instance, or perhaps computed nightly to see what has changed.

That's a bit of a worked example from an earlier scenario on Fire Trucks. If we apply the same principles to the more recent scenario for Employees, we might end up with the model in Figure 67.

The comments are similar. We've got a business-centric Data Vault Satellite, generated from business rules such as renaming Salary to Pay Rate, selectively grabbing Name from whatever Satellite is more trusted, and so on.

Using business rules to populate instances in Hubs

Many people who have developed data warehouses will be familiar with the idea of "conformed" data. I suspect some will more quickly feel comfortable with a conformed Satellite, where a melting pot of data from all sorts of sources is pulled together to create a single, consistent business-centric view. But now let's add a "conformed Hub" to our Employee scenario, where likewise we have Hub instances from several sources but we want to pull the melting pot of instance data together in a more consumable form.

Hub instances can be created not only as a result of loading data from raw source, but also as a result of the execution of business rules. Let's start with the fire truck example from earlier in this book.

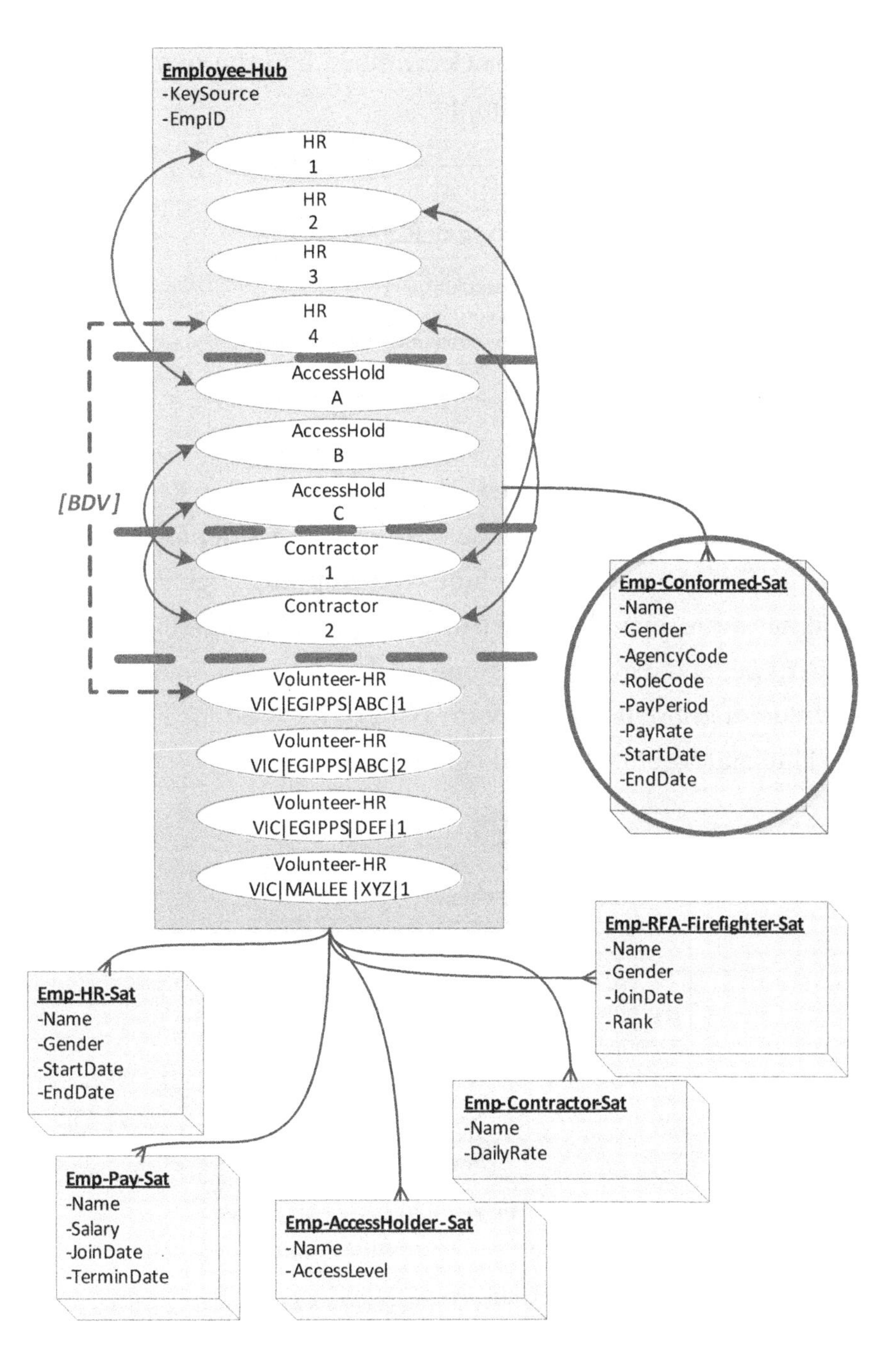

Figure 67: Business Satellite for the Employee Hub

Instances in the Fire Truck Hub had been created as the result of processing source system feeds from the Fleet Management system and the Shared Resource Pool system. The "grain" of the involved parts is the same – Fire Truck. The business concept is a

Fire Truck, the business key is a Fire Truck Number, and the two source system feeds provide data about Fire Trucks. Life's simple.

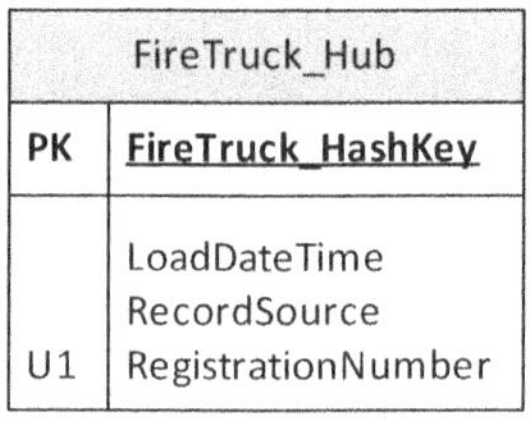

FireTruck_Hub	
PK	FireTruck_HashKey
	LoadDateTime
	RecordSource
U1	RegistrationNumber

Figure 68: Fire Truck Hub (again)

Along comes another source data feed, this time from the Resource Management system. It handles a whole heap of Resources that can be deployed to an emergency event such as a fire. This might include water pumps, generators, bull dozers, chainsaws, and lots more, including fire trucks! This means that (logically) the Resource entity is a supertype, and Fire Truck is one of its subtypes. As a source system data feed, it has a different grain. If we follow the pattern we used for Fire Trucks, we might end up with a Hub and Satellite like that below.

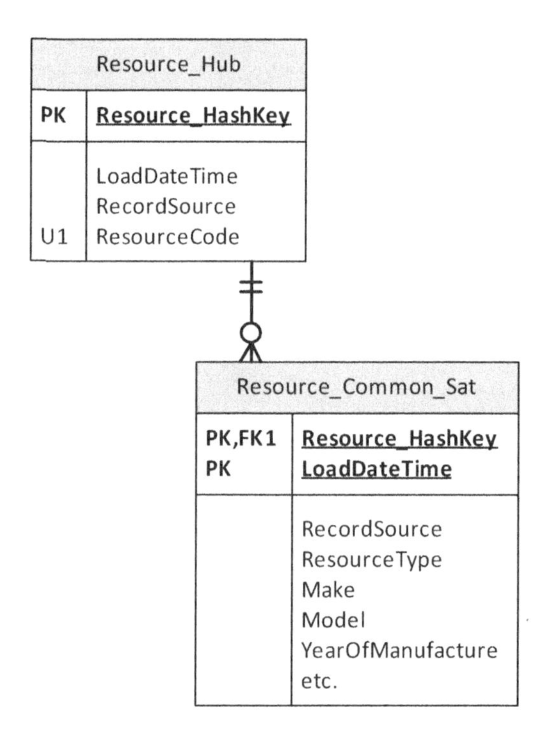

Figure 69: Resource Hub, plus common-attribute Satellite

The Satellite has been included in part to represent those more-common attributes such as Make, Model, and Year of Manufacture, but the important reason for including it is to show the "Resource Type" attribute that classifies Resource instances as a Generator, a Bulldozer, or whatever. There may also be other Satellites (not shown) that may hold specialized attributes peculiar to very specific types of assets.

Now the challenge. We've got Fire Truck instances in the Fire Truck Hub, and also in the Resource Hub. What do we do? Here's one approach, and it's pretty simple:

1. We continue to load data into the Fire Truck Hub from source system feeds at the grain of Fire Truck – these are the Fleet Management system, and the Shared Resource Pool system feed. This is a load of raw source data.

2. We also load data into the Resource Hub from the source system that feeds at the grain of Resource – the Resource Management system feed. This also is a load of raw source data.

3. We then have a business rule whose pseudo code is something like:

    - If the Resource Type in the Resource Hub's Common attributes Satellite is "FT" for Fire Truck, present the Resource Hub's Resource Code (for example, "CCC-333") to the Fire Truck Hub as a Registration Number.

    - If the presented Registration Number hasn't yet been loaded to the Fire Truck Hub, it is loaded as we would for any Hub load!

Note: Just to reiterate, this is a load where the Record Source records a *business* rule as the source, not a raw source system. Now we have instances in the Fire Truck Hub that are "raw", and some instances in the same Hub that are "business"! We can't say that the Fire Truck Hub itself is a "raw Data Vault" table, nor can we say it is a "business Data Vault" table. Instead, we note that *instances* in the Fire Truck Hub can be either raw or business.

Of course, there may be business rules to get Satellite data across from the Asset to the Fire Truck as well, but those principles have been covered in the preceding section.

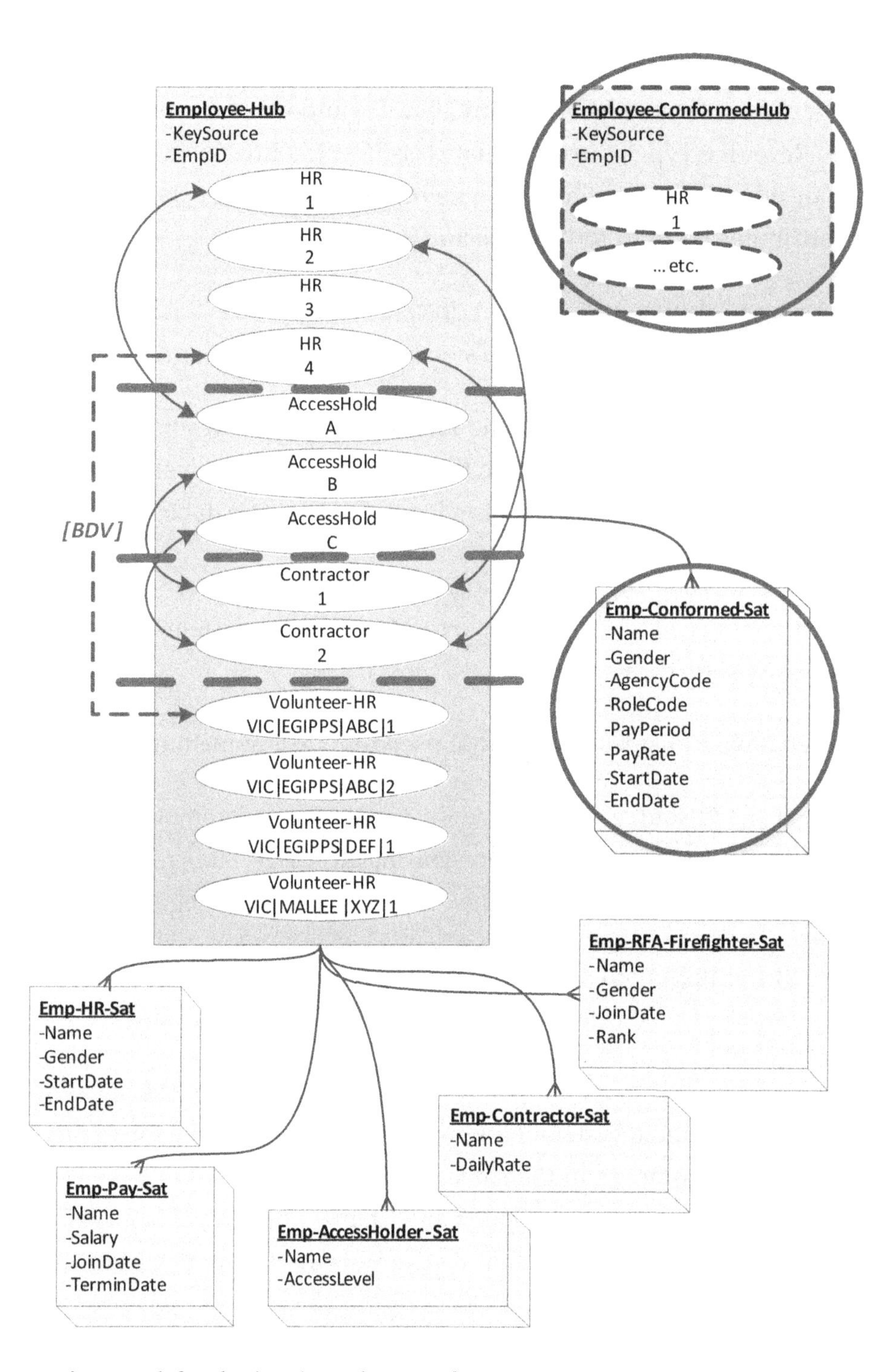

Figure 70: Business Hub for the (raw) Employee Hub

That's one example of having business rules relating to Hub instances, where there are conflicting levels of "grain" (supertype / subtype) across different source feeds. Another common example relates to consolidation of Same-As Links. Sometimes Same-As Links identify accidental duplicates in the same source – one of my clients had customers who deliberately tried to have new customer records created so they could avoid the consequences of unpaid debts under their earlier customer identity! Other times, different source systems create instances using different business keys, but the Same-As Links record that the same real-world entity is known by different key values across multiple systems.

Whatever the reason for ending up with multiple Hub instances that represent the same real-world entity, the business may well ask that the duplicates be *logically* consolidated before being consumed. Please note that I stress the consolidation is logical, not physical. The duplicates, with all of their history, are still retained as raw source loads to the Data Vault. It's just that business rules are used to give the impression that there is only one Hub instance for every real-world employee (or customer, or ...).

Our data is now much better prepared for consumption by the end users, which after all is our primary goal.

Well-formed Links versus "ugly" Links

Preamble

When we set out to design Hubs, we wanted to hear from the business about their business concepts, their business keys, and their hierarchies of types. When designing Links, we are again well advised to go to the business and ask them about the relationships between their core concepts, rather than having our thinking constrained by constructs in the source systems.

The Links the business wants to see for downstream analysis are typically founded on these fundamental business-centric relationships. If we're half lucky, the raw data as supplied to the Data Vault may directly reflect those business object relationships. For example, we might get a data feed that is a simple declaration that a certain employee is the account manager for a certain customer. There are two Hubs (employee and customer), and a simple Link. However, it's more than likely we will get plenty of data feeds that capture complex events or transactions, and the data may be far from normalized. Before it can be consumed by end users, it may need quite a bit of transformation, including untangling the implied relationships. It's interesting that some end users of this data may also want to see the raw transactions as posted. Either way, we simply can't tackle mapping from the raw source data to any enterprise view without having first defined the enterprise view, and thought about how it might map to Hubs, and Links!

When the business and systems views happen to align

We've had a few scenarios to look at so far for the design of Hubs. We've looked at Resources, especially Fire Trucks. We've also looked at Emergency Events, including Fires and Floods. And we've spent quite a bit of time looking at Employees. In one form or another, we've designed Hubs for all of those subject areas, solidly founded on what the business had decided is the right level. That's a really good start. Next we need to "link" them together, starting with Fires and Employees.

When we talked to the business people about assigning employees to emergencies, we heard two things. Firstly, the Human Resources (HR) department can be approached to release employees into a pool of available resources for a particular fire. Maybe they've been asked for one logistics officer, two bulldozer drivers, and three firefighters. They talk to candidate employees, and one by one release them to the fire. The screen they use in the HR operational system might look something like this:

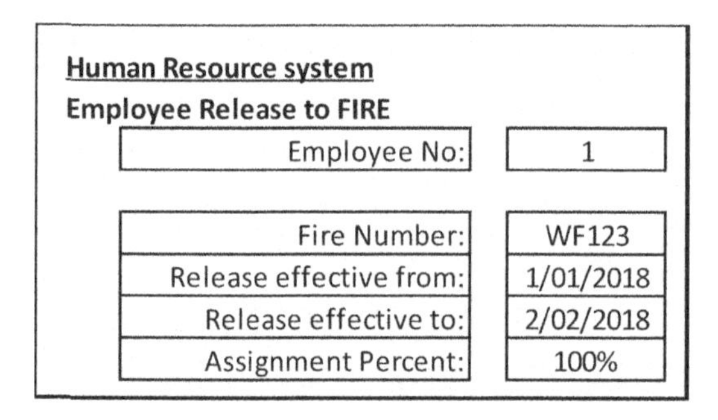

Figure 71: Releasing an employee for fire duty

I call this the "push" scenario. A resource from head office is pushed out into the front line's resource pool.

Now we look at a second scenario. Instead of pushing resources into the pool, an administrative officer working on the wildfire response thinks of particular people he/she would like assigned, and uses his/her screen to log specific requests to pull the nominated people from head office into the wildfire's resource pool.

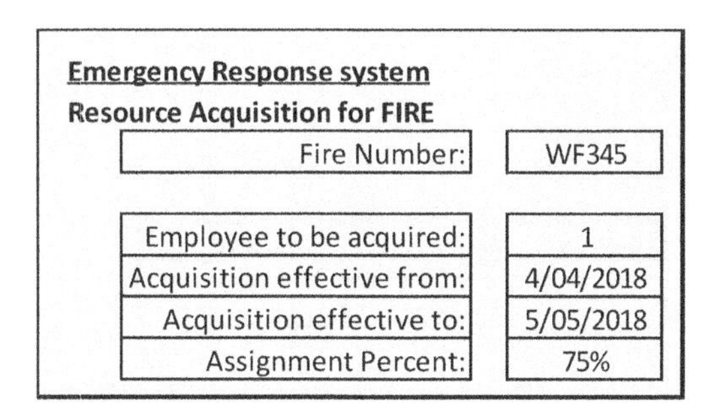

Figure 72: Requesting an employee for fire duty

Interestingly, it's really the same data structure in both cases, even though sourced from two separate operational systems. Nominate an employee (one Hub), nominate a wildfire (another Hub), provide some date and percent assignment details, and the transaction is completed. The enterprise data model takes a holistic view, not a source system view, and represents both source-centric scenarios as one Resource Pool Assignment relationship:

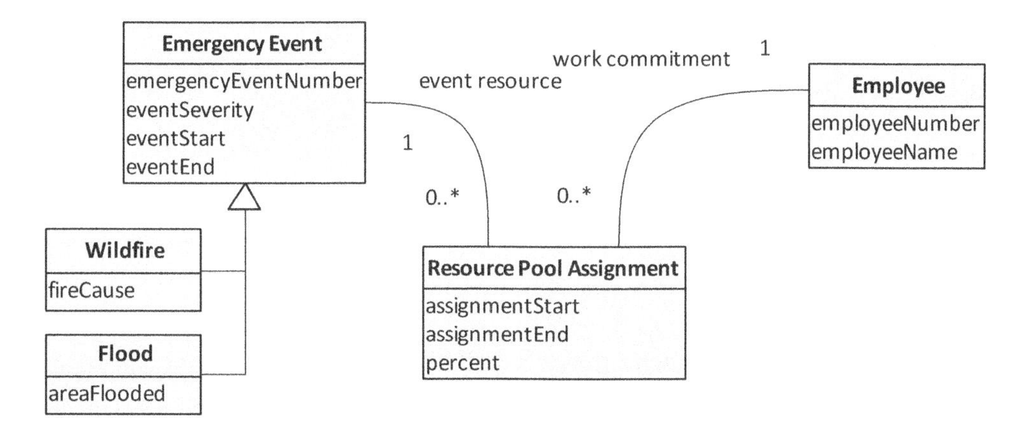

Figure 73: Resource assignment logical data model

If you recall, we chose to design the Data Vault Hubs at the Wildfire and Flood level of granularity rather than at the Emergency Event supertype level. We have taken the relationship that an Employee can be assigned to an Emergency Event, and pushed that supertype relationship down to become a more specialized relationship involving the Wildfire subtype as a Hub. Leaving aside the Data Vault attributes for things like load dates, source systems, and hash keys, a Data Vault model, including Satellites on the Links, might look like this:

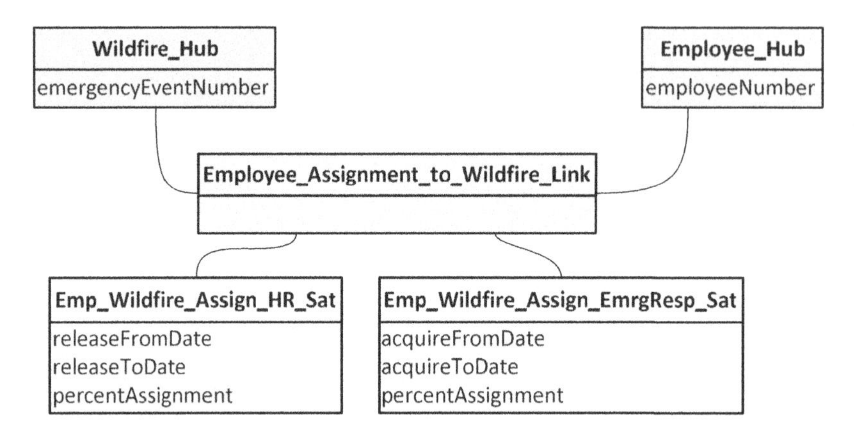

Figure 74: Resource assignment Data Vault model

Note that the Hubs are a direct reflection of how the business sees their core concepts, and that this particular Link is likewise aligned to how the business sees their core data relationships. If only it were always that easy!

When life is a bit more complex

In the real world, and in operation systems, events occur and transactions are executed. Each event or transaction can involve many business objects. Something as common as a sales transaction can involve the customer, the store, the employee, and of course, products.

If the source system is nicely normalized, and if we have Change Data Capture (CDC) turned on in the source system's database, we might be presented with lots of tight little feeds to represent the one sales transaction. For example, the allocation of a salesperson to a store might be triggered by a Human Resources event, and only refer to two Hubs –

the salesperson (an employee), and the store (another Hub). A totally separate feed might associate the order to the customer, and yet another set of individual feeds might associate individual line items to products. That simplicity, especially if each part aligns with agreed business relationships between business objects, was presented in the section above.

Now the harsh reality. Many data feeds triggered by events or transactions in the operational systems deliver data that is not "normalized". Each data feed can reference many Hubs (Customer, Store, Employee, and Product). That's just one example. Another typical example might be an extract from a source system where multiple joins across multiple tables have been performed to get a flat extract file. Let's work through an example related to the Resource Pool Assignment scenario presented in the "When the business and systems views happen to align" section above, but taken from the view of timesheet transactions.

Let's start with the nice, clean enterprise data model view.

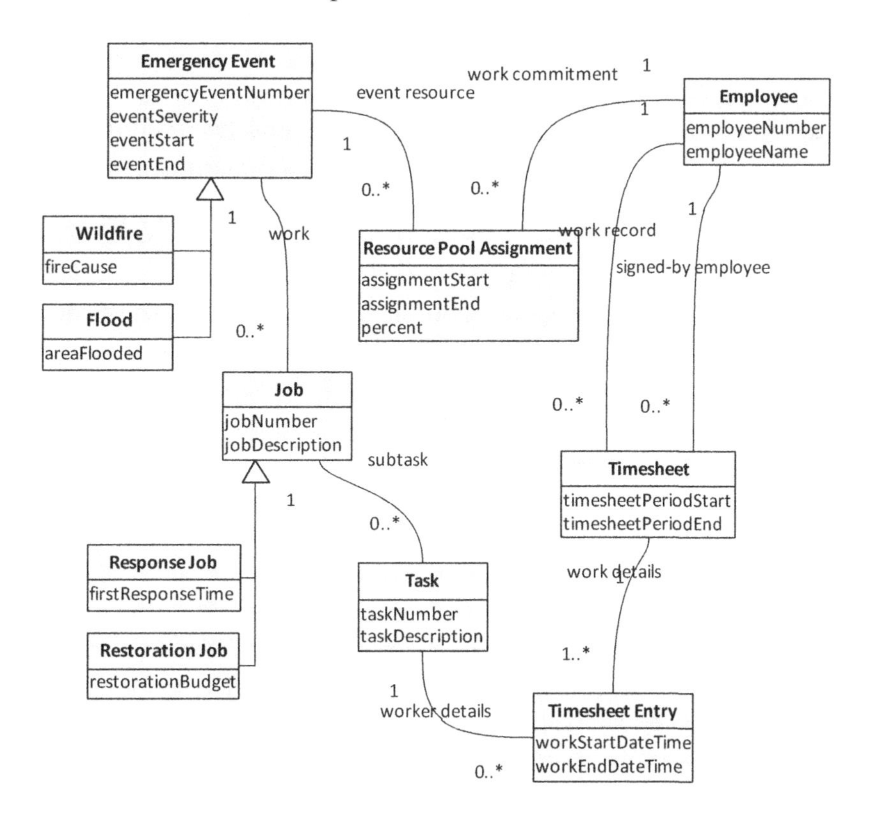

Figure 75: Enterprise logical view of timesheet transactions

We've already seen the assignment of Employees to Emergency Events. Now we can see the idea that large chunks of work called Jobs are done in response to an emergency. These Jobs are broken down into smaller pieces of work, known as Tasks. Timesheets are filled in for Employees working on the Tasks, and signed by other Employees to authorize payment for work done. Each Timesheet Entry (a line on the timesheet) refers to a specific Task the Employee worked on at the nominated time.

An extract from a hypothetical timesheet transaction file follows.

Emp. No.	T'sheet Period Start Date	T'sheet Period End Date	Sign. By Emp. No.	Emerg. Event No.	Job No.	Task No.	Work Start Date	Work Start Time	Work End Date	Work End Time
111	1st Jan	7th Jan	999	WF111	WF111-J1	WF111-J1-T2	1st Jan	9:00	1st Jan	13:00
111	1st Jan	7th Jan	999	WF111	WF111-J1	WF111-J1-T2	1st Jan	13:30	1st Jan	17:30
111	1st Jan	7th Jan	999	WF**111**	WF**222**-J1	WF**333**-J1-T2	2nd Jan	9:00	1st Jan	13:00
(etc.)										

Figure 76: Sample timesheet transactions

We *could* try to "normalize" the input on the way into the Data Vault, breaking it into the relationships represented by the enterprise data model. There are implied relationships between emergency events and their jobs, between those jobs and the smaller tasks they contain, and so on. But notice the highlighted bits of the third row. Maybe these implied relationships may contain bad data. Does the Emergency Event Wildfire WF111 really contain tasks prefixed with Job WF222?

This overly simple example carries a message. If we've got transactions coming into the Data Vault that are not normalized (and hence may reference lots of Hubs), it might be better to create a Link & Link Satellite for storing a faithful, auditable copy of the incoming raw transaction.

The model below holds source-centric Data Vault values. From there we can generate more information as business-centric Data Vault objects – read on.

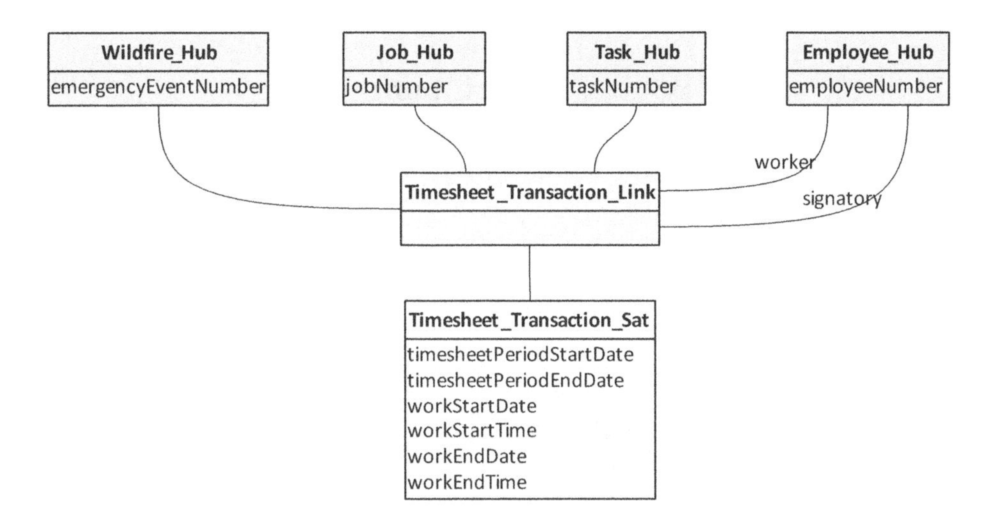

Figure 77: Raw transaction data storage in a Link & Satellite

Business-sourced Data Vault Link and Satellite instances

For the baseline shown in Figure 77 above, we can go on to use business rules to populate business-structured Data Vault Links that represent the enterprise data model's fundamental business relationships, as shown (logically) in Figure 75. These might include the Wildfire-to-Job Link and the Job-to-Task Link, with Satellites as appropriate. We might also be able to imply the Employee-Assigned To-Wildfire Link? And could we (should we) create a Timesheet Hub, implied by all of the timesheet transactions sharing common parentage?

All of these are possibilities we might want to discuss with the business. Here's another one: what if the business later decides that Jobs and Tasks are really the same thing, a bit like Dan Linstedt and Michael Olschimke's example of an aircraft engine,[31] and the engine's parts (turbine, compressor ...) all being just items in the Part Hub. Now we would have one consolidated Hub. Can we populate that Hub from this data? Of course we can. Change the business rules and we're off and running.

[31] Linstedt D. & Olschimke O. (2016) *"Building a Scalable Data Warehouse with Data Vault 2.0", page 131.*

What if we get it wrong?

We have been advocating that we design our Data Vault based around the enterprise data model. We want a single cohesive view. That's a great theory, but what if we get the enterprise data model design wrong? Isn't that a serious risk? Aren't we putting all our eggs in one basket? The answer is that the risk is not as high as it may appear.

1. The fundamentals of an enterprise data model are unlikely to radically change unless the business profoundly changes, as may be true when companies merge. By designing the Data Vault around the business rather than around technology, we start with greater stability. Sure, there will be some business changes, but when they do happen, there are two more saving graces.

2. If the enterprise data model upon which the Data Vault is based is itself constructed using data model patterns, these patterns have been proven again and again to be resilient to change. Len Silverston calls them "universal" data model patterns because of their ability to be applied widely. If you want to read more about data model patterns, David Hay's books[32] [33] and Len Silverston's books[34] [35] [36] are on my recommendation shortlist.

3. Data Vault, by its very nature, is more adaptable to change. I recommend reading Dan Linstedt and Michael Olschimke's book, "*Building a Scalable Data Warehouse with Data Vault 2.0*"[37] for hints on accommodating change.

---

[32] Hay D. (1996) "*Data Model Patterns: Conventions of Thought*".

[33] Hay D. (2011) "*Enterprise Model Patterns: Describing the World*".

[34] Silverston L. (2001) "*The Data Model Resource Book, Volume 1: A library of Universal Data Models for All Enterprises*".

[35] Silverston L. (2001) "*The Data Model Resource Book, Volume 2: A Library of Universal Data Models by Industry Types*".

[36] Silverston L. & Agnew P. (2009) "*The Data Model Resource Book, Volume 3: Universal Patterns for Data Modeling*".

[37] Linstedt D. & Olschimke O. (2016) "*Building a Scalable Data Warehouse with Data Vault 2.0*".

Designing and building a Data Vault is a process. A business-centric design, based on patterns, can reasonably be expected to be closer to the mark from the outset, but it won't be perfect, and even it if was, we need a process for when things in the real world change. Let's look deeper at the last bullet point above on the inherent adaptability of Data Vault, starting with a business view of Emergency Events.

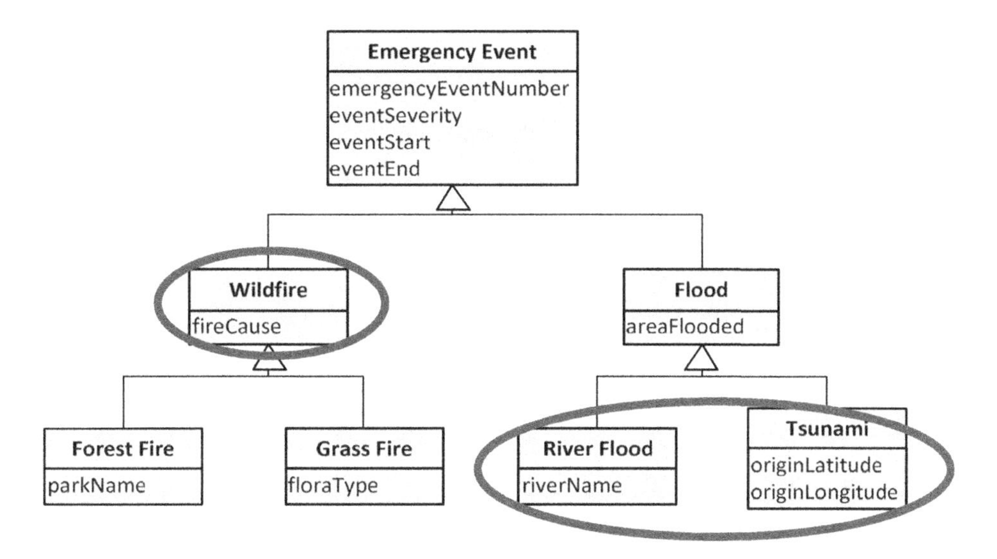

Figure 78: Emergency Event initial subtypes

The hierarchy shows a snippet from the enterprise data model, with Emergency Event having subtypes of Wildfire (further subtyped into Forest Fire and Grass Fire), and Flood (with River Flood and Tsunami as its subtypes). As described in "Finding the sweet spot", discussions are held with the business, and the circled subtypes are chosen for implementation as Data Vault Hubs.

That decision stands for quite some time, but a subsequent decision is made that the two Hubs, River Flood and Tsunami, were too fine grained and should now be just one Flood Hub. And while we're at it, our decision on the Wildfire Hub has gone the other way. We now want to abandon it and instead have two Hubs, one for Forest Fire and one for Grass Fire.

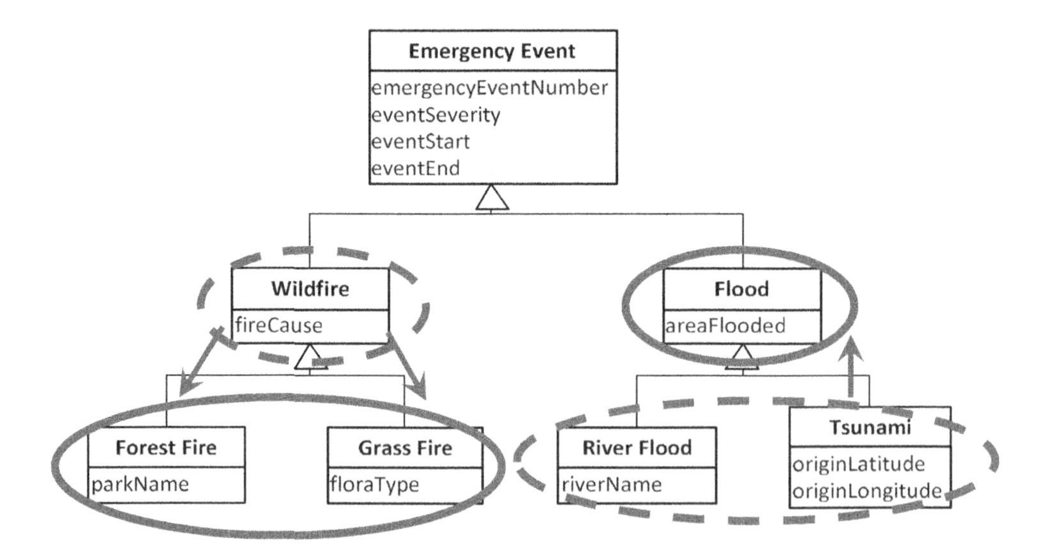

Figure 79: Emergency Event revised subtypes

What do we do? Let's start with the combining of the River Flood and Tsunami:

- Create the one new Flood Hub.
- Redefine the mapping of the incoming data feeds to point to the new Hub rather than the old pair of Hubs, and start loading to it from now on.
- We actually don't need to do anything with the historic data against the old pair of Hubs. Their Satellites won't change in the future as the mapping now directs future feeds to the single Flood Hub.
- Using business rules, we can consolidate the data from the two old Hubs (and their Satellites), merging their two historically separated views with the new single Hub and its Satellites.

The important thing to note is we don't try to change history. We used to load to the River Flood and Tsunami Hubs; now we leave them untouched as a faithful record of the past. All we do is present a new business-centered view of the data as if for all time it had been loaded to the Flood Hub.

Now let's consider the splitting of the Wildfire Hub to create a Forest Fire Hub and a Grass Fire Hub. Our actions follow a similar pattern. Our tasks are:

- Create the two new Forest Fire and Grass Fire Hubs.

- Redefine the mapping of the incoming data feeds to point to the two new Hubs rather than the one old Hub, and start loading to them from now on.

- In a manner similar to the combining of the River Flood and Tsunami Hubs, for splitting the Wildfire Hub we again don't need to do anything to the historic data historically held against the old single of Wildfire Hub; its Satellite won't change as the mapping now directs future feeds to the pair of Forest Fire and Grass Fire Hubs.

- Using business rules, we can split data from the single old Wildfire Hub (and its Satellites), merging its historically single view with the two new Hubs (& their Satellites).

Too easy! But remember, while Data Vault is architected to be flexible, taking such changes on board is made easier by having the design conversations based around the overarching enterprise data model.

CHAPTER 5

Task #3: Map Your Source Systems to the Data Vault Design

We've looked at a case study involving Fire Trucks assigned to Fires. That nice little example may be helpful as an introduction to Data Vault, but it has two huge, gaping holes:

1. It looks at sourcing data for the Data Vault from a single operational system. Arguably one of the most important duties for a Data Vault is to facilitate integration of data from multiple sources. This chapter presents the mechanics of loading data into a Data Vault, and then describes "Task #3" by presenting guidelines for mapping raw source data into the Data Vault.

2. It talks of getting data into a Data Vault, but ignores an essential aspect behind the existence of a Data Vault – getting data assembled for easy consumption by business people, which is where the Data Vault needs to focus if it's going to be applauded for delivery of tangible value to the business. The mechanisms for using "business rules" to transform data are addressed as part of the next chapter, "Task #4".

Understanding Data Vault by understanding data loading

Perhaps it's a bit like peeling an onion – we can learn about how Data Vault works one layer at a time. We've looked at the raw building blocks of Data Vault. We now will reinforce that earlier learning, but importantly we will go further and look at the interaction of multiple sources of potentially conflicting data, considering how data from multiple sources gets stored in the raw Data Vault, and how the sometimes inconsistent values are resolved by applying business rules to generate new instances in the Data Vault.

This section is a bit labored. It aims to offer a view into the internal workings of the Data Vault engine, and to do so takes a scenario and simulates the resultant database contents. If that's the way you like to learn, by lifting the lid and seeing what's happing under the bonnet, please read on. For others, this might be something you are happy to skip. I simply want to give you a choice for a deeper dive if it will assist.

The case study expanded

This time, we've got two operational source systems that provide source data feeds to the Data Vault, and we're going to walk through some explicit source data samples, simulating the act of loading them to the Hubs, Links, and Satellites.

The first source is the Fleet Management system. It records the vehicles owned or leased by the emergency response organization. These vehicles include fire trucks, of course, but also included are vehicles such as the company cars driven by senior management.

The second source system is the Shared Resource Pool system. In my home state, we have government funded emergency response organizations. We also have a volunteer fire brigade, resourced by magnificent men and women who not only freely give their time to protect the community, but they also put their lives at risk, for us. When it comes to responding to a wildfire, it's all hands to the pumps (literally sometimes). For accountability and decision-making purposes, there are clear lines as to which organization is in charge of the emergency response, but for the sake of this example, resources such as fire trucks can be seen as belonging to a shared pool of resources, available for deployment to the most needy emergency.

Then there are other companies who have their own localized fire response resources. For example, out in our west we have massive plantations of pine forests. These forestry companies may choose to make their limited resources available for the common good. It is better for the community to have a fire stopped 20 kilometers from the plantation, and believe me, it's better for the plantation company to stop the fire well before it gets to the edge of their land.

And finally, there are private individuals who sign up to have their equipment made available if required. Yes, that may include fire trucks from individual farmers, but it goes much further than just fire trucks. I had a fire escape route cut through trees on my own place. Phil, the bulldozer driver, has often made his dozer available for emergency response support, but it can get pretty scary. One time winds changed suddenly, and he had to quickly clear away flammable vegetation on a tiny patch of land, then hide behind the dozer's massive blade to protect himself from being killed. He survived, but this is just one of many stories I could share of the brave people behind the simple concept of a Shared Resource Pool system.

The Fleet Management system includes more than just Fire Trucks, as does the Shared Resource Pool, but we will limit the scenario below just to Fire Trucks for simplicity.

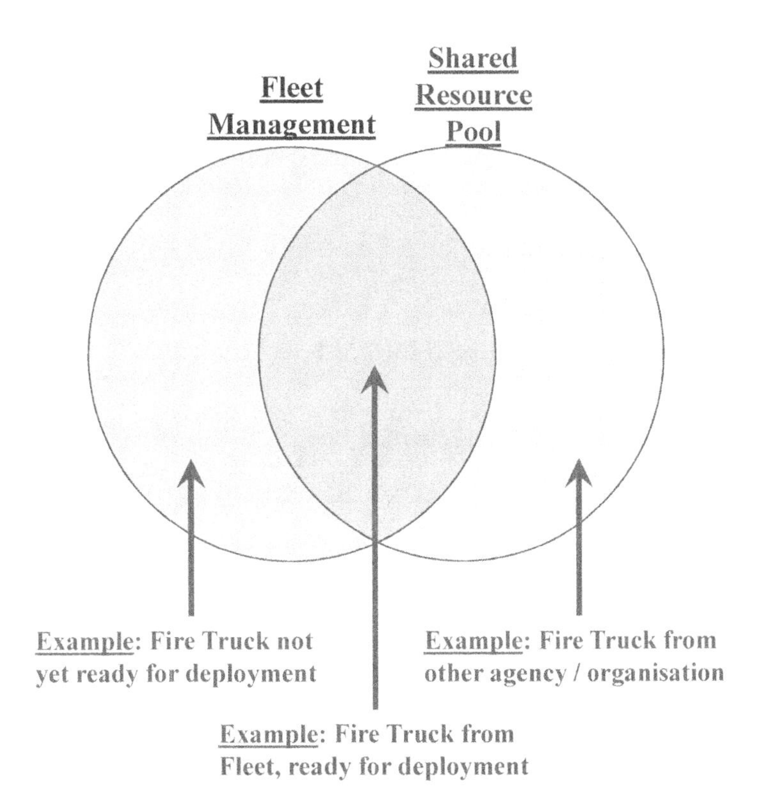

Figure 80: Overlapping data – Fire Trucks

Figure 80 above highlights how separate source system data feeds can share data subject areas, but not necessarily with a 100% overlap; if we've got two systems holding information about fire trucks, not all fire trucks known in one system will necessarily be known in the other. The Fleet Management system might include fire trucks that, at a point in time, aren't also in the Shared Resource Pool system because they're not yet ready for deployment at a fire. Maybe they still need to be fitted with special purpose radios, and have their roof numbers painted. Or maybe they are actually ready for deployment, and the Fleet Management system fire trucks *should* have also been loaded into the Shared Resource Pool system, but the process to synchronize the systems has failed and certain fire trucks are only known in the Fleet Management system.

Conversely, the Shared Resource Pool system will have fire trucks that have been loaded but that are not known in the Fleet Management system, if for no other reason than these shared resource fire trucks are owned by another organization and will never be entered into the prime organization's Fleet Management system.

That's set the scene. Now let's carefully go through some hypothetical data that will expose the next layer of understanding behind a Data Vault solution, by simulating the code for loading the data, and looking at the tables' contents after the load.

Populating Hubs

We go back to where we started, with a Hub for Fire Trucks.

FireTruck_Hub	
PK	FireTruck_HashKey
	LoadDateTime
	RecordSource
U1	RegistrationNumber

Figure 81: Fire Truck Hub

Now we've also got some sample data we want to load to the Fire Truck Hub. We begin with sample data from the Fleet Management system. It is a simple extract of all of the rows in the source system's table. On January 1st, there are only two fire trucks in the entire Fleet Management system. The extract looks like this:

Registration Number	Vehicle Type	Fuel Tank Capacity	Water Tank Capacity
AAA-111	Tanker	200	1,500
BBB-222	Slip-On	55	600

Table 2: Fleet Management source data January 1st

The logic, or pseudo code, for loading any Hub goes something like this for each consecutive row read from the source:

- If the Business Key (in this case, the Registration Number of the Fire Truck) does ***not*** already exist in the target Hub, create an instance in the Hub with the sourced Business Key
- Else (if the Business Key already exists in the target Hub), do nothing with this row

Note that for loading the Fire Truck Hub, only the Registration Number is considered; the other data attributes will come into play when we consider Satellites, but for now we can ignore them.

Pretty simple?

Additional data is provided during the load, such as:

- A computed Hash Key, using the Business Key as input to the hashing algorithm (for the sake of simplicity in this case study, the source text string is shown instead of the long and complex hash result).
- Load Date / Time (again for the sake of simplicity, the values only capture hours and minutes, but not seconds, let alone decimal parts of seconds).
- A code to represent the Record Source (again simplified in this example to the code FM/FT to represent the Fleet Management system's Fire Truck extract).

In this case study hypothetical, the Data Vault (and hence the Fire Truck Hub table) was empty before the load process was run, therefore every Registration Number in the source system must cause the creation of a new instance in the Hub table. The resultant contents in the Fire Truck Hub might now look as follows:

Hash Key	Load Date Time	Record Source	Registration Number
Hash of "AAA-111"	Jan 1st @ 01:00	FM/FT	AAA-111
Hash of "BBB-222"	Jan 1st @ 01:00	FM/FT	BBB-222

Table 3: Fire Truck Hub January 1st

Easy so far? Now we come to the second day. The full extract from the source data feed looks like the following (with some of the more interesting entries highlighted):

Registration Number	Vehicle Type	Fuel Tank Capacity	Water Tank Capacity
AAA-111	Tanker	200	1,500
BBB-222	Slip-On	***60***	600
CCC-333	***Slip-On***	***45***	***450***

Table 4: Fleet Management source data January 2nd

Note:

- Fire Truck AAA-111 has had no changes; the pseudo code will say that the Business Key already exists in the Hub, so there is no action required.
- Fire Truck BBB-222 has had its Fuel Tank Capacity changed from 55 to 60. This can be expected to result in some action in a related Satellite, but the pseudo code for the Hub only looks at the Business Key, BBB-222, which already exists in the Hub, so again there is no action required.
- Fire Truck CCC-333 is new. The pseudo code notes that the Business Key does ***not*** exist, so will add it.

The resultant contents in the Fire Truck Hub might now look as follows, with the entry for Fire Truck CCC-333 showing it was loaded to the Data Vault on January 2nd at 1:00am:

Hash Key	Load Date Time	Record Source	Registration Number
Hash of "AAA-111"	Jan 1st @ 01:00	FM/FT	AAA-111
Hash of "BBB-222"	Jan 1st @ 01:00	FM/FT	BBB-222
Hash of "CCC-333"	Jan 2nd @ 01:00	FM/FT	CCC-333

Table 5: Fire Truck Hub January 2nd at 1:00am

Note that the Load Date / Time for Fire Truck AAA-111 records the "first seen" timestamp of January 1st; it is ***not*** updated to record the fact it was later seen again on January 2nd.

OK, so we've performed a few Hub loads from one source system. How do things change when we introduce a second source? Let's look at a data feed from the Shared Resource Pool system we spoke about earlier. A full extract on January 2nd holds the following information:

Plate No	Body Type	Fuel Efficiency	Water Tank Size
CCC-333	Single-Cab	10	100
DDD-444	Twin-Cab	20	200

Table 6: Shared Resource Pool source data January 2nd

Let's note that, as described in the case study introduction, there are partial overlaps in the Fire Trucks represented by the two systems.

- Fire Trucks AAA-111 and BBB-222 are in the Fleet Management system, but have not (yet) been made available for deployment via the Shared Resource Pool system.

- Fire Truck CCC-333 is in the Fleet Management system *and* in the Shared Resource Pool system.

- Fire Truck DDD-444 may be a privately owned farmer's fire truck. It is available in the Shared Resource Pool system, but because it is not owned or leased by the corporation, it will never appear in the Fleet Management system.

Let's think back to the pseudo code for loading a Hub. Even though Fire Truck CCC-333 is presented to the Data Vault by a different system, the Business Key already exists and no action is required. Fire Truck DDD-444 has not yet been seen by the Data Vault, and it is loaded. If the load time on January 2nd was 1:00am for the Fleet Management system, and 2:00am for the Shared Resource Pool system, the Fire Truck Hub might now look like:

Hash Key	Load Date Time	Record Source	Registration Number
Hash of "AAA-111"	Jan 1st @ 01:00	FM/FT	AAA-111
Hash of "BBB-222"	Jan 1st @ 01:00	FM/FT	BBB-222
Hash of "CCC-333"	Jan 2nd @ 01:00	FM/FT	CCC-333
Hash of "DDD-444"	Jan 2nd @ 02:00	POOL	DDD-444

Table 7: Fire Truck Hub January 2nd at 2:00am

Note that the Record Source for the Fire Truck DDD-444 is "POOL" (a code for the Shared Resource Pool system).

Now here's a trick question. What difference, if any, might be observed if the load sequence on January 2nd was reversed, with the Shared Resource Pool loading first at 1:00am and the Fleet Management system loading afterwards at 2:00am? The answer is below:

Hash Key	Load Date Time	Record Source	Registration Number
Hash of "AAA-111"	Jan 1st @ 01:00	FM/FT	AAA-111
Hash of "BBB-222"	Jan 1st @ 01:00	FM/FT	BBB-222
Hash of "CCC-333"	Jan 2nd @ 01:00	***POOL***	CCC-333
Hash of "DDD-444"	Jan 2nd @ 01:00	POOL	DDD-444

Table 8: Fire Truck Hub (reversed load sequence)

When the Shared Resource Pool load was executed at 1:00am, Fire Truck CCC-333 did not exist, so would have been created. In this variation, the "First Seen" information for Fire Truck CCC-333 would note that the "First Seen" Record Source was "POOL" rather than "FM/FT".

Populating a Hub's Satellites

Hubs are at the very heart of business-centric integration. If multiple sources hold data about the same "thing", all of their data values are held in Satellites that hang off the one central, shared Hub.

The "good practice" default design is to have (at least) one separate Satellite for each source data feed. I say "at least one" because sometimes a Satellite is split further, for example to move attributes with frequently changing values into their own Satellite. But for the sake of simplicity, we will look a bit deeper into how population of Satellites works with one Satellite per source.

We've already seen some sample data, but it's repeated here for convenience, starting with the data that was used to commence the population of the Fire Truck Hub.

Registration Number	Vehicle Type	Fuel Tank Capacity	Water Tank Capacity
AAA-111	Tanker	200	1,500
BBB-222	Slip-On	55	600

Table 9: Fleet Management source data January 1st

When we used this data to create rows in the Fire Truck Hub, we were only interested in the business key values from the Registration Number column. Now the focus shifts to the current values for the Fire Truck's other attributes. We need a Satellite to hold them.

The logic, or pseudo code, for loading any Satellite against a Hub goes something like this for each consecutive row read from the source:

- If attribute values in the source load are different from what's already on file for the Business Key (either because the values have changed since the last load, or because it's the first load and there's nothing there yet!), create a row in the Satellite.

- Else (if the same data values as are found in the source load already exist in the Satellite for the current Business Key), do nothing with this row

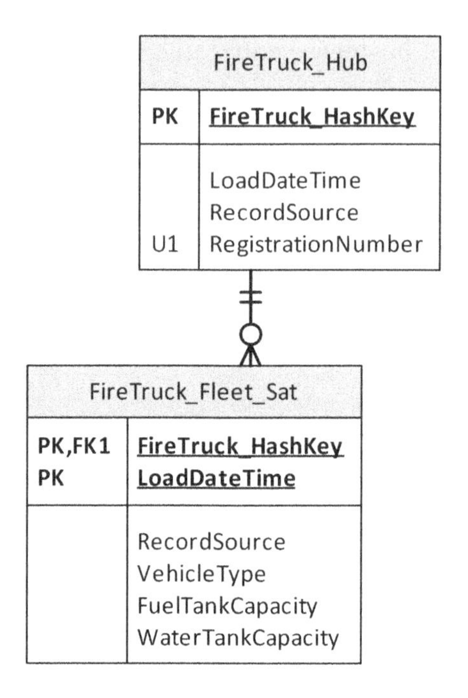

Figure 82: Fire Truck Satellite for Fleet data

Again, the logic is pretty simple, and as for Hubs, we record the Load Date / Time and the Record Source to aid in auditing. Note that the Load Date / Time is part of the Satellite's Primary Key, so we end up with snapshots of the data values each time any of the values presented to the Data Vault change.

Though not shown here, one of the optional extras for a Satellite table is a Hash Difference attribute. The pre-processing in the Staging Area can calculate a hash value across the entire combination of values (in this case, the Vehicle Type *plus* the Fuel Tank Capacity *plus* the Water Tank Capacity as a single text string). If this is stored in the Satellite, next time a new source row comes in (also with its hash value), instead of comparing every attribute to see if anything has changed, comparing the hash value as a single attribute achieves the same result.

The Fire Truck Satellite for data sourced from the Fleet Management system was empty before the first day's processing began, but will now look like this:

Hash Key	Load Date Time	Record Source	Vehicle Type	Fuel Tank Capacity	Water Tank Capacity
Hash of "AAA-111"	Jan 1st @ 01:00	FM/FT	Tanker	200	1,500
Hash of "BBB-222"	Jan 1st @ 01:00	FM/FT	Slip-On	55	600

Table 10: Fire Truck Satellite for Fleet Management, after load on January 1st

That was not too challenging – no data existed prior to the load, so the "first seen" values are simply created. Now things get a little bit more interesting as we load the second day's data. Again for convenience, the second day's data from the Fleet Management system is repeated here:

Registration Number	Vehicle Type	Fuel Tank Capacity	Water Tank Capacity
AAA-111	Tanker	200	1,500
BBB-222	Slip-On	***60***	600
CCC-333	***Slip-On***	***45***	***450***

Table 11: Fleet Management source data January 2nd

Let's think through the logic of the pseudo code for each row.

- Fire Truck AAA-111 has had no changes. The pseudo code will conclude that all of the data attribute values for Business Key AAA-111 already exist in the Satellite, so no action is required.

- Fire Truck BBB-222 has had its Fuel Tank Capacity changed from 55 to 60. The pseudo code will note that at least one value has changed, so will write a new row to the Satellite table.

- Fire Truck CCC-333 is new. The pseudo code notes that the data attribute values have changed (because none existed before!), so will create a new Satellite row.

The resultant contents in the Fire Truck Satellite for data sourced from the Fleet Management system might now look as follows. Note that there are two rows for Fire Truck BBB-222, one being the initial snapshot on January 1st, the other being the more recent snapshot on January 2nd, with one data value (Fuel Tank Capacity) changed from 55 to 60.

Hash Key	Load Date Time	Record Source	Vehicle Type	Fuel Tank Capacity	Water Tank Capacity
Hash of "AAA-111"	Jan 1st @ 01:00	FM/FT	Tanker	200	1,500
Hash of "BBB-222"	Jan 1st @ 01:00	FM/FT	Slip-On	55	600
Hash of "BBB-222"	Jan 2nd @ 01:00	FM/FT	Slip-On	60	600
Hash of "CCC-333"	Jan 2nd @ 01:00	FM/FT	Slip-On	45	450

Table 12: Fire Truck Satellite for Fleet Management, after load on January 2nd

When we looked at loading Hubs, we deliberately introduced a data feed from a second source. A repeated copy of the sample data follows:

Plate No	Body Type	Fuel Efficiency	Water Tank Size
CCC-333	Single-Cab	10	100
DDD-444	Twin-Cab	20	200

Table 13: Shared Resource Pool source data January 2nd

When we load Hubs, the data instances can overlap. For example, Fire Truck CCC-333 is known in both systems. However, when we load Satellites, if we follow the guidelines and we define a separate Satellite for each source data feed, life is simpler. Our data model might look like the model in Figure 83.

Loading the data sourced from the Shared Resource Pool system to its Fire Truck Satellite would result in the following:

Hash Key	Load Date Time	Record Source	Body Type	Fuel Efficiency	Water Tank Size
Hash of "CCC-333"	Jan 2nd @ 02:00	POOL	Single-Cab	10	100
Hash of "DDD-444"	Jan 2nd @ 02:00	POOL	Twin-Cab	20	200

Table 14: Fire Truck Satellite for Shared Resource Pool, after load on January 2nd

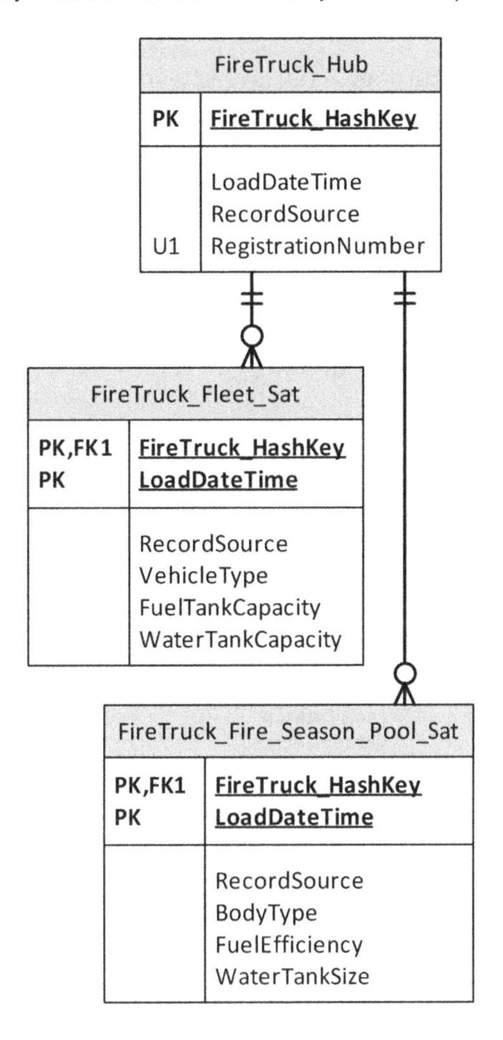

Figure 83: Fire Truck Satellite for Fleet and Pool data

It is worth noting that the types of attributes held about fire trucks are different between the two systems, and even where they appear to be the same, they can have different names for the attributes. Many practitioners suggest that the attributes in a Satellite loaded from a raw source data feed should align with data structures in the source systems rather than use the more business-friendly names we would hope to see in business-centric Data Vault Satellite structures. Two arguments I have encountered for this approach that I think have real merit are:

1. Easier traceability of data back to the source systems (though this should also be achievable by other data mapping mechanisms).
2. Support for data consumers who already have familiarity with source system data structures.

Populating Links

You might remember the skeleton Data Vault model we presented earlier for the introductory case study? When the Satellites are removed, it looked like:

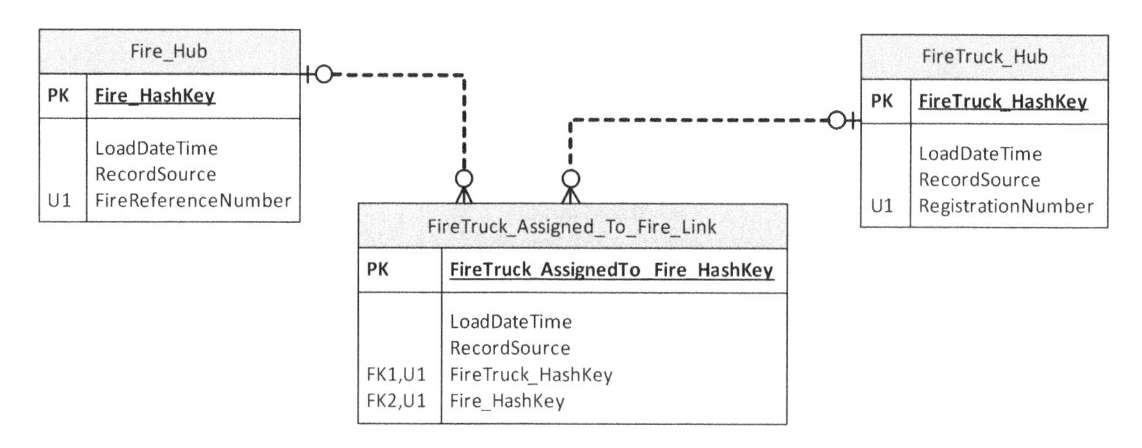

Figure 84: "Fire" data model - Data Vault Hubs and Links

We've been loading Hubs and their Satellites for Fire Trucks. Let's assume we have likewise been loading Hubs and their Satellites for Fires. To bring the two Hubs together, we now need to load the Fire-Truck-Assigned-To-Fire Link.

In the hypothetical case study, there are two ways an assignment of a Fire Truck to a Fire can occur.

The first method is driven by a logistics officer at the Fire itself. He or she sees a need, and submits a request to acquire a Fire Truck from the shared resource pool. They try to "pull" a resource from the pool so that they can put the fire truck under their direct control. Their data entry screen might look something like:

Emergency Response system
- Resource Acquisition function

Fire requiring resources:	**WF123**
Fire Truck to be acquired:	**CCC-333**
Acquisition effective from:	**Feb 2nd**
Acquisition effective to:	***(indefinite)***

Figure 85: Resource Acquisition screen

In this case, the logistic officer has requested the assignment of Fire Truck CCC-333 to the Fire WF123, starting from February 2nd, with the assignment to be indefinite.

(For my northern hemisphere friends, please remember that February is in our Australian summertime. The most recent fire that put my own house at risk was one February when it reached 46 degrees Celsius, or 115 degrees Fahrenheit. And that was in the shade!)

You may remember that the source data for populating the Fire Truck's Hub had lots of data in addition to the Registration Number business key, but for a Hub, we were only interested in the business key, because the attribute values were managed by the Hub's Satellites. We've got a similar scenario here. The assignment transaction provides two business keys (Fire Truck CCC-333 and Fire WF123), and also two contextual data attributes (a "From" date and a "To" date), but for populating the Link, we only need the participating business keys; the attribute values are managed by the Link's Satellites.

To spotlight some of the flexibility of a Data Vault, while we had nightly batch loads populating the Fire Truck Hub, let's assume the resource assignment function needs to be much more dynamic. The sample screen above could be a web-based screen, with the service running on top of an enterprise service bus, in real time. If the operation represented by Figure 85 were to execute at 12:33 on February 2nd, with an almost immediate load into the Data Vault, the resultant Fire-Truck-Assigned-To-Fire Link could look like:

Link Hash Key	Load Date Time	Record Source	Fire Truck Hash Key	Fire Hash Key
Hash of "CCC-333|WF123"	Feb 2nd @ 12:34	ER/RA	Hash of "CCC-333"	Hash of "WF123"

Table 15: Fire-Truck-Assigned-To-Fire Link February 2nd

Just as a refresher on the use of hash keys:

- Instead of storing the actual business key of "CCC-333" for the Fire Truck participating in this Link, we store its hash key value. This is a Foreign Key that points directly to the Fire Truck Hub that contains a row for Fire Truck CCC-333, identified via whatever is its long hashed value.
- Similarly, instead of storing "WF123" for the participating Fire, we store its Foreign Key which is also a hash value.
- Last but not least, we have the Primary Key for the Link itself. In business terms, the Link is identified by combining the business keys of all participating Hubs. We could represent the Fire Truck + Fire resultant text string as "CCC-333|WF123". We then pretend the hashing algorithm takes this text string and spits out some meaningless hash value, which we use as the internal representation of the Primary Key for the Link.

Now to finish off commenting on the contents of this Link instance:

- The hypothetical that says that the Record Source for this Link is code ER/RA, representing the Emergency Response system's Resource Acquisition function.
- The real-time transaction occurred at 12:33, and the Load Date Time for the arrival of this data into the Data Vault was one minute later, at 12:34. In reality, the latency can be mere seconds.

We've looked at one of the real-time functions. It "pulls" resources from the Shared Resource Pool into the control of those managing the fire. Our second hypothetical method for resource acquisition is driven by a resource manager responsible for the shared resource pool. He or she hears of a Fire that's escalating, and sometimes proactively releases one of the Fire Trucks for use by the fire crew. He or she "pushes" one of their nominated resources out to the Fire. A possible representation of their screen follows:

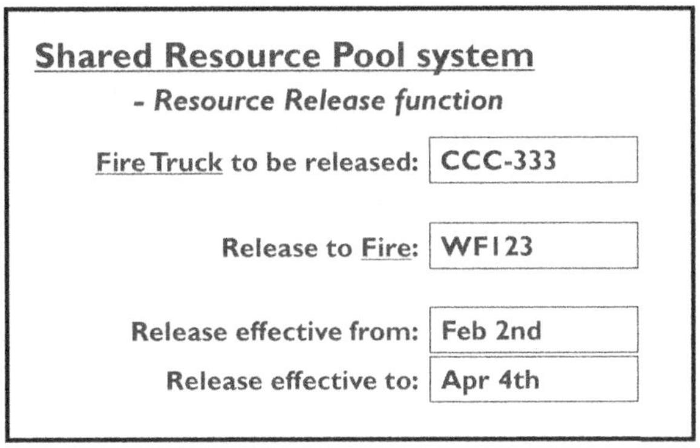

Shared Resource Pool system

- Resource Release function

Fire Truck to be released: CCC-333

Release to Fire: WF123

Release effective from: Feb 2nd

Release effective to: Apr 4th

Figure 86: Resource Release function

In this hypothetical, the resource manager has assigned Fire Truck CCC-333 to the Fire WF123, starting from February 2nd, but with a maximum assignment period, ending on April 4th. This action is performed at 13:57, a bit over an hour after the request had come from the logistics officer belonging to the fire management team.

One thing you may have picked up from the two screen snapshots in Figure 85 and Figure 86 is that they both refer to exactly the same business keys. Maybe the Fire Truck and the Fire attributes appear in a different order on the screen, and the person doing the data entry has a very different "push" versus "pull" view of their world, but at the end of the day, either way Fire Truck CCC-333 gets assigned to a Fire WF123.

You may recall that for Hubs, each Hub instance stores details of "first seen" information; it records the Record Source of the *first* source to present the business key to the Hub, and any other subsequent sources presenting the same business key are ignored. In this scenario, the Link instance likewise stores details of "first seen" information; it records the Record Source of the *first* source to present the set of business keys to the Link, and any other subsequent sources presenting the same set of business key are ignored. The pseudo code for loading Links is very similar to the pseudo code for Hubs. It goes something like this:

- If the set of Business Keys (in this case, the Registration Number of the Fire Truck plus the Fire Reference Number for the Fire), represented by a hash key computation, does ***not*** already exist in the target Link, create an instance in the Link with the sourced set of Business Keys
- Else (if the set of Business Keys already exists in the target Link), do nothing with this row.

It follows that *if* the operation represented by Figure 85 were to execute first (and also at the same time of 12:34), the results would be the same other than with a Record Source code of (say) POOL/RR, representing the Shared Resource Pool system's Resource Request function.

Populating a Link's Satellites

There are some differences of opinion within the Data Vault community on the topic of Satellites for Links, but most if not all accept at least the use of Satellites that record effective periods for the relationship, and for now we will restrict discussions on Link Satellites to this safer ground. Remembering that Satellites, whether for a Hub or a Link, are typically split by source system data feed, we want one Fire-Truck-Assigned-To-Fire Link for the relationship between Fire Trucks and Fires, plus one Satellite for the assignment details when sourced from the Shared Resource Pool's Resource Release function, and another Satellite for the assignment details when sourced from the Emergency Response system's Resource Acquisition function.

We've already looked at the first assignment transaction, depicted in Figure 85. It resulted in the creation of the Link instance as shown in Figure 87. What we now need is a snapshot of the data values at a point in time captured in the Satellite.

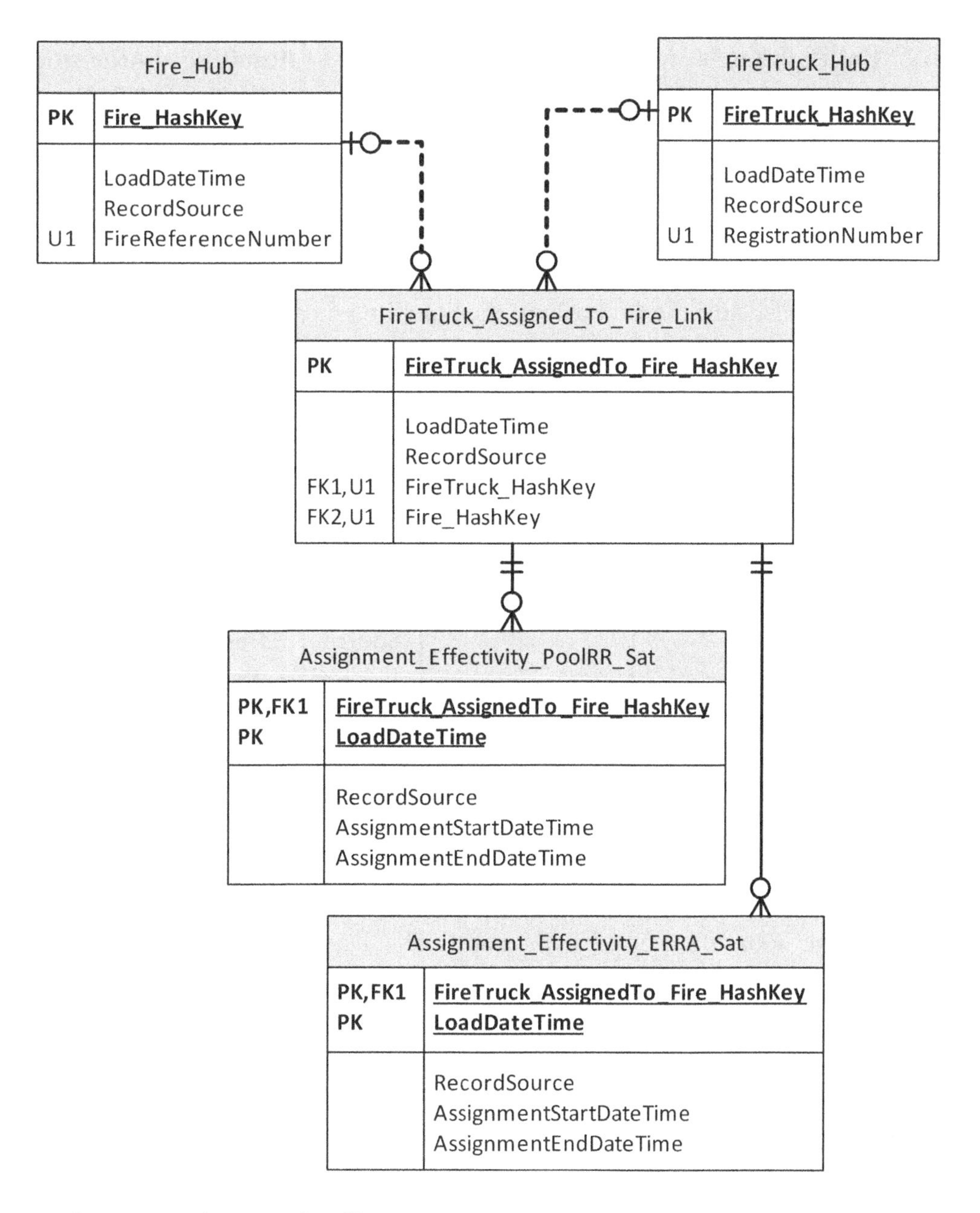

Figure 87: Resource assignment Satellites

The Satellite we want to populate as shown on the Data Vault model in Figure 87 above is the Satellite whose name includes "ERRA", a short-form code indicating its data values are sourced from the Emergency Response system's Resource Acquisition function. As part of the loading of this very first assignment transaction, we end up with the following:

Link Hash Key	Load Date Time	Record Source	Acquisition Effective From	Acquisition Effective To
Hash of "CCC-333|WF123"	Feb 2nd @ 12:34	ER/RA	Feb 2nd	-

Table 16: Assignment Effectivity Satellite for Emergency Response, after load on February 2nd

An hour later, we also add the first row to the Satellite whose name includes "Pool RR", a short-form code indicating it data values are sourced from the Shared Resource Pool system's Resource Release function. It is for the same Link, but has different values in its attributes – the requestor wanted an indefinite assignment, but the Resource Pool's manager said they could have it from today, but only until April 4th rather than indefinitely.

Link Hash Key	Load Date Time	Record Source	Acquisition Effective From	Acquisition Effective To
Hash of "CCC-333|WF123"	Feb 2nd @ 13:57	POOL/RR	Feb 2nd	Apr 4th

Table 17: Assignment Effectivity Satellite for Shared Resource Pool, after load on February 2nd

The two Satellites hold different data that reflects what may be a conflict in the real world as to when the Fire Truck's assignment ends, but they faithfully hold the facts as presented by the source system. That's good. The Data Vault is now positioned to expose any apparent inconsistencies, and action can be taken to resolve the disagreements if required.

We now roll the clock forward. A month later, on March 3rd there's a new fire, WF456. In response, the manager responsible for the Shared Resource Pool makes several decisions:

1. The large Fire Truck, CCC-333, with a highly experienced crew, is reassigned from Fire WF123 and handed over to the new threat, WF456. This action has two parts:

    a. The assignment of Fire Truck CCC-333 to WF123 *was* intended to be up until April 4th, but the assignment is cut short, effective immediately.

   b. The formal assignment of Fire Truck CCC-333 to WF456 is also made.

2. To backfill at the mopping up action for the original Fire, WF123, a smaller Fire Truck, DDD-444 is assigned to that Fire.

The resultant assignment transactions are loaded to the Data Vault:

Link Hash Key	Load Date Time	Record Source	Acquisition Effective From	Acquisition Effective To
Hash of "CCC-333|WF123"	Feb 2nd @ 13:57	POOL/RR	Feb 2nd	Apr 4th
Hash of "CCC-333|WF123"	Mar 3rd @ 14:14	POOL/RR	Feb 2nd	Mar 3rd
Hash of "CCC-333|WF456"	Mar 3rd @ 14:14	POOL/RR	Mar 3rd	-
Hash of "DDD-444|WF123"	Mar 3rd @ 14:14	POOL/RR	Mar 3rd	May 5th

Table 18: Assignment Effectivity Satellite for Shared Resource Pool, March 3rd

Note that the first row is an historic record of the original assignment of CCC-333 to WF123, and that the second row effectively replaces it with updated information. Also note that, over time, Fire WF123 has more than one Fire Truck assigned to it, and likewise, the one Fire Truck CCC-333 is, over time, assigned to more than one Fire. This is a simple example of the many-to-many nature of Links.

Some other data load considerations

Extracts versus Change Data Capture (CDC)

Many of the above examples were based on a full extract of all of the data from the nominated source system, every time. That's safe and simple, but it's not necessarily efficient. Some organizations I have consulted to have had more than ten million customers. If one hundred new customers have been added today, we're processing 10,000,100 rows just to add 100 in the Customer Hub. Data Vault is robust, and doesn't care if we present information it already knows about; it just ignores us! But are there more efficient ways?

Without going into lots of technical details, I will briefly explain two common approaches we may consider.

One approach is to play spot-the-difference in the staging area ("delta" processing), and only pass on to the Data Vault load whatever has changed. The staging area still has to process large volumes, but at least the Data Vault load job is smaller. And we can possibly share the Staging Area workload around a few servers.

Another approach is to turn on Change Data Capture (CDC), or similar, in our source system's database. The database engine can observe inserts, updates, and deletes of rows in nominated tables, and inform the Staging Area of just things that have really changed. That can work well if our relational database management system supports CDC, if it's an affordable feature (some database vendors charge extra for CDC), and if the data we want to present to our Data Vault maps nicely to just one source system table. If not, we may go back to full snapshots, maybe with some pre-processing in the Staging Area.

Restarting the load

Finally, before leaving the topic of loading data into a Data Vault, there's the topic of restarting a load job that has failed to finish successfully. If *none* of the data presented to the Data Vault for processing was successfully loaded, it's like running the load job for the first time. If *all* of the data was actually successfully processed, but we just think the job failed, re-running the load will see no changes needing to be applied, and the attempted re-load will do no harm, even if we run it a hundred times! And if *some* data had been processed and some hadn't been, the bits that were processed will be ignored the second time through, and the bits that got missed will get successfully applied. Data Vault really is robust.

Doing the source-to-Data Vault mapping

Now we've had a closer look at the internal mechanics of a Data Vault as it loads raw data from a source system feed, let's look at the essence of Task #3 – mapping source data to the Data Vault.

We start by taking a snippet from the example of conveyancing (buying and selling of properties). A purchaser need to borrow some money, and the business view of the Data Vault design looks something like the following.

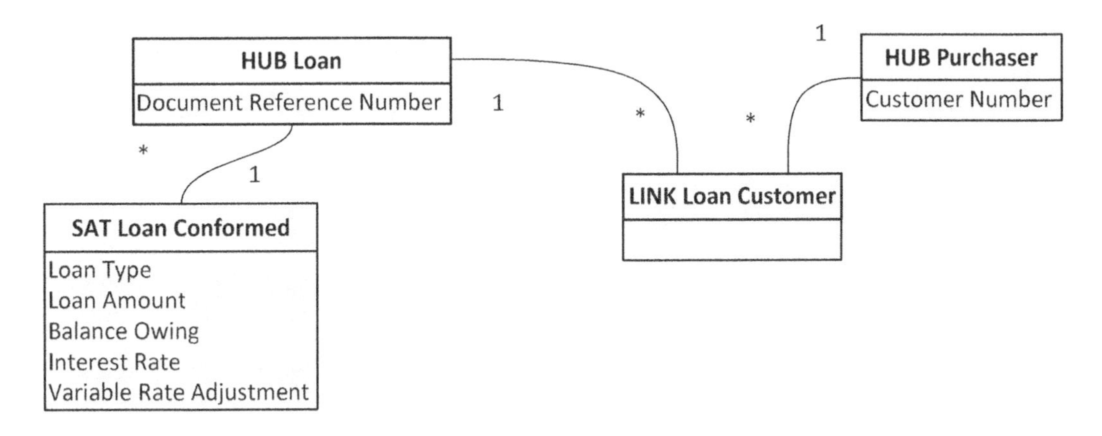

Figure 88: A Purchaser and their Loan

Now let's assume we have a source data feed from the Loan Management operational system. It might look something like the following.

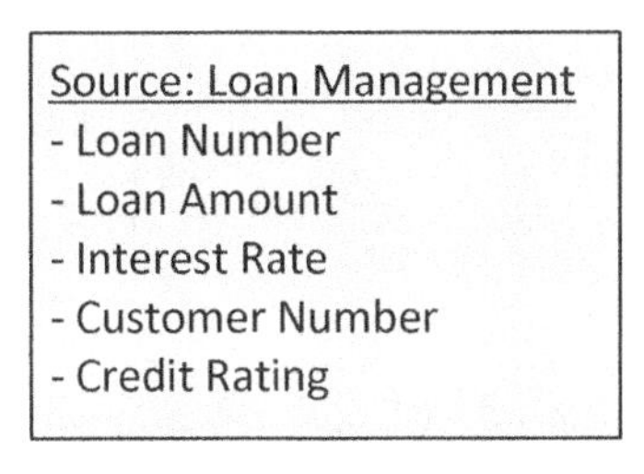

Figure 89: Loan Management source data

If we mentally identify the business concepts and business keys, we can mark up the source data feed with "BK" (business key) tags.

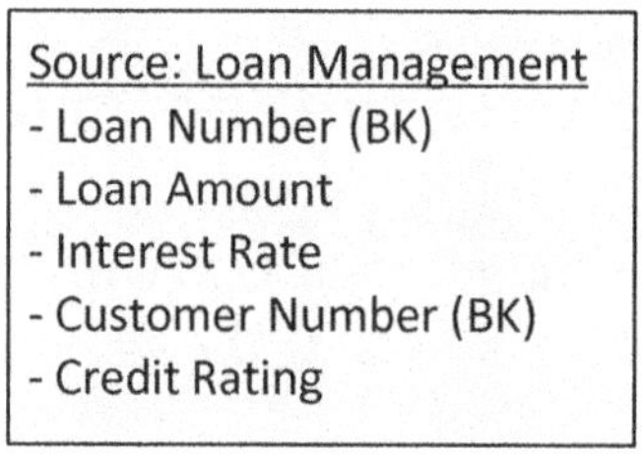

Source: Loan Management
- Loan Number (BK)
- Loan Amount
- Interest Rate
- Customer Number (BK)
- Credit Rating

Figure 90: Loan Management data, with Business Keys identified

Before we go any further, we can map the source feed to the Data Vault Hubs. Assuming we've got some tools to take our mapping and generate code, we've already got enough to drive the population of Hub instances.

HUB Loan
Document Reference Number
HUB Purchaser
Customer Number
LINK Loan Customer
SAT Loan Conformed
Loan Type
Loan Amount
Balance Owing
Interest Rate
Variable Rate Adjustment
1
*
Source: Loan Management
- Loan Number (BK)
- Loan Amount
- Interest Rate
- Customer Number (BK)
- Credit Rating

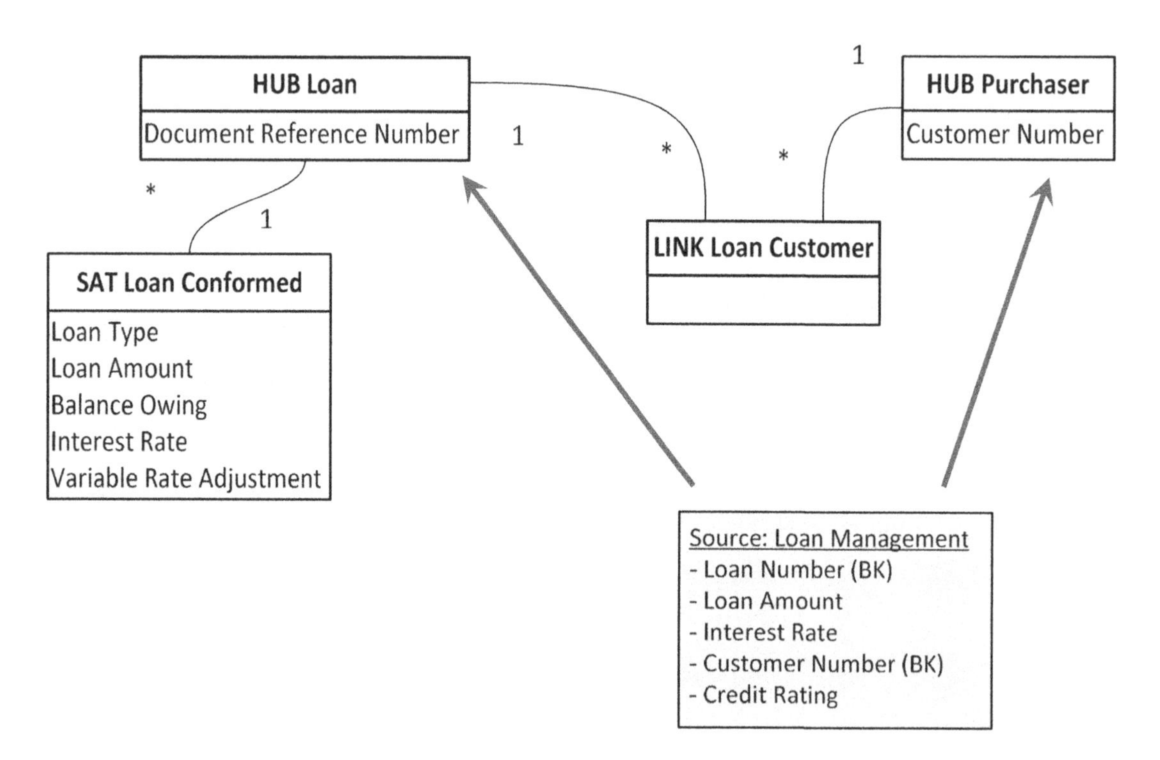

Figure 91: Mapping raw data to (business-centric) Hubs

Next we note that the two Hubs identified by the business also have a Link identified by the business as a fundamental "business relationship". We are in luck. The raw source has the same level of "grain" – the business-centric Link relates to two Hubs, and the raw source data feed also relates to the same two Hubs. It is not always so, but in this hand-picked example, we can map the raw source feed directly to a business-centric Link.

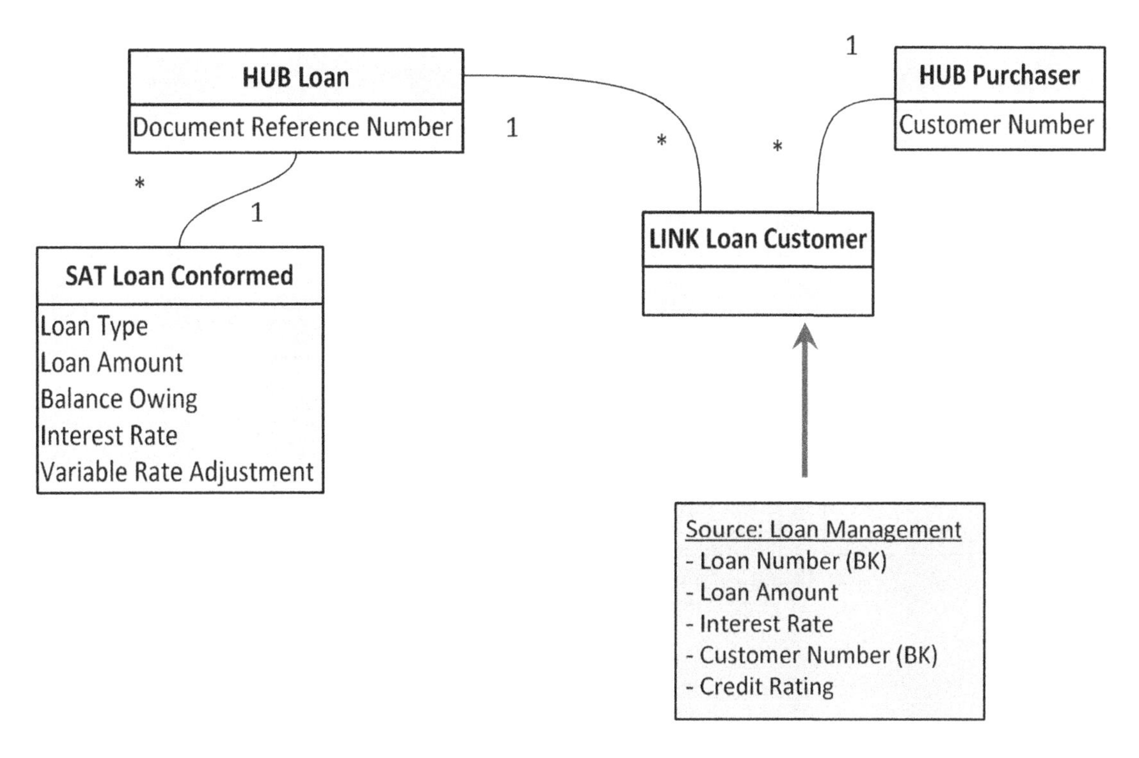

Figure 92: Mapping raw data to a (business-centric) Link

Now we've got some data in the raw source that needs to go in a Satellite somewhere. We've already designed a "business-centric" Satellite for the Loan Hub, called the Loan Conformed Satellite. If we could guarantee that the Loan Hub was only ever going to be fed from one source, maybe we could treat the Conformed Satellite as if it were the Satellite from a single source. However, we expect that the Loan Hub will have data coming in from multiple sources, with each source being given its own source-specific Satellite, so we design a new Satellite just for the "LMgt" (Loan Management) source, as shown in "Figure 93: Mapping raw data to a Satellite". Though not shown in Figure 93, we would do likewise for a Satellite holding the Credit Rating attribute, hanging off the Purchase Hub.

It's nice when life is simple, but it's not always that way. If you've ever bought or sold a house, there's the exciting day when "settlement" occurs (see Figure 94). And it can be pretty complicated. Behind the scenes, you've got the buyer ("Purchaser") and the seller ("Vendor"). At the table, you might have the legal representatives for each of these two parties, and maybe their two banks. The vendor might reference a mortgage to be discharged, and the purchaser might reference a new mortgage to be registered. Then at the center is the land title being transferred. And maybe the purchaser's mum and dad as guarantors for the loan, and on and on.

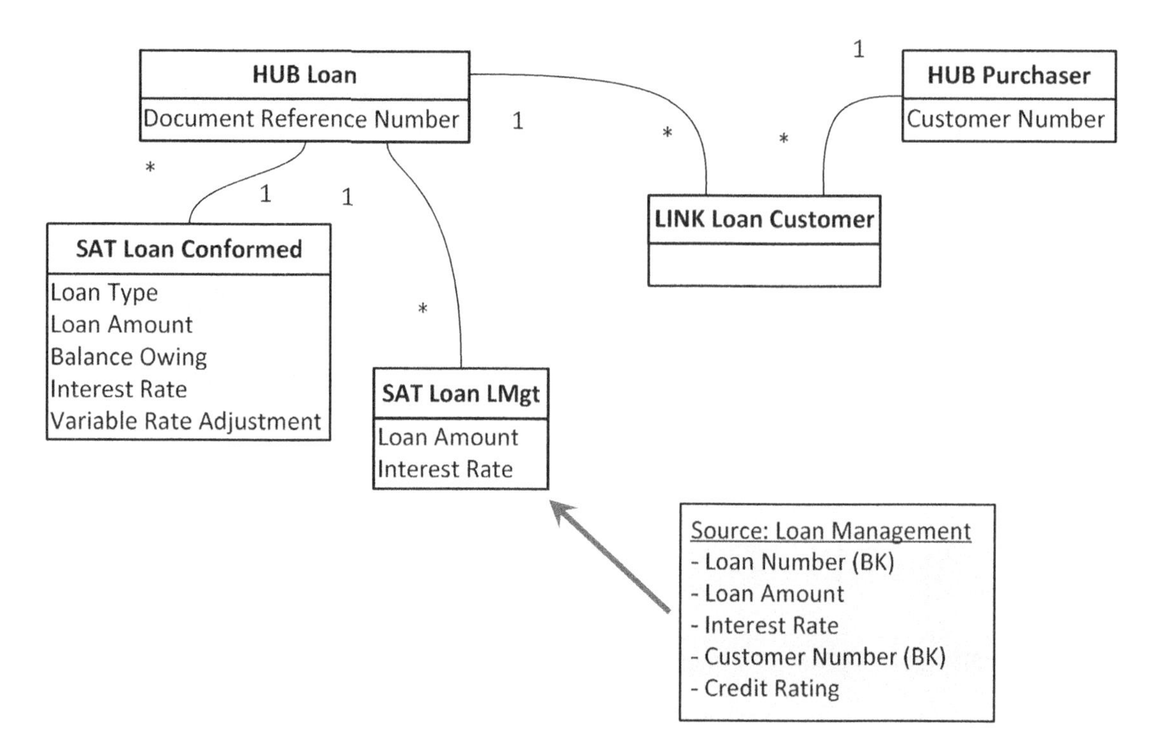

Figure 93: Mapping raw data to a Satellite

It's no wonder that there are times settlements "fall over" on the day because some small but vital part doesn't line up. A subset of this complexity is presented below, where a source system data feed has been marked up with Business Key (BK) tags.

Figure 94: Complex source data feed

In this feed alone, there are nine business keys identified. If we try to find a Link to match, you may hear people refer to a Link with a "grain" of nine. Realistically, the chances of finding a business-centric Link that perfectly matches are low. The solution? One approach we can adopt is to create a source-centric Link (with a Satellite) that matches the event / transaction being presented to us for mapping.

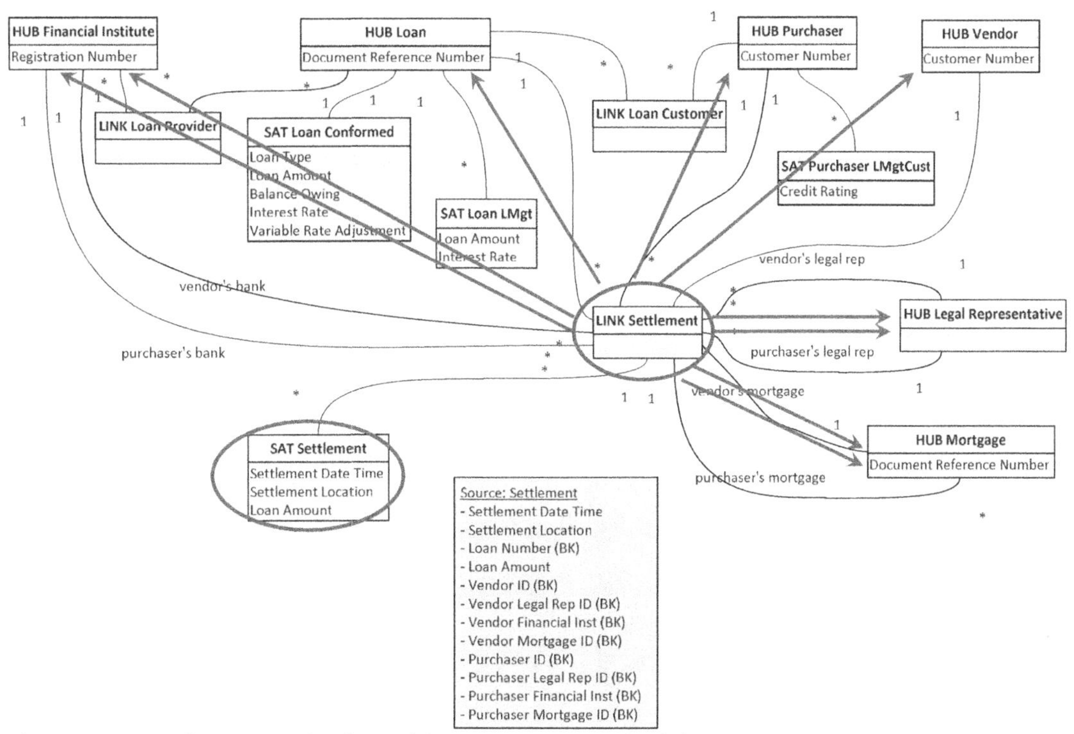

Figure 95: Complex source feed requiring a source-centric Link

The diagram is detailed, ugly, and hard to read. But the message is simple. If the business had already identified the Settlement transaction as a business concept with its own business key, it may have modelled Settlement as a Hub. But in this scenario, we have no such luck. Settlement is merely a transaction with no business key, and so it's a Link, tied to a multitude of Hubs.

We've captured the data, and that's good. But we may want to map some of the data to objects that are more business centric. For example, maybe the Loan Amount should be in a Satellite hanging off the Loan Hub, and maybe we want to record the business relationship between the Loan and the Purchaser in the business-centric Loan Customer

Link. How do we do this? By using business rules to do some transformation of data. Please read on.

CHAPTER 6

Task #4: Using Business Rules to Close the Top-Down / Bottom-Up Gap

Business rules, and the "Transformation" bit

You may well be familiar with the concept of ETL – Extract, Transform, Load. In the introductory section of this book titled "A bit of data warehouse history", there was a very brief mention that in the Data Vault world, we flip the order around and do ELT – Extract, Load (into the so-called "raw Data Vault"), then Transform (by applying soft business rules to create business-centric Data Vault objects).

The business-centric Data Vault objects require business rules that are tailored according to the mandate of the business people. Some simple examples were provided in "Business-sourced Hub and Satellite instances", especially in the text following "Figure 66: Business Satellite for the Fire Truck Hub". Examples shown there included renaming attributes, choosing between two candidate sources for a value, and computing derived values (converting gallons of water to liters of water, and computing how far a fire truck can travel based on its fuel efficiency and the size of its fuel tank). A wider use of the concept of business rules includes things like decision tables, and this approach may also be required in some cases.

The business rules are often first expressed in natural language (English for many I interact with) by people from the business themselves, and then turned into executable code. The code will often be SQL operating against a relational database, so the natural language expression might be interpreted by SQL developers; this interpretation has the possibility of things being lost in the translation.

Better still is if the business folk can enter the rules directly themselves. I've encountered "business" people whose skill with SQL outshines the capabilities of many IT professionals. They could happily express their business rules directly in code.

A half-way house might be a tool that offers click-&-point facilities something like the ability within Microsoft Access to create a query visually, while at the same time, under the covers, formulating SQL. Failing that, it's probably back to swivel-chair translation of free text business rules into executable code, based on the best efforts of programmers to interpret the sometimes imprecise expressions by the business.

One comment here that's vital. If we want end-to-end traceability of data lineage, from business query results right back through the Data Vault to source systems, we need to manage these business rules. And that includes keeping history of past rules that produced past results.

The business-rule sourced Data Vault instances can include data in Hubs, Links, and Satellites (plus things like Point-In-Time tables and Bridge tables that are explained in the section aptly titled "Point-In-Time (PIT) and Bridge tables"). Let's look at a scenario we can use to show how these various elements can interact.

We take a hypothetical bank, and look at how it manages risk.

We start with something that might surprise you – a "country" is a Hub, not a reference data set. There's a separate section on modelling "Reference data" a bit later, but for now we want to model country as its own regular Hub. This is because it's got a lot more data than just a "code-&-description" reference construct. In particular, it has a number of attributes that record aspects of perceived "risk" against that country. For example, right now there are some countries where the geo-political situation is more than a little shaky. Lending money secured by housing in such countries certainly carries risk.

The hypothetical presents two source systems that provide customer data for loading into the Customer Hub, and its Satellites – a Billing system, and a Marketing system. One would expect the Satellites against the Customer Hub to be split by system, and they are.

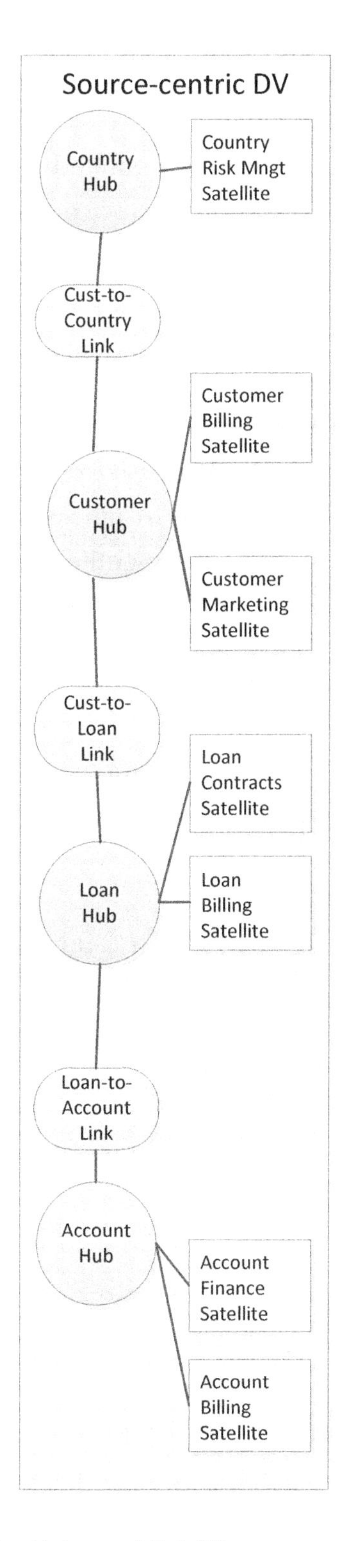

Figure 96: Bank source-centric Hubs, Links, and Satellites

We also have a Hub for Loan (sourced from a Contract system and a Billing system), and a Hub for Account (sourced from a Finance system and a Billing system). In this model, a Loan is the agreement (a "contract" entered into by the participating parties), and the Account is the mechanism for holding the current balance of money owed. And of course, we have appropriate Links between these Hubs. Now let's add some Point-In-Time (PIT) and Bridge tables, plus some simple "conformed" Satellites.

The samples for the Point-In-Time (PIT) tables and the Bridge table are pretty straightforward. Note that the lines with arrow-heads show how data that already exists in one or several Data Vault objects is used as input in building new Data Vault instances. For example, the time-stamps on instances in the Customer Billing Satellite and the Customer Marketing Satellite are essential input into creating the Customer Point-In-Time (PIT) table's instances. Similarly, the hash key values in the Customer, Loan and Account Hubs, plus their associated Links, are essential data values in building the Customer-to-Loan-to-Account Bridge.

The conformed Satellites are also quite simple – some business rules might, for example, rename some attributes, and consolidate values when two source systems provide conflicting perspectives. Note:

- The Country Hub has only one Satellite, and the decision was made that a PIT table wasn't warranted.
- The Bridge table spans the relationships between three Hubs – the Customers, Loans, and Accounts.
- The Loan and Account Hubs each have a simple PIT table and a Conformed Satellite.
- The Customer Hub has two conformed Satellites, one focusing on attributes related to the customer's address, and another focused on personal attributes.

These first four conformed Satellites "belong" to their parent Hubs. Lines to show the relationship to their "parents" are not shown. Instead, arrowheads are shown to demonstrate how, in this case, the PIT tables are used to efficiently identify the Satellites that need to be consolidated ("conformed") at a point-in-time.

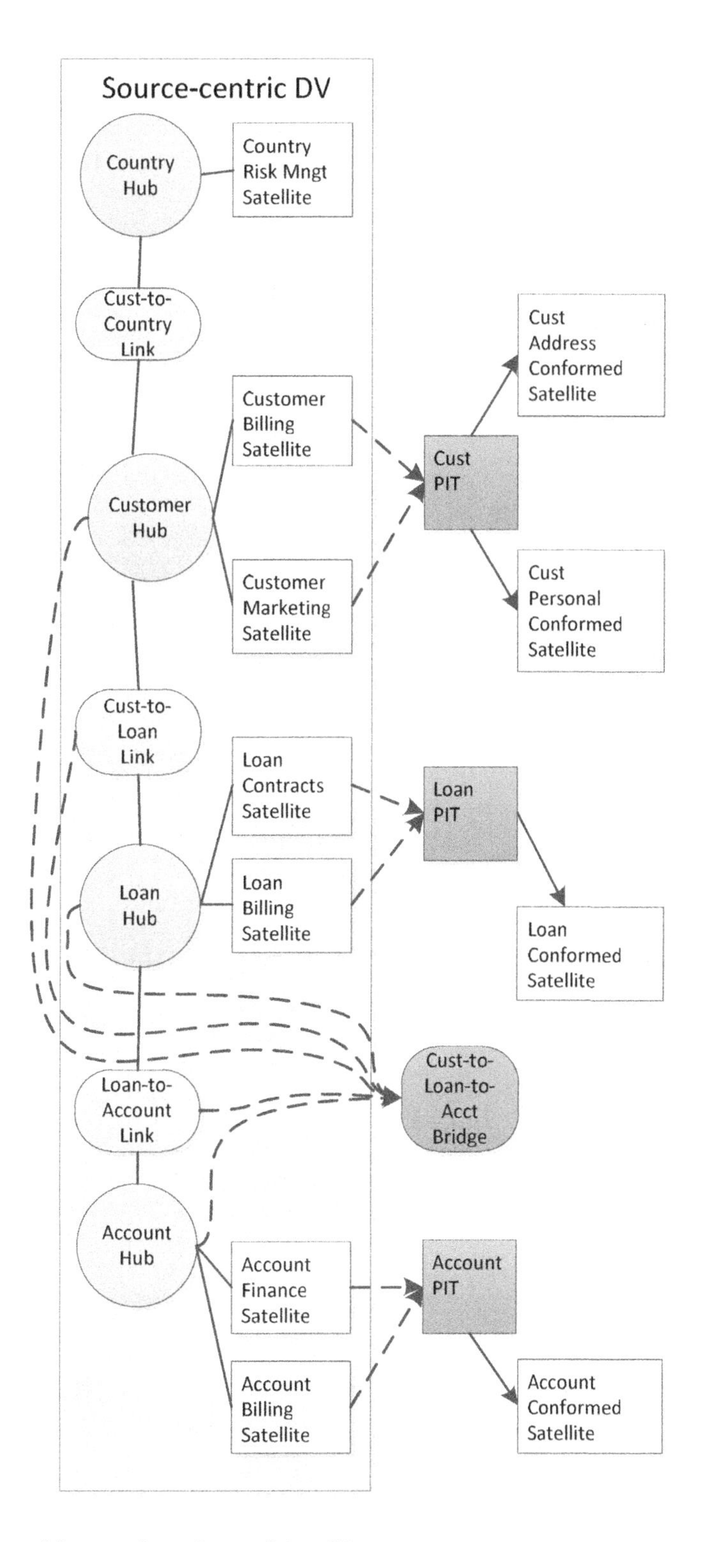

Figure 97: Bank PIT, Bridge, and Conformed Satellites

Now let's look at some additional layers in the business-rule sourced Data Vault.

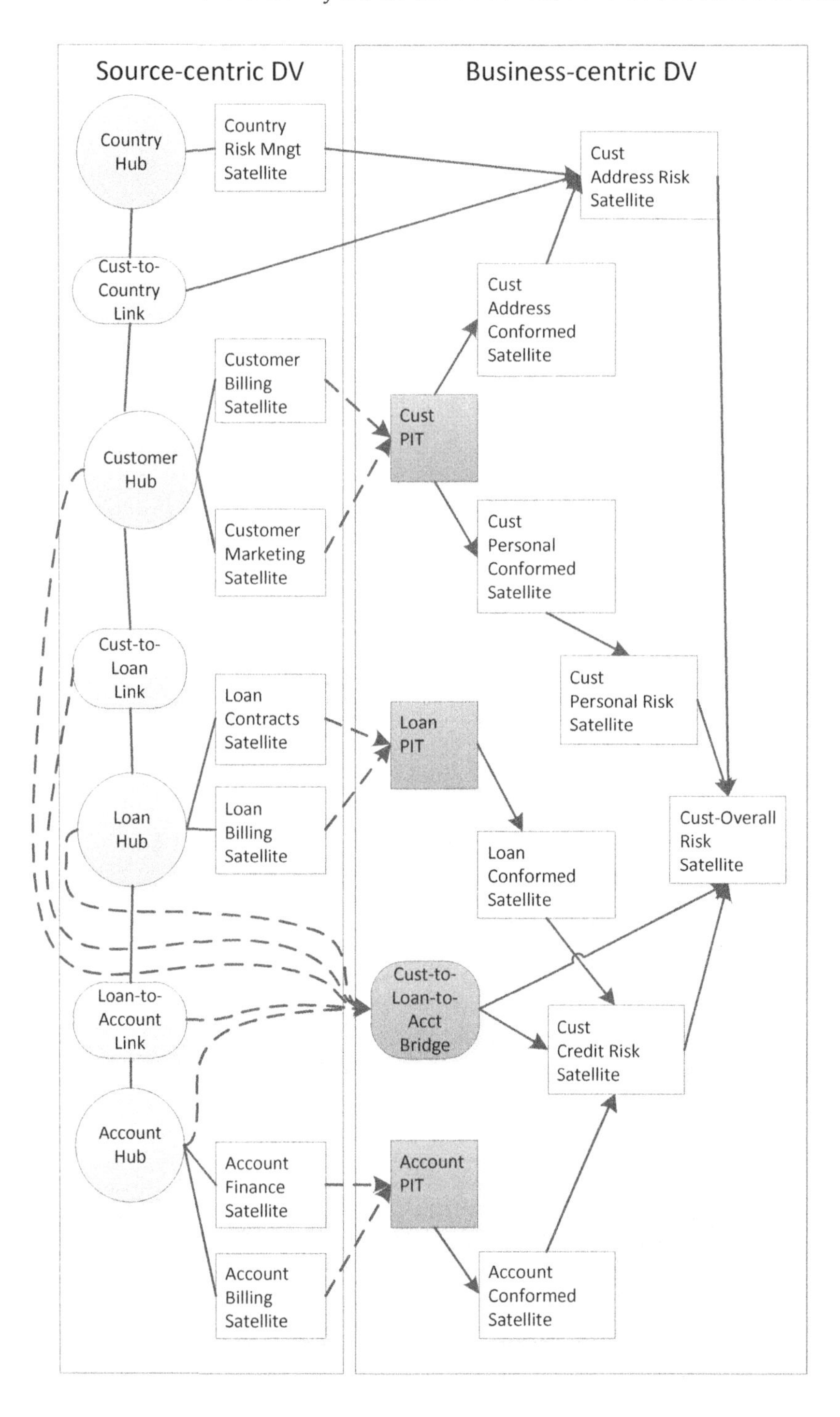

Figure 98: Bank "risk" Satellites

We want to assemble a Satellite that evaluates information about the loan risk for a customer, based on a combination of factors relating to the customer themselves ***and*** their country of residence. We create a new Customer Address Risk Satellite for this purpose. The business rules look at data from the customer's Address Conformed Satellite, and using the Customer-To-Country Link to locate the associated Country Hub, the business rules also look at attributes in the Country Risk Management Satellite. Some complex algorithms are applied to the collected data, and new attributes such as an address-based risk score are computed.

Likewise, we want to assemble a new Customer Personal Risk Satellite for information that looks at the loan's risk from the perspective of the individual customer, separate from the address-based considerations mentioned in the preceding paragraph. This time, the Customer Personal Conformed Satellite has all of the information needed for the algorithms.

Now we want to focus just on the customer's loan and account information. We are grateful that the Customer-to-Loan-to-Account Bridge has provided the associations we need between customers, their accounts, and their loans. Using that Bridge for navigation, and then using the Loan Conformed and Account Conformed Satellites, we again apply some fancy algorithms to compute values for the Customer Credit Risk Satellite.

It's interesting to note that Data Vault instances created by business rules can have the business rules operate directly on raw sourced-generated Data Vault instances, but can also use the results from other business-rule generated Data Vault instances. In this scenario, the bank wants an overall customer risk computation, and it uses the three other risk computations (as held in the Customer Address Risk Satellite, the Customer Personal Risk Satellite, and the Customer Credit Risk Satellite) to generate values in the Customer Overall Risk Satellite!

The computation of this final score may be hugely complex, but I have simplified it for this scenario by making baby-steps in the business-rule generated Data Vault instances. Though not shown, I have ensured traceability via the data lineage. The final twist in this scenario is that some algorithms in end-user analytics tools may execute using the rich data from the Data Vault, and store their results which can then become another raw source system for feeding back into the Data Vault!

Applying business rules to "close the gap"

If we think back to the example in Task #3's description on "Doing the source-to-Data Vault mapping", you may recall that we had loaded a complex "Settlement" transaction. To hold the data, we had created a Settlement Link with its associated Settlement Satellite. We may want to create a simple Satellite directly on the Loan Hub to hold the Loan Amount attribute as recorded in the Settlement transaction. Likewise, we may want to untangle the complex Link and simply record the Loan-to-Customer Link. Let's look at the diagram below.

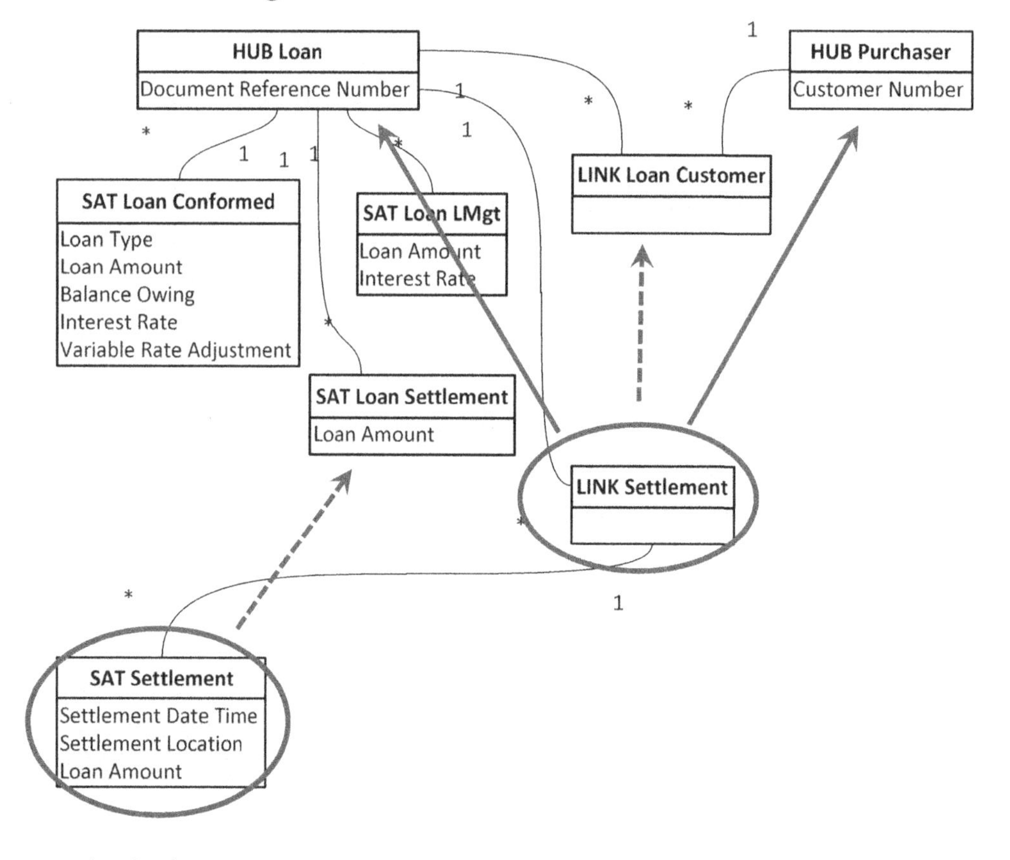

Figure 99: Using business rules to populate a Satellite and a Link

The diagram has the original source data objects circled.

The business rules really aren't that complicated.

For the Loan Settlement Satellite, we take the instance in the Settlement Satellite, grab its Loan Amount value, and populate the Loan Settlement Satellite that belongs to the Loan Hub related to the Settlement Link.

For the population of the Loan-to-Customer Link, we go to the Settlement Link, determine its associated Loan Hub and Purchaser Hub, and use this data to populate the Loan Customer Link.

Too easy?

The point is that if we've designed the Data Vault in a top-down manner, the final closing-the-gaps tasks can be relatively simple. Compare this to a bottom-up approach where maybe 50 Purchaser Hubs exist, one per source, each with one Satellite. Let's say we've then got 40 Loan Hubs. And then goodness knows how many Loan-to-Customer links spanning all sorts of relationships between 50 Purchaser Hubs and 40 Loan Hubs. Then you need business rules to consolidate all of this. That's hard. And that's why I strongly endorse Dan's position to drive the Data Vault design from the perspective of the enterprise ontology!

CHAPTER 7

Tying Off a Few Data Vault Loose Ends

A quick glance at some more advanced topics

The basic building blocks for a Data Vault have a delightful elegance – there are just Hubs, Links, and Satellites. I love the pattern. But within this simplicity there are many variations. Perhaps one could compare Data Vault to Lego® bricks. The Lego I first encountered some years ago had a few limited sizes, and a few colors, and that was it, yet there was enormous potential to create all sorts of structures.

Data Vault, too, has several recognized ways of putting together the basic building blocks. A few are mentioned below, but there are more. I do encourage you to buy the books, attend the courses and conferences, and participate in forums. This Data Vault primer is most definitely not intended to replace any such formal knowledge acquisition. But the following topics may prove to be helpful in building your foundations for Data Vault success.

Hierarchical Links

In traditional data modeling, we encounter self-referencing relationships, where a Foreign Key points to the Primary Key of another row in the same table.

A simple example might be a table of Employees, with Employee Number as the Primary Key. Each Employee (other than the most senior "boss") may identify their manager by using their manager's Employee Number in a Foreign Key relationship. [Some might argue that the employment hierarchy should involve an Employee table and a Position table, but that's a separate topic. For the sake of introducing Hierarchical Links in Data Vault, I am choosing to present a simpler model.]

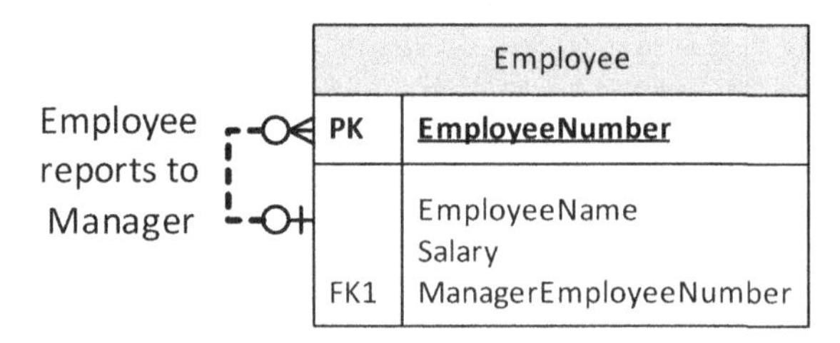

Figure 100: Employee hierarchy - operational

Another example might be an Organization Unit table, where individual Organization Units reference another Organization Unit to which it "belongs".

The Data Vault equivalent of these operational system self-referencing relationships is a Link known commonly as a "hierarchical" Link. In almost every aspect it really is just an ordinary Link, but with each instance in a hierarchical Link pointing to two Hub instances in the *same* Hub table, for example an Employee Hub instance for a subordinate and an Employee Hub instance for the related manager.

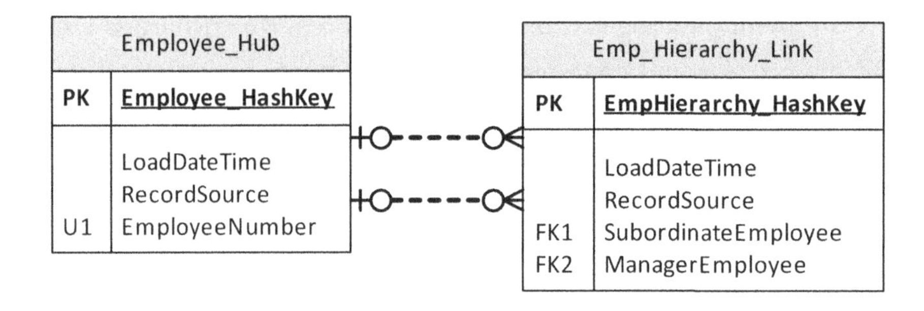

Figure 101: Employee Hierarchy – Data Vault

Same-As Links

One commonly quoted usage of a Same-As Link is to associate multiple customer instances in a Customer Hub that actually represent the same real-world customer. Maybe a few years ago Sam Smith dealt with the company, using Customer Number Cust123. Now, some years later, Sam turns up again and starts buying. The "correct" process may be to recognize Sam as the same person, and get them to use the old

Customer Number, but the process breaks and Sam gets a new Customer Number Cust456.

The Data Vault ends up with history for purportedly two separate customers. Subsequently, a cleanup initiative involving the source systems spots the duplication, or maybe an operator identifies and records the duplication. We don't want to rewrite history by merging data in the Data Vault. That breaks the trust in its audit trail. So what do we do? It's simple. We create a Same-As Link that has two Foreign Key relationships, one to point to the "old" Customer Number, and one to point to the "new" Customer Number.

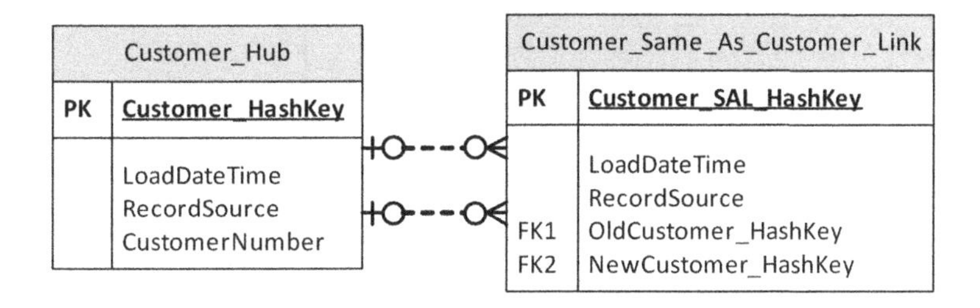

Figure 102: Customer Same-As Link

Reference data

Often our IT systems have what many call "reference data". Examples could include a collection of country codes and names, a collection of order status codes and names, or a collection of employee gender codes and names. There are a variety of ways to manage reference data within a Data Vault. Let's begin the discussion by looking at an example from a banking scenario. In the operational system, we've got Customers, and they are classified according to some Customer Type reference data. A simple reference table could look like this:

	Customer_Type
PK	CustomerTypeCode
	CustomerTypeName CustomerTypeDescription

Figure 103: Customer Type - no history

We've already decided that the Customer from the operational system is to be loaded to a Data Vault Hub. But where do we load the Customer Type reference data?

One of the first questions to ask is whether or not the history of changes is to be kept. We could use the data structure from the above operational table structure directly in our Data Vault if we only want the current values for a given code. As an alternative, if we want our Data Vault to hold the history of slowly changing values in our reference table, the following table structure might do the trick. Each time a Customer Type Name or Description changes, we can add a new row holding a snapshot of the new values, while retaining the previous values, too.

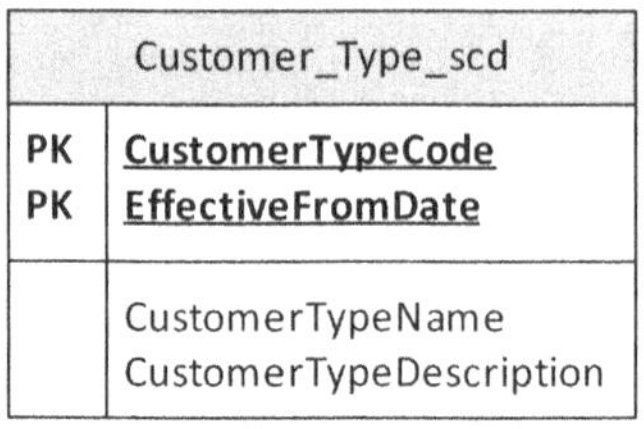

Customer_Type_scd	
PK	**CustomerTypeCode**
PK	**EffectiveFromDate**
	CustomerTypeName
	CustomerTypeDescription

Figure 104: Customer Type - slowly changing history

Maybe Country is another reference set for customers, recording their country of residence. In this scenario for the bank, let's assume that Country is not just a simple code-&-description reference data set. Instead, it is its own business concept with a recognized business key, and its own rich set of attributes, including recording the currency for each country, a geopolitical classification, a perceived risk of lending to customers in that country, whether or not the bank's head office recognizes political sanctions on trading with that country, and more. In such a case, maybe "country" could be seen as a Hub in its own right, especially if it has its own rich set of relationships with other Hubs.

The below diagram shows both scenarios. Country is modeled as a completely standard Data Vault Hub-&-Satellite structure, with a Link associating it to the Customer Hub. In contrast, the Customer Type Code attribute in the Customer's Satellite holds just the code, and this *can* be joined to the identical code in the Customer Type table.

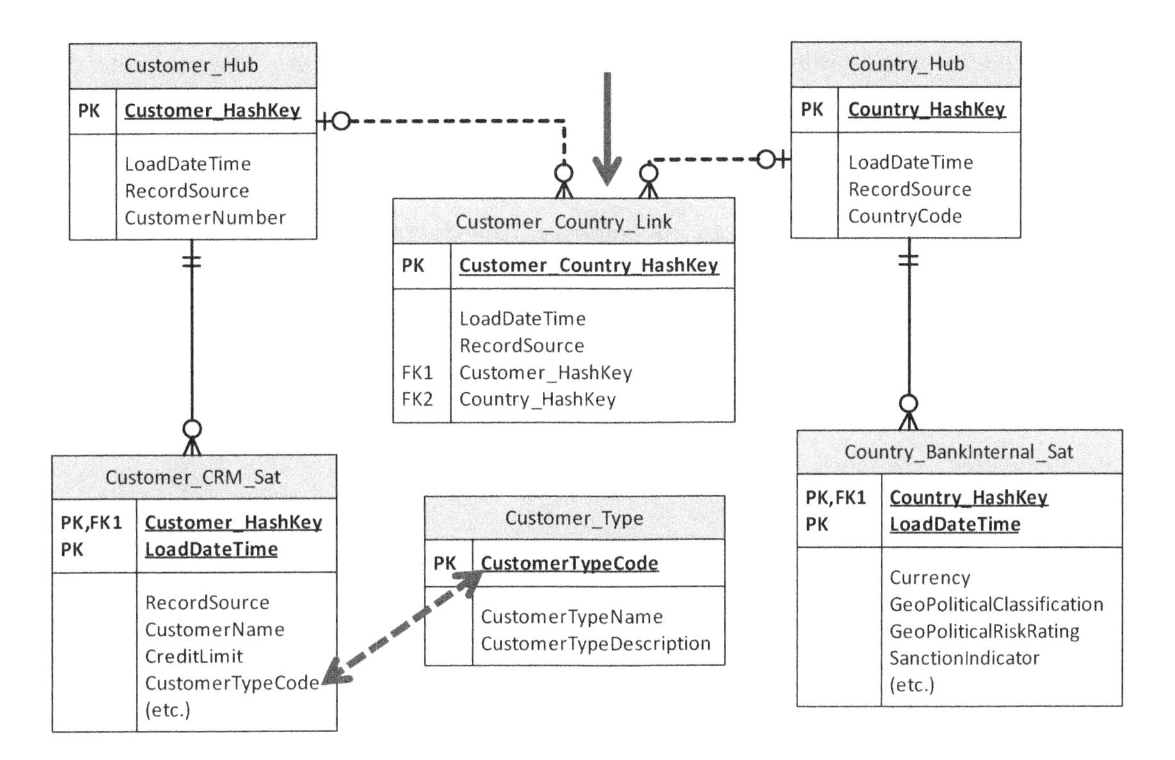

Figure 105: Reference data in a Data Vault

Two things are to be noted:

1. The Customer Type table can be assumed to be a table within the database that also holds the Data Vault Hub, Link and Satellite tables, even though it does not follow the Data Vault construct.

2. The dotted line does *not* represent a Foreign Key relationship defined within the database. It is a logical construct – the codes can be joined, and perhaps we may wish to create a relational view involving these codes, but in a Data Vault's Satellite we most definitely do not want a Foreign Key definition, let alone attempt to enforce referential integrity. The reason for this is we don't want to have expectations on what codes are "valid", and have "invalid" codes rejected. Let's take an example. Let's say we have Customer Types of Manufacturer, Bank, and Retailer defined in our reference table. If we load a customer nominated as having a Customer Type of Primary Producer, if we enforced rejection of invalid records, that one would not get through. We don't want the record rejected (in this case because our reference data is incomplete). Codes can

arrive in the Satellite that don't have a matching code in the reference table, and that's OK – it is just a representation of reality.

There's another variation that is commonly practiced. The Customer Type table can be replaced by a Hub-&-Satellite pair. As shown in the diagram, it is not connected by a formal Data Vault Link (it's now become an "unconnected" Hub) but it has the advantage of having all the standard Data Vault mechanisms for data loading and recording audit trails.

Deletions

The baseline functionality of a Data Vault is great for capturing *inserts* into source system databases. A new Fire Truck is created, and it goes into a Hub. A new relationship between Fire Truck and a Fire is created, and it gets loaded into a Link, and any attributes describing these new instances get loaded into appropriate Satellites.

The baseline functionality of a Data Vault is also great for capturing *updates* as they occur in source system databases. The changes are reflected by new rows in the affected Satellites.

But *deletions*? If a Fire Truck is deleted in an operational system, how does a Data Vault respond? A bare-bones, minimalistic Data Vault will do nothing, but don't get concerned – there are features within Data Vault for recording such activities if we need them.

Before we go any further, let's see if we can get some clarity about so-called "deletions". Some of the variations that may be of interest to us are listed below.

1. There can be <u>physical</u> deletions at a database level. We've got a Fire Truck table, and one of the Fire Trucks has been sold, so perhaps we simply delete its record.

2. There can be <u>logical</u> deletions within an application. If an Employee terminates, we are unlikely to physically delete their record straight away, but instead we might record their Termination Date.

3. Within a Data Vault environment, the Staging Area can be set up to keep a record of what things were seen at the time of the previous full-snapshot load, and what things are seen in the latest full-snapshot load. For example, yesterday's batch load of Employees had 10,000 rows. Today's load has 10,005 rows. At first glance, that looks like we've got five new employees, but instead maybe we've got seven new employees, and two that we saw yesterday weren't included in today's extract. They are "No Longer Seen" – a form of implied deletion.

Now let's immediately get one misconception out of the way. If we know something has been deleted in a source, we don't try to mimic that action in our Data Vault. Data Vault architecture is intended to be "insert only". We insert new Hub and Link instances to represent new business objects and new business relationships or new transactions. We insert new Satellite rows to represent observed updates. But if a deletion occurs back in the source system, we don't *delete* the history for those things from the Data Vault. What we can do is *insert* some data so that we can keep a record of the fact that a "deletion" has been occurred.

There's one other foundational matter regarding "deletions" that needs to be communicated. Any perceived "deletion" is a perception told to the Data Vault from a nominated source. Independent of the type of deletion (logical, physical, no longer seen), each and every source system can inform us of *their* different perceptions, at different times. The Human Resources system can, for example, tell us that an employee has been logically deleted on Monday by setting a termination date for last Friday. The Payroll system might inform us a year later of the termination, after the lucky ex-employee has received a year's pay without doing any work! Then the source system for managing building access to employees has a different view, as does the system for managing computer network logins.

How is this separation of perceptions managed in the Data Vault? It's simple, really, and it's handled by Satellites. The recommended practice for Satellites hanging off a Hub (or Link) is that each source has its own Satellite. If we've got four sources of Employee information, we can expect at least four Satellites to be hanging off the Employee Hub. Let's look quickly at the three types of "deletions" noted in the bullet list above.

Logical deletions such as an employee's termination date are recorded in data, along with all sorts of other attributes. The dates can be put in an ordinary Satellite along with the other attributes, or if we like, we can split the Satellite out to create a so-called "Effectivity Satellite". Either way, it's just data from a source system feed ending up in a regular Satellite.

Physical deletions can be identified by mechanisms such as Change Data Capture (CDC) on a source system's relational table. If we physically delete a row for an Employee from a system responsible for recording building access permissions, that action may be captured by the database CDC mechanism. If we subsequently expose the CDC results to the Data Vault, we can record the precise moment in time when the deletion occurred. Data Vaults can use what is called a "Status Tracking Satellite" to capture not only physical deletes, but also physical inserts and updates. Some CDC mechanisms even offer the ability to capture the details for each time a row is read!

No-Longer-Seen observations also have a standard Data Vault mechanism, known as a "Record Tracking Satellite".

Status Tracking Satellites, Record Tracking Satellites, and Effectivity Satellites all have different structures. Some people may prefer a single structure to record "deletions". This can be achieved as follows:

- Instead of Status Tracking Satellites, a simple solution is to let the Staging Area do some pre-processing to change the structure (*not* the content) of the incoming data feed, and flip it around so that a Status Code and a Status Date are supplied as simple data to be loaded into a Satellite just like any other Satellite.

- Instead of Record Tracking Satellites, the Staging Area which is already responsible for detecting changes between successive full extracts, can go one step further and create a Status Code and a Status Date in a similar structure to that used by the replacement for Status Tracking Satellites above.

- For Effectivity Satellites, we keep the standard Data Vault mechanism for handing the effective-from and effective to dates.

If we make the Staging Area work a bit harder, as described above, we *could* present different types of "deletions" in one standard data structure. We *could* go one step further and put all these "deletion" tracking milestones into one physical Satellite, even if they come from different sources. If we actually implemented the Tracking Satellites this way, there would problems. Standard Satellite update mechanisms simply wouldn't work with (1) multiple source data feeds populating the one Satellite, and (2) even for one source data feed, having the data presented in a Name/Value Pair construct. It is *not* what I am suggesting. (Instead, I recommend one Tracking Satellite per source, with appropriately named specific columns.) However, for the sake of simple presentation in the worked example that follows, the data is presented as if all new data is added to the single, shared Tracking Satellite. Let's look at an example.

There are only perhaps a dozen single-row data feeds, so the scenario isn't too vast, but it has some interesting and subtle twists and turns. I encourage you to carefully follow the story as it unfolds. The details are a bit technical. If you are happy with the standard Data Vault mechanisms of Status Tracking Satellites, Record Tracking Satellites, and Effectivity Satellites, please read up on them in Dan and Michael's book.[38] However, if you have struggled with these basic building blocks and are looking for another way, there's an alternative presented below. Either way, the following scenario will still be helpful to understand how these things fit together, even though the data structure presented below is the simplified one used to hold all types of deletions in a single form.

Also note that while the focus of this section is on capturing "deletions", we could use the same mechanism to capture "insertions" by source system (as compared to the single-source "first seen" Data Vault dates and times). This can assist in constructing a whole-of-life view for nominated objects (Hubs or Links) in the Data Vault. Like with "deletions", these "insertions" can capture logical insertions (via an Effective Start Date attribute), physical insertions (by using CDC records), and First-Seen insertions based on comparison of consecutive full batch extracts as seen in the Staging Area.

The worked example starts with a person successfully being accepted for a 9-month engagement. Some hard-working individual in the Human Resources (HR) department

---

[38] Linstedt D. & Olschimke O. (2016) *"Building a Scalable Data Warehouse with Data Vault 2.0", pages 143-149.*

comes in on New Years' Day (Monday January 1st), and loads the details for the expected new employee into their HR system. Employee Number 111 is assigned, and an intended start date of Monday January 8th is entered.

The Data Vault Satellite to capture this new employee's dates is shown below, followed by an explanation of how the data got assembled. For the sake of brevity, date-&-time stamps are abbreviated to just month and day.

Employee Hub Hash Key	Load Date Time	Record Source	Status Code	Status Date
Hash of "111"	January 2nd	HUMAN RES	First Seen Date	January 2nd
Hash of "111"	January 2nd	HUMAN RES	Effective Start Date	January 8th

Table 19: Tracking Satellite after HR load on January 2nd

A batch job fires up a bit after midnight each night to take a full snapshot extract from the HR system. The Staging Area persists a copy of "active last time" Employee Numbers. Its pre-processing function for this batch noted that Employee 111 wasn't in the last extract, but is now. It generated a row of data for loading to the Data Vault with a Status Code of "First Seen Date", and its own Staging Area run date-&-time to declare that Employee 111 was first seen by the Staging Area at 1:00am on Tuesday January 2nd.

The intended Start Date for Employee 111 is just a piece of data that can be mapped to a Satellite. The Staging Area's pre-processing simply assigns a Status Code of "Effective Start Date". No End Date is nominated for the Employee, so the logic simply ignores a NULL value and does nothing in the way of generating an "Effective End Date" row.

After loading a new instance in the Employee Hub (a given), we also added rows to our special shared-records Satellite.

Now we swing our attention to the source system that issues passes to permit access to buildings. Instead of using a batch job for a full extract, this system runs on a database with the ability to generated Change Data Capture rows. The HR system had created a record for the new employee a week ahead of the expected start date. The person responsible for creating new building access passes normally waits until a new employee actually turns up on their first day. The source system then, by default, issues cards for six months from the actual date of the card's creation. The Effective From and Effective To dates are generated and stored.

However, the person who issues cards is taking Monday off, so instead creates the access card ahead of time, on the Friday, and forgets to override the Effective From date, giving the impression that the new employee actually commenced on Friday the 5th. It's a data quality mistake, but one that the Data Vault will faithfully record. On Friday January 5th, a new row is created in the Building Access system, and a CDC "insert" row is automatically generated by the CDC mechanism. Again we look at the Data Vault results, and then discuss them in more detail.

Employee Hub Hash Key	Load Date Time	Record Source	Status Code	Status Date
Hash of "111"	January 5th	BUILDING ACCESS	CDC Physical Insert	January 5th
Hash of "111"	January 5th	BUILDING ACCESS	Effective Start Date	January 5th
Hash of "111"	January 5th	BUILDING ACCESS	Effective End Date	July 5th

Table 20: Tracking Satellite after Building Access load on January 5th

The Staging Area pre-processing function generates a row of data for loading to the Data Vault with a Status Code of "CDC Physical Insert", and the precise date and time, to a fraction of a second (not shown), when the physical insert actually took place in the source system. The Staging Area pre-processing also generates rows for the Effective From and Effective To dates.

Most employees like to get paid, but that doesn't usually happen on day 1 of their employment. While company policy is to get the HR records loaded before the new employee arrives, and to create the building access card on their arrival, creation of the Payroll records can wait a bit. On Tuesday January 9th, the Payroll records are created, and exposed to the Staging Area early the next morning, Wednesday January 10th. Just like the HR system, a full extract is provided as a batch job. Like the HR system, the "First Seen Date" is generated, as is the "Effective Start Date", matching that of the HR system. The Payroll worker also provided an "Effective To Date" of Monday October 8th to reflect the 9-month employment contract.

Employee Hub Hash Key	Load Date Time	Record Source	Status Code	Status Date
Hash of "111"	January 10th	PAYROLL	First Seen Date	January 10th
Hash of "111"	January 10th	PAYROLL	Effective Start Date	January 8th
Hash of "111"	January 10th	PAYROLL	Effective End Date	October 8th

Table 21: Tracking Satellite after Payroll load on January 10th

Now the drama begins. Things haven't worked out as expected in the relationship between the organization and the worker. The planned 9-month contract is being cut short. On Friday February 2nd, notice is given of premature termination, with an end date in a few weeks (February 23rd). This information is loaded into the HR system, which in turn is loaded to the Data Vault on Monday February 5th.

Employee Hub Hash Key	Load Date Time	Record Source	Status Code	Status Date
Hash of "111"	February 5th	HUMAN RES	Effective End Date	February 23rd

Table 22: Tracking Satellite after HR load on February 5th

In the turmoil of the unexpected departure, nobody thought to tell Payroll what was happening. The employee may no longer be active in the HR system, but is very much active in the Payroll system! They have continued to pay the ex-employee. It's now July, in the new financial year.

The logic in the "full" batch extract of HR records isn't actually a *full* extract. The extraction code says that if we're in a new financial year, and an ex-employee was terminated in the previous financial year, exclude them from the extract. This is a beautiful example of one of the differences between a physical delete and "no longer seen". As of the first working day in the new financial year (Monday July 2nd), Employee 111 is still in the HR system, but not in the extract file. When the file hits the Staging Areas and the business key comparison is performed, 111 is "no longer seen", with the implication it may have been deleted.

Employee Hub Hash Key	Load Date Time	Record Source	Status Code	Status Date
Hash of "111"	July 2nd	HUMAN RES	No Longer Seen Date	July 2nd

Table 23: Tracking Satellite after HR load in July

A Data Vault is capable of executing business rules. Let's assume that one very valuable rule is to generate an alert when a person has disappeared from view in the HR system but appears to be still active in the Payroll system. It is discovered on Tuesday 3rd July that in fact the ex-employee has continued to be paid since termination in February. Oops! Amongst other things, their Termination Date in the Payroll system is set after-the-fact back to February 23rd, and this information is loaded into the Data Vault early the following morning.

Employee Hub Hash Key	Load Date Time	Record Source	Status Code	Status Date
Hash of "111"	July 4th	PAYROLL	Effective End Date	February 23rd

Table 24: Tracking Satellite after Payroll load in July

Another belated action is taken, this time by the Building Access system. The record for Employee 111 is physically deleted on Friday July 6th. They could have first updated the End Date, but if the record is being deleted, who cares.

Employee Hub Hash Key	Load Date Time	Record Source	Status Code	Status Date
Hash of "111"	July 6th	BUILDING ACCESS	CDC Physical Delete	July 5th

Table 25: Tracking Satellite after Building Access load in July

If the scenario above seems a bit complicated, sadly it is a direct reflection of the complexity that sometimes occurs in the real world. So here's a bit of good news. When the real-world systems disagree as to the "facts", the Data Vault is well positioned to contribute to the resolution of data quality problems observed in source systems.

There's another bit of good news. As noted earlier, the mechanisms put in place for tracking "deletions" can also track "insertions", contributing to the building up of a picture of entity life cycle, as seen by multiple source systems with sometimes conflicting perspectives. This feature hasn't been shown in the example, but it would be easy to add.

And the last bit of good news is that the three patterns described in this section (logical inserts/deletes, physical inserts/deletes, and first-seen/no-longer-seen), while requiring three separate bits of code, are a pattern for reuse across all Hub and Links, not just Employees as highlighted in this scenario.

Point-In-Time (PIT) and Bridge tables

Dan Linstedt has commented that Point-In-Time (PIT) tables and Bridge tables are "*... the two most misunderstood, and misused, and misapplied modeling techniques in the Data Vault landscape today.*"[39] He elsewhere also stresses the value of these artifacts, especially to assist with simplicity and response time performance of queries for downstream users. So they're important, but what do they look like?

Let's start with PIT tables. I've come across people who really struggle to understand or explain them, but the fundamentals really aren't that hard to grasp.

We'll paint a hypothetical picture. Chris is an employee of Acme. The Data Vault has an Employee Hub, with two of the source systems being the Payroll system and the Human Resources (HR) system. The Hub has Satellites not only split by source system, but also by general topic and/or expected rate of change for the attribute values. A snippet of the Satellites and their values over time for Chris follows.

The first Satellite is from the Payroll system, and holds "Personal" slowly changing attributes such as Date-Of-Birth, Gender, Country-Of-Birth, and Name. Date-Of-Birth may never change unless a data entry mistake was made. Gender may change, but the Data Vault modeler does not expected this to be a frequent change. Country-Of-Birth may possibly change if the country itself changes name, but again this won't be frequent. Finally, the Name attribute is expected to have occasional but infrequent changes for some employees. For the sake of simplicity, it is assumed that the only attribute in this set that changes for Chris is the Name, and this is the only attribute shown in the sample for the Payroll-sourced "Personal" Satellite.

---

[39] https://danlinstedt.com/allposts/datavaultcat/datavault-models-business-purpose-data-as-an-asset/.

	Payroll / Personal	Payroll / Rate		HR / Personal		HR / Role	HR / Phone	
Date	Name	Grade	Weekly Pay	Name	Education	Job Title	Home	Mobile
1/01/2001	C.Smith	2	$1,111	C.Smith	Batch'r Engin'g	General Maint	9876-5432	0404-111-111
2/02/2002							9876-5432	0404-222-222
3/03/2003		2	$1,222					
4/04/2004							9876-5432	0404-333-333
5/05/2005				C.Smith	Masters Engin'g			
6/06/2006		3	$1,333			Consult Engineer	9876-5432	0404-444-444
7/07/2007	C.Jones			C.Jones	Masters Engin'g		8888-7777	0404-444-444
8/08/2008		3	$1,444					
9/09/2009	C.Smith						6666-5555	0404-444-444

Figure 106: Point-In-Time (PIT) sample data

The other Payroll Satellite holds many payroll "Rate" attributes such as frequency of pay (weekly or fortnightly), bank account details, grade and weekly pay rate. Chris, and all of the employees, hope that the pay rate is a frequently changing attribute! Again, only a subset of these attributes are shown in the table above.

Similarly, the Human Resource system's data feed is split, this time into three Satellites, with some of the attributes shown.

Let's walk through the timeline.

- At the start of 2001, Chris joins Acme. On his first day (1/1/2001), the Hub instance is created, along with values in all of the HR and Payroll Satellites.

- In February 2002, Chris gets a new mobile phone, and instead of transferring the old number to the new phone, gets a new mobile phone number. A new row is created in the HR / Phone Satellite. Note that, as is true of all Satellites, the unchanged values (in this case, the Home phone number for Chris) are captured in the new snapshot.

- March 2003 brings some good news – Chris gets a pay rise, moving from $1,111 per week to $1,222 per week. Only the Payroll-sourced "Rate" Satellite is needed to record this change.

- April 2004 comes around – time for another new mobile!

- May 2005 is another milestone for Chris, with completion of the Masters' degree in Engineering, recorded in the HR-sourced "Personal" Satellite.

- … and the new qualification pays off. In June 2006 Chris gets a promotion from General Maintenance work to a Consultant Engineering role. This also means a regrading from 2 to 3, and a pay rise to $1,333. And to celebrate, why not get a brand new mobile phone? Several Satellites capture this happy scenario.

- July 2007 brings another major change, this time personal. Chris gets married and chooses to take the spouse' family name, recorded in both the Payroll system and the HR system. The new matrimonial arrangement means Chris has shifted, and has a new Home phone number.

- August 2008 brings another pay rise.

- Unfortunately, the marriage doesn't work out. Chis moves out (resulting in a new Home phone number), and reverts to the birth family name, which is recorded in the Payroll system but not updated in the HR system.

Now we get downstream users who want to submit queries.

Someone wants to compare the situation as at end of June this year (2009), for all employees. But focusing just on Chris, what is Chris' Name (according to *both* systems), Grade, Weekly Pay, Education, Job Title, Home phone and Mobile phone as at that date?

	Payroll / Personal	Payroll / Rate		HR / Personal		HR / Role	HR / Phone	
Date	Name	Grade	Weekly Pay	Name	Education	Job Title	Home	Mobile
1/01/2001	C.Smith	2	$1,111	C.Smith	Batch'r Engin'g	General Maint	9876-5432	0404-111-111
2/02/2002							9876-5432	0404-222-222
3/03/2003		2	$1,222					
4/04/2004							9876-5432	0404-333-333
5/05/2005				C.Smith	Masters Engin'g			
6/06/2006		3	$1,333			Consult Engineer	9876-5432	0404-444-444
7/07/2007	C.Jones			C.Jones	Masters Engin'g		8888-7777	0404-444-444
8/08/2008		3	$1,444					
9/09/2009	C.Smith						6666-5555	0404-444-444

Point-In-Time as at end June, 2009

Figure 107: Point-In-Time = end June 2009

When we look at the point-in-time line through the Satellite values, we can easily see the answer. But the code for finding the active Satellites at a given point-in-time can be a little trickier. So what if we construct that code, execute it, and store the results? We could hold all of the actual attribute values (Name = C. Jones, Grade = 3 …), but to avoid a bloated data set, a baseline Point-In-Time table instead holds the set of foreign keys that point to the Satellites that were active at the point-in-time.

That's one example, based on a query for end of June, 2009. Maybe we might want to keep PIT rows for the end of every financial year, or for every month, or for every time any values changes in any of the Satellites. That's fine. We can do that, too.

That's the good news, but there's a caution. The "point-in-time" relates to timestamps in the Data Vault recording when the data was loaded. These are technical dates, and shouldn't be used for constructing a business view of when things happened. For that perspective, we need to look at dates in the Satellites' data.

Now let's talk about Bridge tables.

Earlier in our fire truck example, we saw a pair of Hubs, and one associated Link. It is copied below, with a "Bridge" table added.

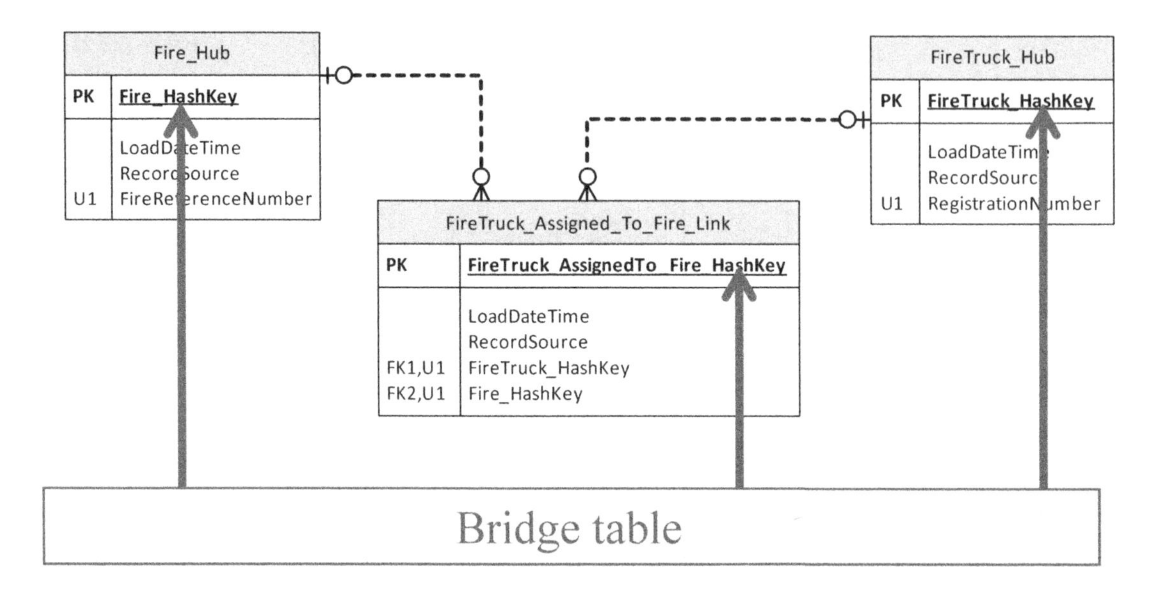

Figure 108: Bridge table

In its simplest form, a Bridge table holds a set of foreign keys pointing to related Hubs and their Links, plus a date that records when the associations were applicable. The example shows two Hubs and one Link; the scope of a Bridge table can be much wider, involving lots of Hubs and Links.

Like for Point-In-Time tables, they exist primarily to improve performance. The heavy lifting for complex joins is resolved in a set of keys, ready to be used to support end-user queries.

There's a bit more to PIT and Bridge tables, but for the Data Vault modeler, it might be enough to have a broad understanding of what they are and where they fit. If you want to read more, Chapter 6 in Dan Linstedt and Michael Olschimke's book[40] goes into greater (and more technical) detail.

---

[40] Linstedt D. & Olschimke O. (2016) *"Building a Scalable Data Warehouse with Data Vault 2.0"*.

Using a Data Vault to Shine Some Light on the "Process" World

Gap analysis using a Data Vault

We've already recognized the role of processes to assist in understanding, challenging, and extending the enterprise model. That's an example of a process view of the world making a contribution to the Data Vault world. But can a Data Vault pay back the favor by making a contribution to the "process" world?

The answer is a resounding, "Yes", and one way it does this is by giving us a measured and reliable view into the process world. Dan says, *"Data Vault models are representative of business processes and are tied to the business through the business keys."*[41] So how does this work, and how can we leverage Data Vault to deliver value?

I did some work at a water utility. At first glance, the business was so very simple. One way we could look at it was that they had two products. First, they sold clean water for drinking, cooking, and bathing. Second, they charged, in one way or another, for taking away less-than-clean water, including after people pressed the flush button. But they did have some problems they wanted help with, and water meters were at the heart of their issues.

Sometimes data people and process people don't see eye to eye. Tommy was different. He's a really nice bloke, and he's great at his process stuff. Importantly, he understands "data" as well, and welcomed the opportunity for the two of us to work together. He asked if the Data Vault could provide some metrics to help track actual progress through a number of business processes.

---

[41] Linstedt D. (2011) *"Super Charge your Data Warehouse: Invaluable Data Modeling Rules to Implement Your Data Vault", page 7.*

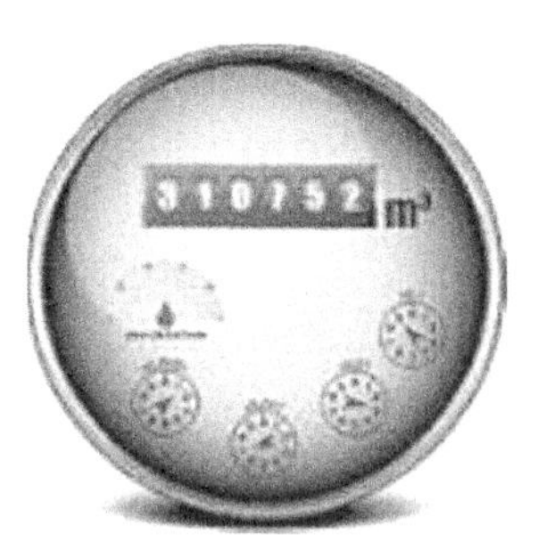

Data Vaults are great at seeing when business keys (in Hubs) are created, when the relationships between them (in Links) are created, and when the Satellites that hold data about them reflect an update. They also have mechanisms for recording when things are deleted (logically or physically) in a source database. Let's take an example of how we might use a Data Vault to inspect some business processes.

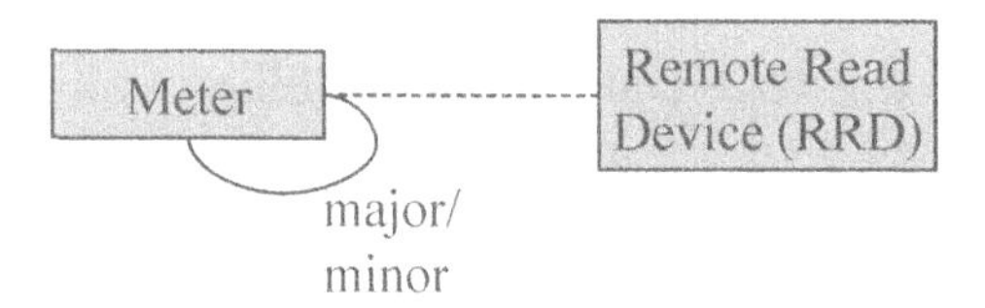

Figure 109: Data Vault objects for a water utility

We start by looking at the Data Vault model. We've got a couple of Hubs (shown as boxes):

- Meter: This is a physical device, installed at a customer's premises, to measure the amount of clean water consumed, or waste water taken away.

- Remote Read Device (RRD): An attachment to a meter to allow electronic reading of the meter when we can't safely get in to read the meter.

I've got lines representing relationships between the Hubs, and these would be implemented as Links in the Data Vault.

One is for a connection between major and minor water meters as might occur in a block of flats. The major meter measures total flow for the overall property, and the minor meters measure flow for individual houses. The difference between the sum of the minor meters and the total flow for the major meter records "property" use, perhaps for watering of the common garden.

The other relationship, shown as a dotted line between the Meter and the Remote Read Device (RRD), is for the relationship between a water meter and the remote read device. Please refer to the notes in "Hubs with more than one business key" for further details of this relationship.

Now let's look at a selected subset of business processes related to meters.

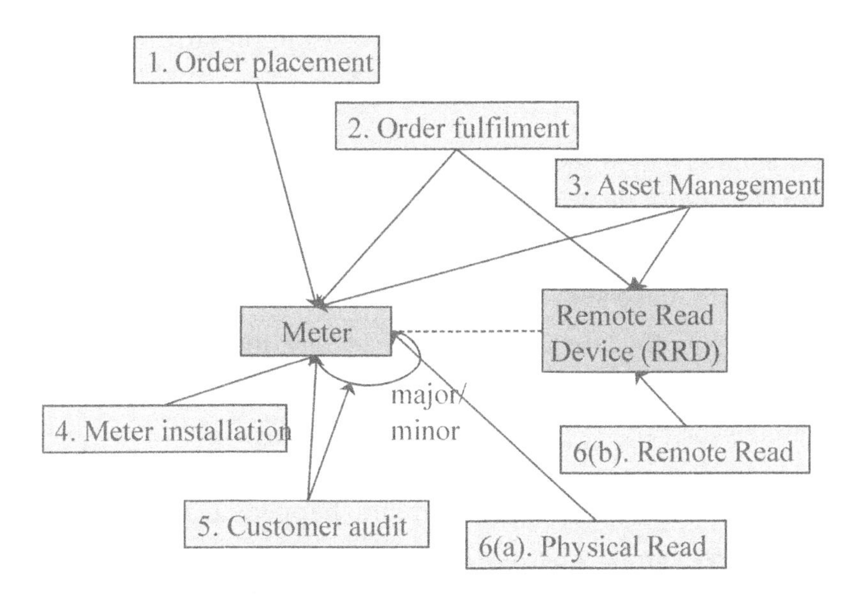

Figure 110: Data Vault and water utility processes

The sunny-day picture goes something like this.

The water utility holds a number of spare meters, and spare remote read devices, in stock. When the levels start to get low, the Order Placement process kicks in. The thing that's unusual about this process is that the water utility orders ahead of time what the meter numbers are to be for the yet-to-be-manufactured meters. Most manufacturers deliver products with their own serial numbers assigned; here, the manufacturer delivers products with the customer's serial numbers physically stamped on the meters. So the water utility's internal records in the operational system (and in the Meter Hub in the Data Vault) can record meter instances before they are even manufactured!

If all goes according to plan, two weeks later the Order Fulfilment process records the delivery of the ordered meters and remote read devices, and they go into the warehouse. Almost immediately, the Asset Management system updates its records.

This IT system is responsible for all corporate assets (company cars, laptop computers, ... and yes, water meters and remote read devices). Even though it uses its own Asset Number business key for all assets, it also records the Meter Number for water meters and Remote Read Device Number for the RRDs. That's taken care of the incoming assets. Now we engage with water utility customers. An order comes in for a Meter Installation. After the Meter Installation process is completed, additional details about the meter (in Satellites) and additional Links (for example, to the Customer) can be added.

If the meter is a simple, single meter for a residential customer, there is no need for a Customer Audit. However, if it's for a large block of units, a factory, or a hospital, where there are multiple meters involved in the installation, an audit will be performed, amongst other things to make sure that the records are correct as to what meter number is connected where. Now the customer has connections, the schedule for meter readers is updated to include the new meters, and in due course, either Physical Reads or Remote Reads are performed.

That's the sunny day scenario. But what might happen in reality? Orders can get placed, but the delivery can be way beyond the expected two weeks. Deliveries can be made, but the Asset Management system fails to "almost immediately" record the new assets (or maybe it never gets around to recording the new arrivals). Meters can be installed, but in situations where an audit is mandated, the audit process slips through the cracks. And though it may sound impossible, a customer can be connected, but the bills for usage never arrive because the meter is never read.

So how might a Data Vault help? In a blog,[42] Dan Linstedt shares the following glimpse of hope: "*The* **original Data Vault model** *provides pure business value by demonstrating the* **gaps** *between the business* **perception** *(of the way they THINK their business is running) and the* **reality** *(the way the data is actually captured and processed through business processes and systems).*"

---

[42] https://danlinstedt.com/allposts/datavaultcat/datavault-models-business-purpose-data-as-an-asset/.

Dan and Michael go into more detail in their book, in the section titled *"The value of bad data"*.[43] My attempt at summarizing their position goes like this:

- The business has a *belief*, and expectation, as to what is happening within their organization.
- IT systems record the data *actually* captured as business processes interact with those systems.
- A bit of analysis of the captured data might reveal that there is a gap between the business belief and the reality of what the IT systems reveal.

A Data Vault can be used to track what's happening in source systems, facilitate comparison around business keys, and offer the results for downstream analysis. For the water utility, some simple examples follow:

- The Order Placement process records the creation of a Hub for meter 123 on the first of the month, some time last year. The Order Fulfilment process adds a Satellite for that Hub on the 22nd of the same month, three weeks later. A simple comparison of the dates recorded in the Data Vault indicate that the expectation of a 2-week turnaround from order placement to order fulfilment was not met.
- A Satellite (and associated Links) indicate that in January of this year Meter 123 was installed at a customer's premises. Six months later, there are still no readings for use related to the meter. Seeing bills are meant to be produced quarterly, something looks wrong. A process somewhere seems to be broken.

They may be examples of pretty obvious sorts of analytics we could perform. A bit of good old fashioned detective work by Tommy found some more anomalies.

My first story relates to changes in subdivision plans. Maybe a property developer originally intended to build five houses on a large block of land, and to assist the builders, five water meters and taps were installed. Subsequently, the developer decided to build four larger houses instead of five crammed shoe-box dwellings.

---

[43] Linstedt D. & Olschimke O. (2016) *"Building a Scalable Data Warehouse with Data Vault 2.0"*, pages 521-523.

Permission was given for the changes, and the titles office and the local shire council knew about the new plans, but the water utility was not informed. We've got five meters now on four blocks, and one is never going to be connected.

Now the twist that will make you smile. The five meters get scheduled for reading. In due course, readings are taken, and of course, the one that's not connected has a reading of zero usage. There's another process that kicks in at this time. Sometimes meters get stuck and won't turn. Water is still being delivered, but not billed, so there's a targeted process to replace faulty or blocked meters with a brand new ones. The field worker does his or her job, and replaces the zero-read meter, but no one wakes up to the fact that it's not turning because it's not connected. And in due course, the new meter that also records zero usage is also replaced. And the new one also reports a zero read ...!

To understand "Process", we need more than a Data Vault

For us to deliver the full potential of performing analysis on processes, I suggest we need at least three things. The first is to see raw data in all of its glory. Some other approaches to data warehousing aim to clean up the data on the way in. In contrast, I've heard Dan talk about capturing "all the data, all the time". Warts and all, the whole philosophy behind loading source-centric raw data into the Data Vault is to not hide perceived anomalies from view. That's a tick for the first of my three requirements. Next, we want to perform analytics by source. The bare minimum of Data Vault capture of dates does provide some insight, but it might not be enough. For example, the Meter Hub will record the source of the first data feed to present Meter Number 123 to the Data Vault, and the date it was loaded, but it doesn't record what other sources have also had visibility of Meter 123, or when. More advanced aspects of Data Vault, such as Status Tracking Satellites or Record Tracking Satellites, can provide insight into business keys, and their creation dates and even "deletion" dates, by source. This is what I wanted.

Lastly, we need to recognize that IT systems, the data they capture, and this data that then gets moved to a Data Vault, is only part of the picture. Yes, it's important that a Data Vault is capable of faithfully capturing what's being entered into the source systems. But things can happen in the business that are not even visible in the source systems. People do work-arounds. They capture stuff in spreadsheets. They have totally manual processes that breach the rules. This is the reality.

Dan and Michael are very precise when we look closely at what they say on this topic. They claim (emphasis mine) that, "*… source systems provide the truth about* ***the data being collected*** *and what is really happening* **from a data perspective**".[44] In this quote, Dan and Michael are not claiming that the source systems represent the truth, the whole truth, and nothing but the truth for processes that occur outside the view of the source systems.

I remember doing some data quality work for one of Australia's largest telecommunications companies. The lead consultant, Bill, had a PhD in mathematics. He held the view that we could get *some* insight by looking at the data in IT systems, and comparing them. If two systems disagreed on a person's date of birth, he concluded that at least one was wrong, but maybe both were wrong. The way to check was to go back to the real world. I remember a comparison across four systems, three of which agreed. One person at the company concluded that the three must be correct, and the fourth wrong. Bill challenged this assumption, and went on to prove that three were wrong, and one right. Bill had a sense of humor. He got a coffee cup made that portrayed him being at the company's reception desk, with the receptionist saying something like, "Bill, you can't be you – three out of four of our systems record the fact that you're dead!"

Two more stories from my time working with Bill. The first was where a data analysis showed a spike in errors for the IT systems' data from one phone exchange. Bill dug a bit deeper, and uncovered the fact that the staff at that particular exchange never updated the central records because they had all of the information they needed on a spreadsheet. Then there was the time when Bill's dogged pursuit of the truth uncovered an illegal hard-wired patch between two telephone exchanges.

A number of us have seen less dramatic examples of where the IT systems don't capture the facts. Maybe a "standard" process doesn't work in fringe cases, so people

---

[44] Linstedt D. & Olschimke O. (2016) *"Building a Scalable Data Warehouse with Data Vault 2.0"*, page 522.

"break the rules" to get the job done. A recent client is involved in forensic analysis related to deaths that the coroner wants investigated. I won't confront you with the sad background, but sufficient to say that the central IT system simply can't cope with some of the tragic real-world scenarios. To do their job, workarounds are absolutely essential, and totally ethical. But the key message is that if we were to load the data from operational systems into a Data Vault and then analyze it in isolation from the "real world", we could come to some dangerously wrong conclusions. To try to protect the community by learning from the past, we must have solid analysis. In this forensics setting, lives depend on it.

What's the key message from all of this? That while the Data Vault can facilitate data analytics by triggering lines of investigation, or providing detailed insight as the analyst drills down, we need to have a healthy skepticism and challenge what the data is telling us. A capable human being is required to drive what Dan and Michael call "gap analysis". Don't underestimate the value that the Data Vault can add to the equation in providing an integrated view, and dates that challenge how processes are really working, but I do encourage you to dig deeper. Bill used to require his team to "ride the trucks", even if that meant crawling around a dirty, dusty phone exchange to understand what was really happening.

A bit on projects

Agility

Data Vault has the potential to be "agile", but agility doesn't just happen because someone thinks it's a good idea. There's a lot of stuff that needs to be in place for agile to succeed. Just some of the things we might need for any agile software development project include:

- Some idea of the goals. No, not hundreds of pages of excruciatingly detailed requirements' specifications, but a broad idea of what success might look like.

- Some tooling. What's the development environment (Java, .NET …)? Have we got an interactive development environment? What about automated / regression testing tools? Can we easily do DevOps rapid promotion to production? Have we got something as fundamental as a database to store our data! And on and on.

- A team. Pretty obvious? But in agile, it's not about having a bunch of technical propeller-heads locked away. The business needs to be on board, too. And agile projects recommend the team be co-located, which leads to …

- Facilities – a work area, probably a whiteboard, some collaboration tools (even if they're Post-it notes), computers already loaded with required software, … And a good coffee machine?

- Training. Sure we can learn on the job, but if we want to hit the ground running, have at least some of the team proficient in the languages, tools, and processes.

- Permission. You might wonder why I raise this, but I've seen projects threatened by people who say things like "You can't have access to that data" or "You can't use those tools" (because they're not authorized by head office, so the resultant code will not be permitted to be moved to production) or "You can't have Sam on the project because something more important has just come up".

Much of the list above applies to any agile project, whether it is for a Data Vault build or not.

Platform & tooling projects versus the Data Vault project

There are two threats to Data Vault projects I've observed that relate to muddying the waters on project scope.

The first threat is confusing the project to build required infrastructure with the project to build a Data Vault. Maybe we want Hadoop as part of our architecture? Fine. And we need a project to get it in place in our organization? Fine again. And we want to fund and manage the Hadoop implementation as part of the Data Vault project? That's where I see red lights and hear warning bells clanging.

No matter what the new software components might be (Hadoop as described above, or real-time mechanisms, or service-oriented architectures, or …), if they're part of our strategy, identify the interdependences, but consider funding and managing them separately.

There's an option we might want to consider: perhaps we can at least start the Data Vault project on an interim platform, deliver tangible value to the business, and accept we may have some technical debt to pay back when the other projects catch up with us. After all, much of the metadata we need (including for the design of Hubs, Links, and Satellites, and source-to-target mapping) should turn out to be relatively stable even if the underlying technology changes.

The second threat is similar, but closer to home for the Data Vault project, and it's about confusing the Data Vault delivery project with the tool evaluation / acquisition / build project. Sooner or later (probably sooner), we will want to use a tool for moving the data from layer to layer, doing extract/transform/load, though not necessarily in that order!

We may choose to buy a tool, and that strategy has lots of merits. I encourage you to check out what's on the market. Evaluate the candidates. Do we need to specifically model columns such as Source and Load Date-&-Time stamps, or is the tool smart enough to know these are part of the Data Vault package? Can we define, manage, and execute business rules? Do they integrate with our testing tools and DevOps strategies, or maybe they even include them? Lots of questions. And if we can find a tool that meets our requirements, or is at least "sufficient", that's great.

Alternatively, we might decide to build our own tool, or at least hard-code some bits while we do a Data Vault proof-of-concept.

I consulted to one organization that was very altruistic. It wanted to gift its entire Data Vault (less the data) to others in the same industry, and not have them need to get a license for the Data Vault toolset. They chose to develop the tools in-house so they could give them away. I take my hat off for their generosity. But I simply want to warn that building you own toolset does come at a price. And like with establishing other software infrastructure, I recommend that the build of a tool be separately funded and managed.

A few hints

OK, we've got everything in place. We've got the team, they're trained, we've got the complementary software, a tool, and we're ready to go. I've got a few final hints for us to consider as we build our Data Vault:

- At the very outset, check out the infrastructure bits we've been given to work with by creating a "walking skeleton" – some tiny bits of code that exercise the architecture, end-to-end. Yes, agile is meant to deliver business value as part of each iteration, but treat this as a technical spike to try to eliminate the possibility of architectural show-stoppers.

- Next, do something similar to give end-to-end visibility of some business data. Pump a tiny bit in from a source, and push it all of the way through to end-user consumption. Again, perhaps this might provide minimal business value, but it shows the business how the whole thing works. More importantly, it provides a baseline on which we can build to progressively deliver incremental business value.

- Now for the remaining iterations, keep delivering end-to-end, focused on tangible business value.

There's one phrase that appeared in all of the above bullet points. It's "end-to-end". Why do I see this as being important? I've unfortunately seen tool vendors, and Data Vault consultants, who impress with how quickly they can load data into the Data Vault, but fail to give enough focus on actually delivering against business expectations. The good will that might be won by demonstrating a speedy load will sooner or later evaporate unless business value pops out the other end of the sausage machine.

One more suggestion. In the earlier section titled "Is "agile evolution" an option?", I shared a confronting story. The lack of a data model hampered an agile project. The team took one iteration to assemble a relatively stable data model. Subsequent iterations resulted in a 12-fold increase in productivity.

My conclusion? For a Data Vault project, I suggest that the data modeler(s) on the team try to think about what's coming up, at least one sprint ahead of the development.

A few controversies

There are a number of well-recognized voices in the Data Vault community in addition to that of Dan Linstedt, the founder of Data Vault. I've heard a joke that goes something like this: "If you've got three data modelers in a room, you'll get at least four opinions." Oops.

I take heart from the PhD of Graeme Simsion on a related matter, as adapted for publication in his book, "*Data Modeling Theory and Practice*".[45] I can't do an entire book justice in a few sentences, but here's my take-away from his work. If we've got a bunch of data modelers, and each one thinks there can only be one "correct" solution for a given problem, don't be surprised if there is heated disagreement. Conversely, if all accept that several variations may actually "work", a more balanced consideration of alternatives and their relative merits is possible.

I think it is healthy if there is room for respectful discussion on alternatives to Data Vault modeling standards. For me, my baseline is the Data Vault 2.0 standard, but I

---

[45] Simsion G. (2007) "*Data Modeling Theory and Practice*".

welcome objective consideration of variations, especially as they may suit specific circumstances. Dan Linstedt also welcomes the standards being challenged. He just, quite rightly, warns against changes without due consideration as to unwelcome side effects.

Modeling a Link or a Hub?

We may encounter debates as to when something could or should be modeled as a Hub versus modeling it as a Link. I know this is contentious in some quarters. Part of me would prefer to not even raise the topic, as whatever position I take, I suspect someone will disagree. Nonetheless, avoidance of the issue won't make it go away, so I will stick my neck out, hopefully in a manner that is respectful of the views of others.

I would like to share two scenarios that might help shed some light on this topic.

In the first scenario, there is an accident on a highway. Cars are damaged, drivers are upset, insurance companies may be faced with claims, but thankfully no one has died. From the perspective of one of my clients, there may be a police report with "links" to cars and their registration numbers, drivers and their driver's license numbers, health practitioners who may assist, police force members identified by their member number, and so on. The "key" message (pun intended) is that there is no business key for the accident itself. However, in our Data Vault, we can create a Link (and maybe a Satellite – see the next "controversy" for comments on Links with Satellites) to associate the accident with the cars, drivers, health practitioners, police members, and more.

In the second scenario, a fatality occurs and forensic examination of the deceased is required. A "Case Number" business key is assigned. In the Data Vault, there is a Case Hub. We can create an instance in the Case Hub, populate its Satellite, and also populate Links to the cars, drivers, health practitioners, police members, and so on.

Which model is correct, or are both models OK? Here are my starting-point rule-of-thumb guidelines for choosing Hubs versus Links, at least as they relate to business views of the world:

- If the thing to be modeled is recognized by the business as a tangible concept, with an identifiable business key, it's a Hub.

- If the thing to be modeled looks like an "event" or a "transaction" that references several Hubs via their business keys, but doesn't have its own independent business key, it's a Link.

There we are. Some nice, clean guidelines.

But what about an event or transaction that also has a clearly recognized business key? It seems to span my two definitions; it's an event so it's a Link, but it has an independent business key so it's a Hub! For example, maybe an engineering workshop has "transactions" that are work orders, with a Work Order Number.

If the work orders are "recognized by the business as a tangible concept, with an identifiable business key" (such as a Work Order Number given to the customer so he/she can enquire on progress), then to me, the work orders look like they belong to a Hub. (If something walks like a duck, quacks like a duck, and swims like a duck, maybe it is a duck.) *But* if the transaction didn't have a Work Order Number and was identified by nothing more than the collection of business keys in related Hubs, the work orders look like they belong to a Link.

Even if my guidelines are helpful, please recognize that, as noted by Graeme Simsion's research, there might still be times when experienced modelers may have to agree to disagree, take a position, and see how it works.

Roelant Vos also adds a valuable perspective. We can start by modeling at a higher level of abstraction, capturing how the business sees their world. From this position, if we have flexible tools, we may be able to generate variations of the physical Data Vault tables while having a single, agreed logical view. That approach may actually defuse some of the tension in the following topics. Thanks, Roelant!

Modeling a Satellite on a Link?

I've got another controversy to share at this point. Some suggest that a Link should never have a Satellite, apart from maybe an "Effectivity Satellite" that has a From Date and a To Date to record the period the relationship was active. Those who hold this view seem to suggest that if a "thing" has attributes, it has to be a Hub.

Conversely, others happily model Satellites against Links.

For a moment, I want to step back to traditional data modeling, then to the Unified Modeling Language (UML) to see if we can get some clues to help us decide which way to go.

In a traditional data model, we have relationships, and these somewhat approximate a point-in-time equivalent of a Data Vault Link. If an operational system has a one-to-one or one-to-many relationship, the relationship itself is represented by the presence of a Foreign Key in one entity. This type of relationship is unlikely to have associated attributes, and if it does, they will be mixed in with other attributes in the entity holding the Foreign Key. If data from this operational system maps to a Data Vault Link, there is probably no data to even put in a Satellite off the Link.

Conversely, if the relationship is a many-to-many relationship, modeled as a resolution entity, it can have attributes in addition to the Foreign Keys that point to the participating "parent" entities. When we map this resolution entity into a Data Vault, I think most if not all people are happy that the additional attributes go into a Satellite. But is it a Satellite hanging off a Link, or a Satellite hanging off a Hub?

Before we make a decision, let's quickly look at the UML Class Diagram notation – a modeling style with some correlation to a data modeler's Entity-Relationship Diagram. A UML class approximates an ERD entity, and a UML association approximates an ERD relationship. Now if the association has its own attributes, a new type of object appears – an "association class". It's an association (a relationship) that can have its own attributes in a dedicated class (entity). It looks something like a data modeler's resolution entity, but can hold attributes for an association (relationship) even if the cardinality is not many-to-many.

So where does all of this lead us? One answer is that there are many answers! Dan Linstedt's Data Vault 2.0 standard of allowing Satellites to hang off a Link looks like it's got good company with data modeling resolution entities, and with UML association classes. Others may argue that the UML association class gives us a hint that the moment an association / relationship has attributes, it needs a class, and does that hint at a Hub in the Data Vault world?

OK, I will share my opinion; for me, I like to start by considering whether a "thing" looks like a Hub or a Link (see the section immediately above), *independent* of whether it has its own attributes or not. And if it turns out to look like a good Link, and it has attributes, I am happy to create a Satellite on the Link. I think this approach is clean, simple, consistent, and it aligns with much of what I observe in both data modeling and class modeling (UML) practices.

Having said that, you may reach a different conclusion, and hopefully we can still be friends!

Normalization for Links, and Links-on-Links

We may encounter guidelines on Links that encourage the structure to be "de-normalized". A purist data modeler may look at the examples, and suggest that in fact the structures are being "normalized".

In some ways, it's simply not worth the debate. Very few can quote precise definitions for first, second and third normal form, let alone Boyce-Codd normal form, or fourth or fifth normal form. And I suspect few care about such abstract terminology anyhow. It is arguable that a working knowledge of these levels of normalization is more important than their definitions. In another way, precision as to whether something is normalized or not does matter. But before we get to that, let me note that the examples I've seen on Data Vault modeling sometimes touch on the more advanced levels of normalization, such as 5th Normal Form (5NF). That may sound scary to some, so let me please share a very simple example from a cut-down model for the airline industry. The examples given in the text below the diagram are not meant to be necessarily correct, but just indicative of the types of information that could be held.

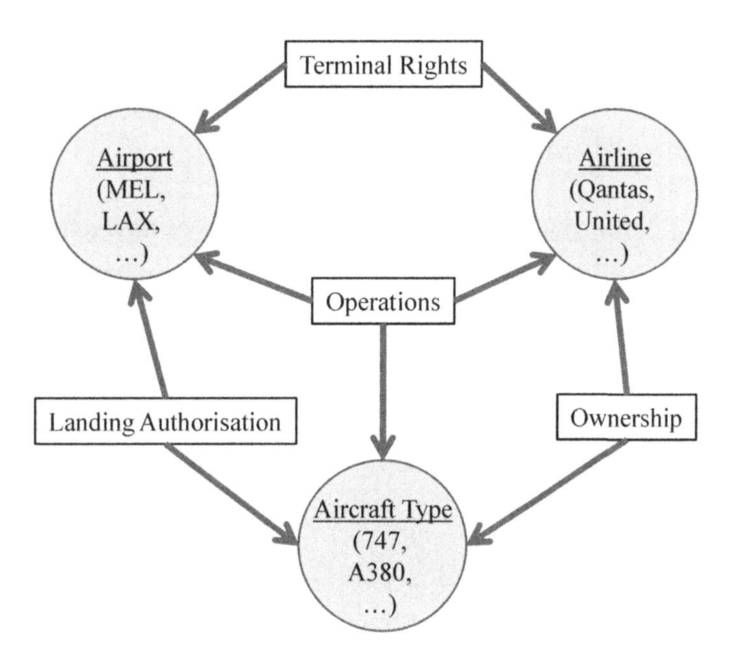

Figure 111: Example of normalization for Links

The large circles represent core business concepts for airlines. They could be relational tables in an operational source system, or Hubs in a Data Vault.

- The Airport table/Hub holds instances for the airports of interest – Melbourne, in Australia (MEL), Los Angeles in the USA (LAX), Heathrow in the UK (LHR), and even the tiny airport I've used in a remote part of Australia, the Olympic Dam airport (OLP).

- The Airline table/Hub holds instances for participating airlines such as Qantas, United, and British.

- The Aircraft Type table/Hub holds instances for types of aircraft such as Airbus A380, Boeing 747, Being 767, and maybe the Cessna 172.

Forming an outer ring are three boxes with arrows to the core entities. They could be many-to-many resolution entities in the operational system's relational database, or Links in a Data Vault.

- The Terminal Rights table/Link holds pairs of codes from the Airport and Airline entities, defining which Airlines have terminal rights at which Airports.

Examples might include that Qantas has landing rights in Melbourne and Los Angeles, United has rights in Los Angeles, and British Airways has rights in Heathrow and Melbourne.

- The Landing Authorization table/Link holds pairs of codes from the Airport and Aircraft Type entities, defining which Aircraft Types are authorized to land at which Airports. Examples might include that Airbus A380s and Boeing 747s are authorized to land at Melbourne airport. ***Not*** in the list might be Cessna 172s at Heathrow (emergencies aside, it's too busy to permit regular use by light aircraft), and Boeing 767s at Olympic Dam (it's just a dirt airstrip next to an outback mine).

- The Ownership table/Link holds pairs of codes from the Airline and Aircraft Type entities, defining which Aircraft Types are owned by nominated Airlines. Qantas owns A380s, …

Each of the above three tables relates to just two "parent" tables. They are normalized. If we tried to have a single three-way table that held the Cartesian product of all combinations from the three separate tables, it would not only cease to be normalized, but it may hold combinations that are not valid. For example:

- Maybe Qantas has landing rights in Melbourne (MEL), Los Angeles (LAX), and Heathrow (LHR).

- Maybe Qantas owns Boeing 747s, 767s and Airbus A380s.

- Maybe Melbourne (MEL), Los Angeles (LAX), and Heathrow (LHR) can handle Boeing 747s, 767s and Airbus A380s.

But a Cartesian product of all of these data sets may be misleading. Perhaps Qantas chooses to only operate its A380s between Melbourne and Los Angeles (not its 767s). Maybe it operates 767s between Melbourne and Heathrow (not its A380s). It is misleading to create a 3-way Link between the three Hubs, based on possible combinations; retaining the set of three 2-way Links is actually holding the relationships in a normalized form.

Now we turn the example on its head.

The single 3-way Operations table/Link holds triplets of codes from the Airport, Aircraft Type, and Airline entities, defining which Airlines actually operate which Aircraft Types out of which Airports. One of the examples above was Qantas operating its A380s into and out of Los Angeles.

It was dangerous to assume we could take all combinations of the three 2-way Links to generate a single 3-way Link to represent which airline flew what aircraft types in and out of what airports. Likewise, we can't simply take the single 3-way Link and assume it represents all combinations for the other 2-way Links. Maybe no airlines actually operate out of Roxby Down with a Cessna 172, but the Airport is capable of handling them. This time, retaining the single 3-way Link is actually holding the relationships in a normalized form!

We could have included another Link on the diagram, showing Flights. It would be a 4-way Link, involving the Airport table/Hub twice (From, and To), plus the Airline and the Aircraft Type. It too would be normalized for this purpose. So what are the take-away messages?

1. The logical model of the business concepts and the business relationships should be assembled as a normalized view.

2. The Data Vault model can have multiple Links that in part share common "parent" Hubs, and that's fine. There is no need to have Link-to-Link relationships – keep them separate, just like the 3-way Link and the set of 2-way Links have independent lives as shown in the diagram.

Closing comments on controversies

I've seen divisive debates on alternative approaches. My own opinion is that while the differences are important, there is much in common. Let's leverage off what is truly common, and respectfully and objectively evaluate the differences.

More uses for top-down models

Remember that Dan Linstedt said that if we have an enterprise ontology, we should use it? That's great if we have one. But what if we don't? The section of this book titled "Task #1: Form the Enterprise View" was written to help people who didn't already have an enterprise data model to create it quickly, without comprising the quality.

But can the same enterprise data model be used for other purposes? The good news is there may be many initiatives within an organization where an enterprise data model can potentially make a contribution. Some of these are listed below.

- Strategic planning: I've participated in several projects where strategic planning, for the entire enterprise or just for the IT department, was assisted by the development and application of an enterprise data model. In each case, a "sufficient" enterprise (top-down) model was developed in a few weeks.

- Enterprise data integration: One of my clients was involved in the merging of 83 separate organizations. The management did an amazing job given the pressing time frames mandated by an act of parliament. But after the dust settled, an enterprise data model gave them a long-term framework for integrating the multitude of data to provide a single, consistent view.

- Master Data Management (MDM) and Reference Data Management (RDM): It's probably a self-evident fact to say that management of data as a corporate asset requires a corporate vision! An enterprise data model can provide the consistent framework for Master Data Management and Reference Data Management initiatives.

- Benchmarking candidate IT package solutions: A company engaged me to develop an independent view of their data. They didn't want their target model to be influenced by assumptions consciously or unconsciously incorporated in any vendor software packages that had been shortlisted for selection. The top-of-the-list package was ruled out when compared to the essential features of the benchmark model. It was estimated that the cost savings from this insight could be measured in millions of dollars.

- Facilitating IT in-house development solutions: One client wanted an enterprise data model to drive the design for their service-oriented architecture, particularly the data structure of the data payloads in XML. Another wanted a UML class model to drive a Java development, and the enterprise model (using the UML notation), was the kick-start they needed.

- Facilitating communication: Most if not all of the above uses have a technical aspect. What I have seen again and again is the participation of business *and* IT people in the development of an enterprise data model delivering a massive beneficial side effect – the two sides now talk the same language!

- Process modeling: Further to the above, the existence of a common language can facilitate the development of process definitions.

... and last but not least, we return to the catalyst for this book – using the enterprise data model to shape a Data Vault design.

So an enterprise data model can be used for many purposes. But what happens when it is used for more than one of these reasons, in a single organization?

Even if our motivation for pursuing top-down big-picture enterprise modeling had been for only one of the above reasons, that's enough. But if the model is used across two or more such initiatives, the multiplier effect kicks in as the investment in one area contributes to another related area. For example, if several agile in-house development projects also produce source data that will be required in a Data Vault, why not base all such projects on a common data architecture? Everybody wins.

In conclusion

Australia has some cities that grew somewhat organically, and their origin is reflected in some chaotic aspects! Australia also has some major cities that were planned from the outset, where the designers articulated a vision for the end-state, and the authorities defined a clear path to get there.

Some Data Vault practitioners appear to follow a simplistic bottom-up raw source-centric Data Vault design and hope the business-centric Data Vault solution will magically appear. Like the source-driven tool vendors, they can impress with their speedy delivery of something, but subsequent delivery of tangible business value may be much slower, and the project, and therefore the Data Vault initiative, may fail.

Of course, the Data Vault is flexible, adaptive, and agile. You *can* create source specific Hubs and Links, and later create business-centric Data Vault artifacts to prepare the raw data for business consumption. But if you head down this route, don't be surprised if you experience an explosion of source-specific Hubs, followed by a matching explosion of source-specific Links.

Data Vault is about integration. Just because Data Vault *can* use the business rules layer to untangle a messy gap between source-specific Hubs and Links, and ready-for-consumption artifacts, why should it? Why not create a small number of clean, agreed, business-centric Hubs, and then define business-centric Links around them to represent the more stable business relationships? If you take this approach of identifying business-centric Hubs and Links, the source-specific Data Vault Satellites can now be loaded happily against this framework, immediately providing a useful level of integration.

The good news is that this can be done. By properly designing the Data Vault, from the very outset, based on an enterprise data model, you can expect to reduce "business debt". And hopefully this book will help you achieve tangible business value both initially and in the longer term.

And now a parting thought. While Data Vault is capable of contributing to the cleaning up problems in the source operational systems, let's not forget the role of data governance in moving resolutions back to the source where reasonably possible. Operational staff who use these source systems will thank you. But to guide such an endeavor, you'll benefit if you start with a top-down enterprise model.

APPENDIX

Common Data Model Patterns – An Introduction

Below is a collection of light-weight data model patterns that can be used as a jump-start for modeling. For some, they may be sufficient, and no further details may be necessary. Some others may need to drill down a bit deeper, and for them I highly recommend the publications of David Hay and Len Silverston that have been mentioned several times in this book.

The Unified Modeling Language (UML) notation has been used, in part because of its increasing use for a wide variety of purposes. If we use the patterns to drive (say) a physical implementation in a relational database, some logical-to-physical adaptations may be required. An example relates to my direct representations of many-to-many associations which, in a relational world, would need to be converted to resolution entities.

Please note that these patterns represent a logical view of data, typically implemented in an operational system, and typically representing a single point in time. This is in direct contrast to a Data Vault model that represents data changes over time. Nonetheless, these patterns can be used effectively for shaping a Data Vault, starting with Task #1 to assemble the enterprise view, and continuing onto Task #2 as they contribute to shaping the Data Vault model.

Pattern: Party & Party Role

Please note that this appendix does not include many aspects of the Party pattern as it has already been presented in the "Could I see an example, please?" section earlier.

Pattern: Position

Some simplistic models for reporting hierarchies within organizations depict employees reporting to employees. For example, if Alex is the manager of Brooke, an Employee class can have a simple self-referencing relationship from the subordinate employee's record to that of their manager.

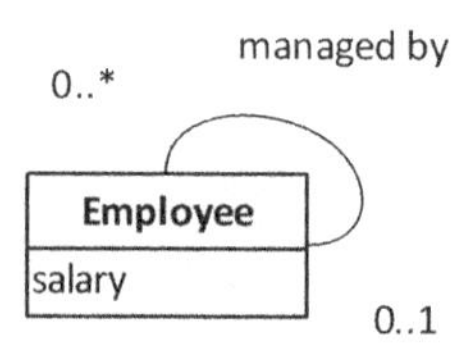

Figure 112: Simple employee-to-manager relationship

A widely recognized improvement on this model is to explicitly model a Position class.

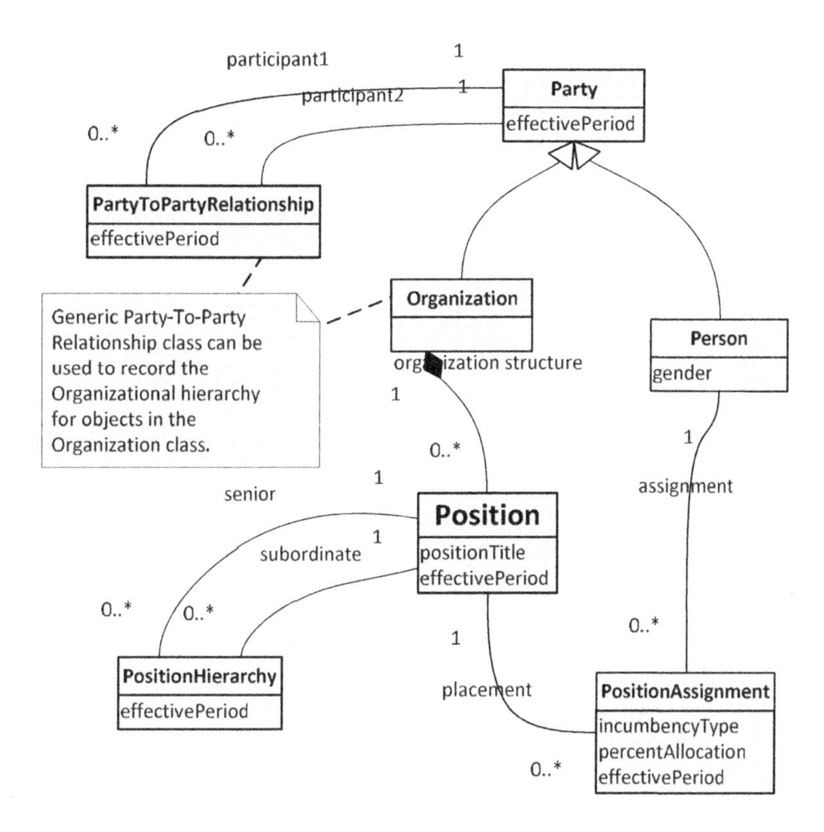

Figure 113: Position pattern

Organizations have structure. They may have departments, sections, divisions, and so on, relating to each other in a hierarchy. Positions also have structures. One Position reports to another, which in turn reports to an even higher Position. And Positions are created within Organizations!

Rather than trying to accommodate both hierarchies in one structure, the model intends to allow both to coexist. For example:

- There may be a hierarchy of Positions, all within one Organization unit.
- A Position "belonging" to one Organization unit may report to a Position "belonging" to another Organization unit.

Within this framework, employees can then be assigned to these Positions. In this model, rather than a Person reporting to their manager (as portrayed in Figure 112), a

Person is assigned to a Position that reports to a Position to which their manager is assigned!

This may appear to be a bit more abstract and difficult to grasp, but arguably it has greater flexibility. For example, one Person may fill multiple Positions at the same point in time. Similarly, at a given point in time, a Position may be vacant because it has no employee assigned, while at another point in time, it may have more than one Person assigned.

Recording the management hierarchy via its Positions typically provides greater stability. The incumbents of a Position may change relatively frequently, but it might be reasonable to expect that the Position relationships are relatively stable.

These assignments are managed via the Position Assignment class. Its attributes include the following:

- The Incumbency Type, such as "Acting in role" during the absence of the primary person, or "Shared" for a job-sharing situation.
- The Percent Allocation, which defaults to 100%, but could record, for example, one Person being allocated for 60% of the time and another Person allocated for 40% of the time.
- The effective period, for example used to record a short-term allocation while the primary incumbent is on leave.

Note also that the common Employee / Position pattern assumes that people assigned to positions are actually employees. However, it is possible to have people assigned to positions that are not necessarily considered "employees" in the traditional sense. That is why the above model associates the Person class to the Position Assignment class rather than a more specific employee class.

Pattern: Agreement

An Agreement (or "contract") represents some formal or informal arrangement between parties. Examples of formal Agreements might include lease contracts for vehicles, or employment contracts. An example of an informal Agreement might be the recording of Dan's willingness to chair tomorrow's design review meeting.

An Agreement may be "typed" via the Agreement Type class, or if specific attributes are required, it may be typed as a subclass, such as the Employment Contract shown as an example.

An Agreement may be further detailed through its Agreement Item class. For example, an Agreement to purchase some products may have items to detail each intended product purchase.

Agreements have an interesting relationship with the Document class, which is responsible for managing instances of hard-copy or electronic documents. Not all Agreements require collection of "documentary evidence" for the Agreement, but where they do, the Document class comes into play. The Document class has its own pattern, and is described separately. This Agreement class is responsible for managing the *structured* data related to Agreements. Examples of attributes recorded might include date signed, status, reference number, and the involved parties and their roles.

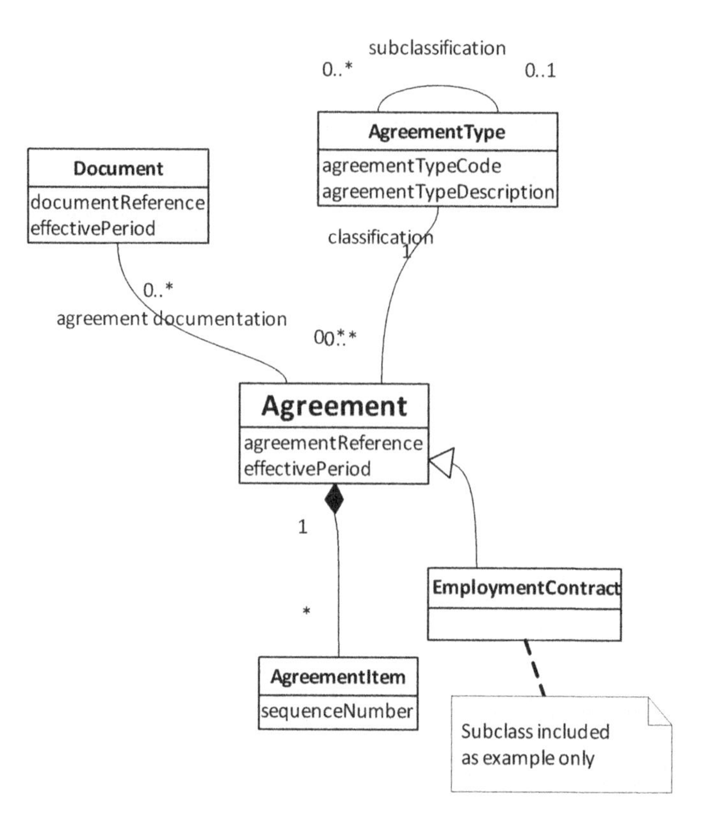

Figure 114: Agreement pattern core

As shown in Figure 115, Agreements are typically associated with the Party class or the Party Role class that records the parties involved in the Agreement, and their roles. For example, an employment contract could be expected to have the employer and the employee involved. A transfer-of-land agreement might involve the vendor(s), the buyer(s), solicitors for both sides, banks for both sides, perhaps a guarantor, a witness, and so on.

As explained in the Party Role pattern (refer to "Figure 37: Party Role pattern", and its supplementary text), the participants in the Agreement can have declared roles such as the role of the real estate agent, or contextual roles such as the witness to the signature.

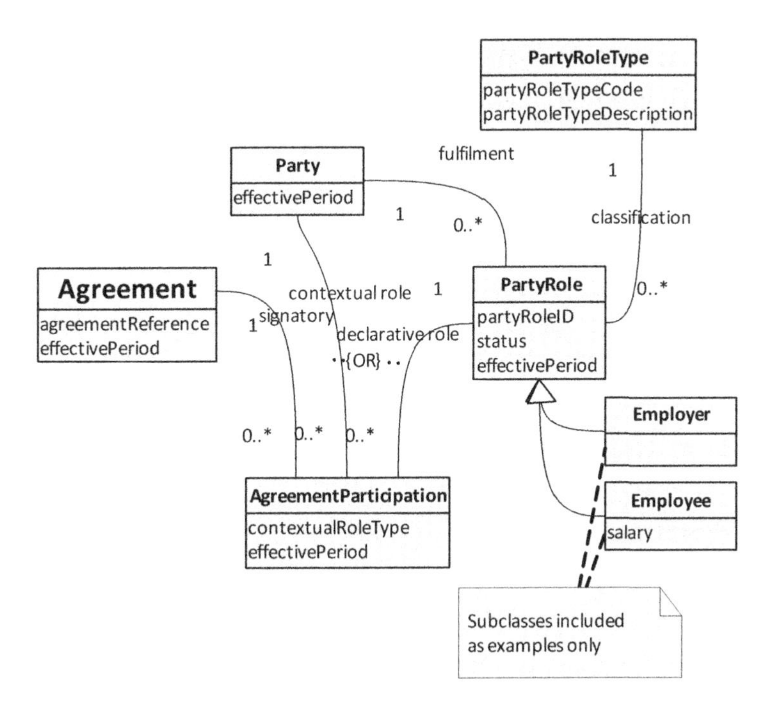

Figure 115: Agreements pattern and associated Parties

Agreements can be associated to other associated Agreements. For example, a subcontract may be associated with the larger, overarching contract, or one Agreement may be the updated replacement for the now-obsolete version.

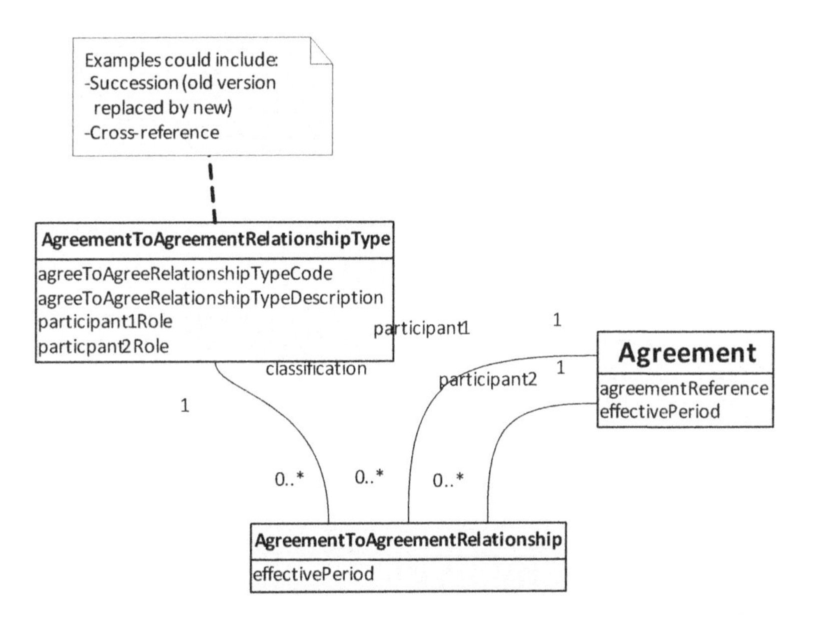

Figure 116: Agreement pattern inter-relationships

The Agreement To Agreement Type class defines allowable types of interrelationships, and the roles of each participant. For example, if the type of relationship between Agreements is a "Replacement" relationship (one Agreement is the replacement for another), the Participant 1 Role might be defined as "Obsolete Version" and the Participant 2 Role might be defined as "Replacement Version".

Pattern: Resource

The concept of a Resource is sometimes also known as an asset. Examples could include buildings, computers, company cars, consumables, and much more. The model below gives several examples from a wildfire emergency response scenario. It is interesting to note that from a wildfire logistic officer's perspective, people *could* be seen as "just" resources! The Human Resources people might disagree.

Typically, the Resource class is subclassed when there is a requirement for specific attributes and/or associations. It must be noted that some Resources do not require any specialization and hence may be treated using the generic Resource class (with a resource type – see the associated Resource Type class).

The concept of a Resource may be relatively straightforward, but its relationships may be more complex. One of the inter-relationships between types of Resources is shown below, where there is a relationship between a slip-on four-wheel-drive tray vehicle and the slip-on tank-&-pump unit that is attached to the vehicle in summer. Other types of relationships for a Resource might include a number of types of objects, all of which are patterns in their own right:

- An association with its geospatial Location.
- Its association with Events, such as a fire truck involved in an accident.
- Its involvement with Agreements, Accounts, and Parties (e.g. the association of a helicopter leased from a United States supplier).

- Its assignment to certain Tasks, such as a fire truck assigned to a work on firefighting activities.

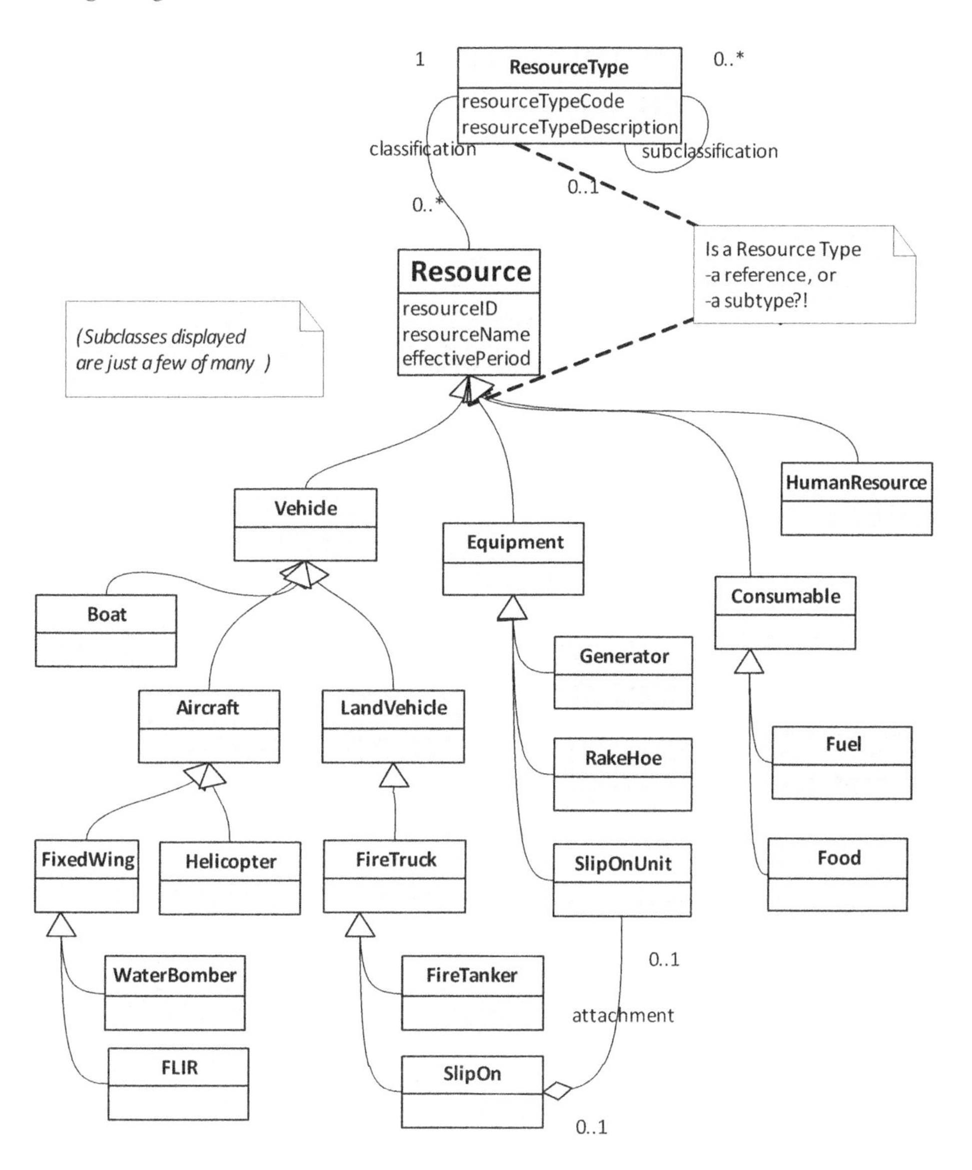

Figure 117: Resource (also known as Asset) pattern

Pattern: Event

The idea behind an Event is "something noteworthy" that happens at a point in time. Maybe going for a cup of coffee is an event of importance to me, but it is probably not considered to be noteworthy from a corporate perspective. In an emergency response setting for wildfires, the outbreak of a fire is a major event. A hopefully infrequent but still vitally important event is an occupational health and safety "personal injury" event if a firefighter is hurt.

When something happens that the business deems to be "noteworthy", a record of that business event is created.

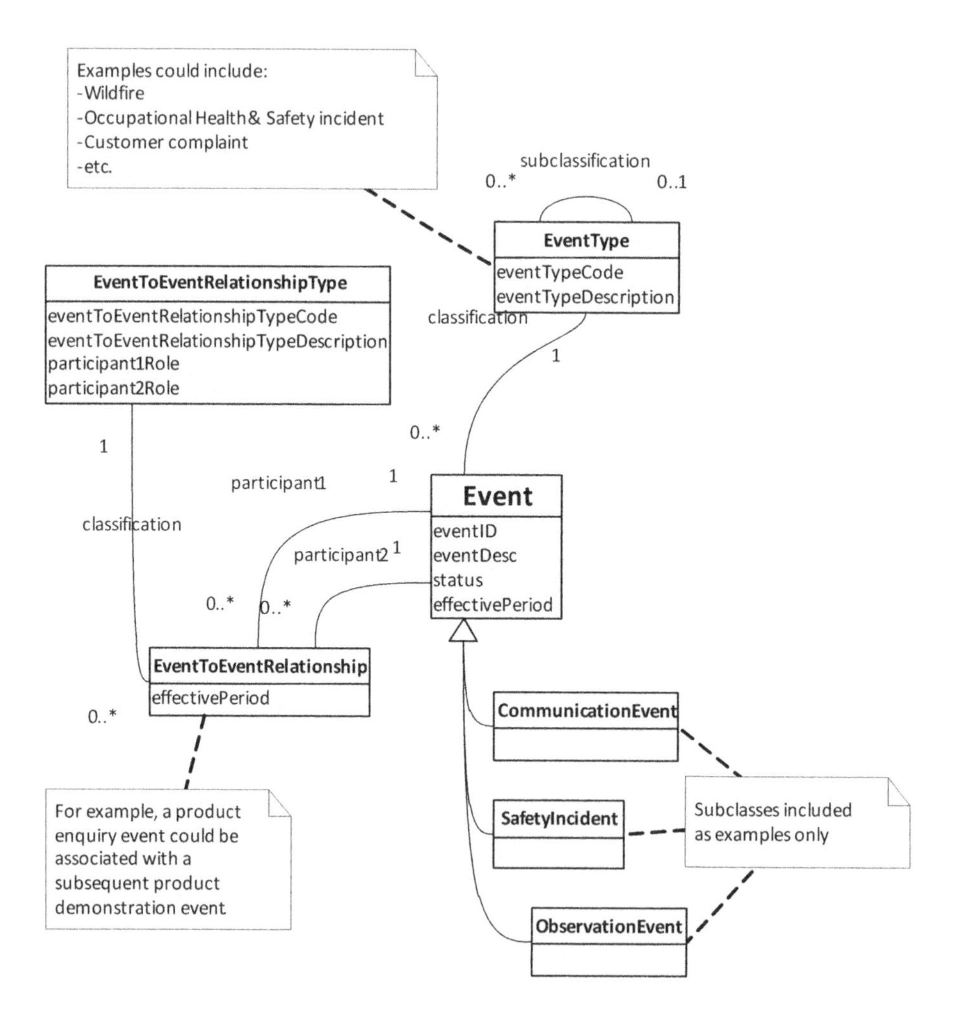

Figure 118: Event pattern

An Event may be "typed" via the Event Type class, or if specific attributes are required, it may be typed as a subclass, such as the Communication Event shown as an example.

Sometimes Events are related to each other. Maybe a customer phone call to make a product enquiry may be a considered noteworthy. This enquiry Event could be followed by another Event such as an on-site product demonstration. These two Events could be associated with each other. Such associations can be managed via the associated Event To Event Relationship class.

The Event To Event Relationship Type class defines allowable types of interrelationships, and the roles of each participant. For example, if the type of relationship between Events is a "Succession" relationship (one Event is succeeded by another), the Participant 1 Role might be defined as "Predecessor" and the Participant 2 Role might be defined as "Successor".

Within computer science there is the concept of event-driven architectures. A gross simplification suggests that the occurrence of an event such as the clicking of the "Commit" button is observed and published by one piece of software, and separate pieces of software consume this knowledge and react accordingly.

Somewhat similar relationships can be observed in the business world. Business events occur, they are noted, and appropriate business responses follow, which may be recorded as "tasks" (work done). Often a series of tasks triggered by an event reach a milestone that can be recorded as a noteworthy event. There is an elegant bi-directional relationship between the business events and the corresponding business responses. Let's take a look at a model of this synergy.

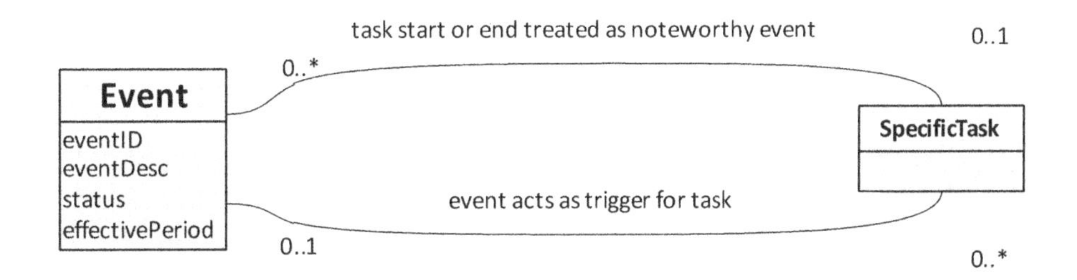

Figure 119: Event pattern & Task pattern synergy

An example of this synergy between Events and Tasks follows.

Someone reports smoke – that's a noteworthy Event. One of the two types of relationships between Events and Tasks is an Event acting as a trigger for a Task. The "smoke reported" Event triggers Tasks relating to the deployment of the initial response team.

The team arrives and evaluates the situation. This may be where the "task start or end treated as a noteworthy event" relationship may come into play. If it's a smoky barbeque and all is under control, the completion of the evaluation Task may be treated as a noteworthy Event of type "false alarm", and it's all over. However, if it's a genuine wildfire which is already running fast, the evaluation Task may result in recording of a "fire confirmation" Event. The evaluation team may sometimes also record a "suspicious cause" Event if it looks like the fire was deliberately lit.

Now the two-part cycle really kicks in. The "fire confirmation" Event may trigger a whole series of response Tasks, and the "suspicious cause" Event may trigger separate forensic investigation Tasks. And each of these sets of Tasks may have subsequent Events that in turn trigger more Tasks!

Pattern: Task

The idea behind a Task is typically some work to be done. A Task can represent a small unit of work. An example might be a simple checklist item ("make sure that someone rings the client back to notify them of a delay", "perform a credit check on the prospect" ...). A Task can also represent a large and complex unit of work such as a major project or even an entire program of work. Of course, some of these may require specialized attributes. For example, a project may have a budget and a project manager. Nonetheless, they are all represented by a generic Task, which can be extended by appropriate subclassing.

The Task class has two subclasses, namely the Specific Task class and the Template Task class:

- Template Tasks define an overall profile of Tasks that occur frequently. For example, it would be reasonable to expect that a template would be defined that describes a profile for day-to-day responsibilities such as responding to a product enquiry. Templates have a profile, but are not related to any calendar dates / times, and may describe generic deployment of *types* of resources, but will not typically nominate *specific* resources.

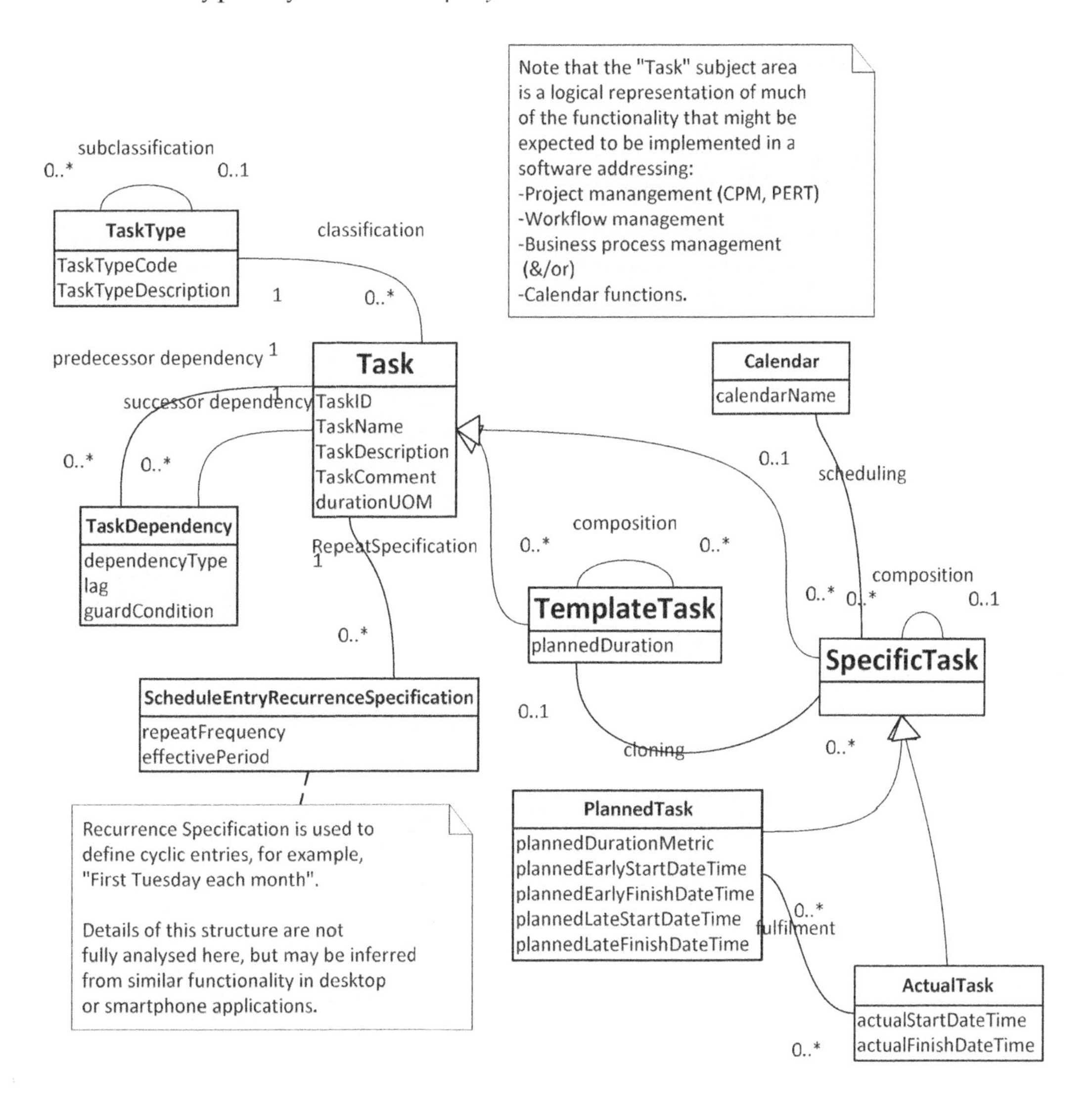

Figure 120: Task pattern

- Specific Tasks are instances of Tasks that have been "attached" to a Calendar. [A placeholder class is modeled for the Calendar class, but details are not modeled.] Whereas there might be a generic template for responding to a product enquiry, each planned and/or actual enquiry would be one specific Task ("At 9:17 am today we commenced processing a product enquiry initiated by Dan Daniels"). The Specific Task class typically records details either for some work to be done in the future – a Planned Task – or some work already started if not yet already completed – an Actual Task.

As part of a business process, a Template Task can be identified as being applicable, and then cloned to create a Specific Task.

The first volume[46] of Len Silverston's series represents many of these concepts within the "Work Effort" set of patterns.

Some features of Tasks are listed below:

- Tasks may be components in larger Tasks and/or may be broken down into finer-grained Tasks – refer to the "composition" relationships in the model.
- Tasks may have dependencies on other tasks, perhaps the most common being a "finish-to-start" dependency. That is, the first task must finish before the second task can start. Attributes of the Task Dependency class include:
    - The Dependency Type: Typically "FS" (finish-to-start), but may be "FF", "SF", or "SS".
    - Lag: Gap between two activities with a dependency. For example Task 2 is to start when Task 1 finishes, but with a delay of four days. (Note that the lag can be negative e.g. Task 2 is to start two days before the expected finish of Task 1.)
    - Guard Condition: Boolean condition on the commencement of the successor task.

---

[46] Silverston L. (2001) *"The Data Model Resource Book, Volume 1: A library of Universal Data Models for All Enterprises"*.

- Tasks have durations, and this model separates the metric, for example a duration of "3.5", from the unit-of-measure (UOM), for example "Hours".

- Some Tasks require the specification of recurring tasks entries, for example a task that occurs on the "First Tuesday each month, starting next January, and going until June". The Schedule Entry Recurrence Specification class is a placeholder for this functionality, but full details of this structure are not included here. However, details may be inferred from similar functionality in desktop or smartphone applications.

We have introduced patterns for Tasks. Now we look at what we need to do to assign "resources" to Tasks.

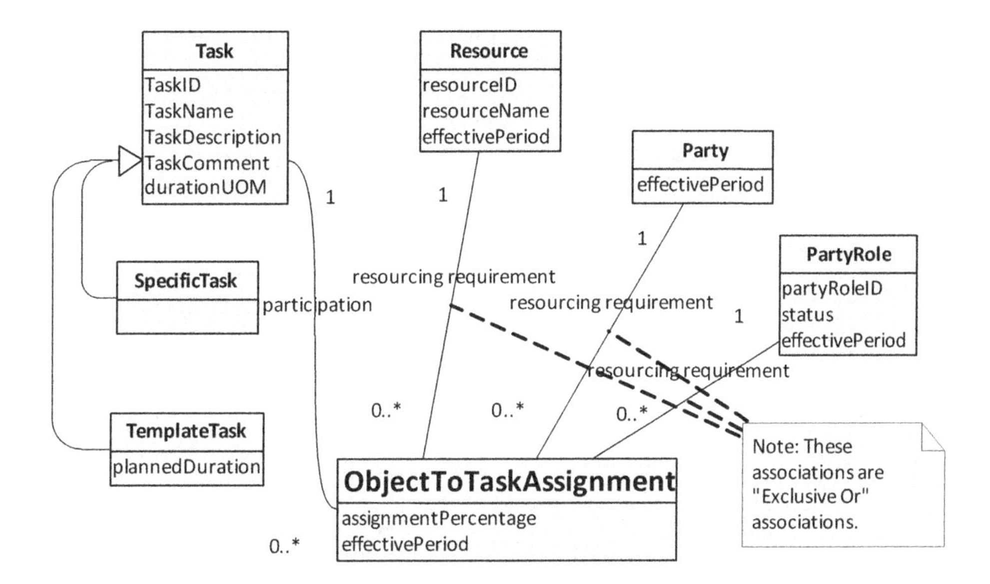

Figure 121: Objects assigned to a Task

Those familiar with project management tools such as Microsoft Project will be aware that, in that context, the term "resource" is inclusive of physical resources (such as cars and computers) and human resources. In the model displayed above, a subtle distinction is made between the resources represented by the "Resource" class, and what we have modeled as Parties and their Party Roles.

As an example, a specific task for firefighting commencing tomorrow at 9:00am might have assignments that include:

- The fire truck with registration ABC-123 (from the "Resource" class).
- Acme Catering (an organization, a subtype of "Party").
- Dan in the role of Driver (a party in a "Party Role").

This example relates to assignment of resources to a Specific Task. The diagram does also permit assignment of resources to Template Tasks, for example Acme Catering may be the catering company nominated in a Template Task as the default organization for every Specific Task instance created from the Template.

Not only can *instances* of resources (a specific fire truck, a specific organization, a specific driver) be assigned to Tasks, but resource *types* can also be assigned rather than resources instances, party *types* rather than party instances, and party role *types* rather than party role instances.

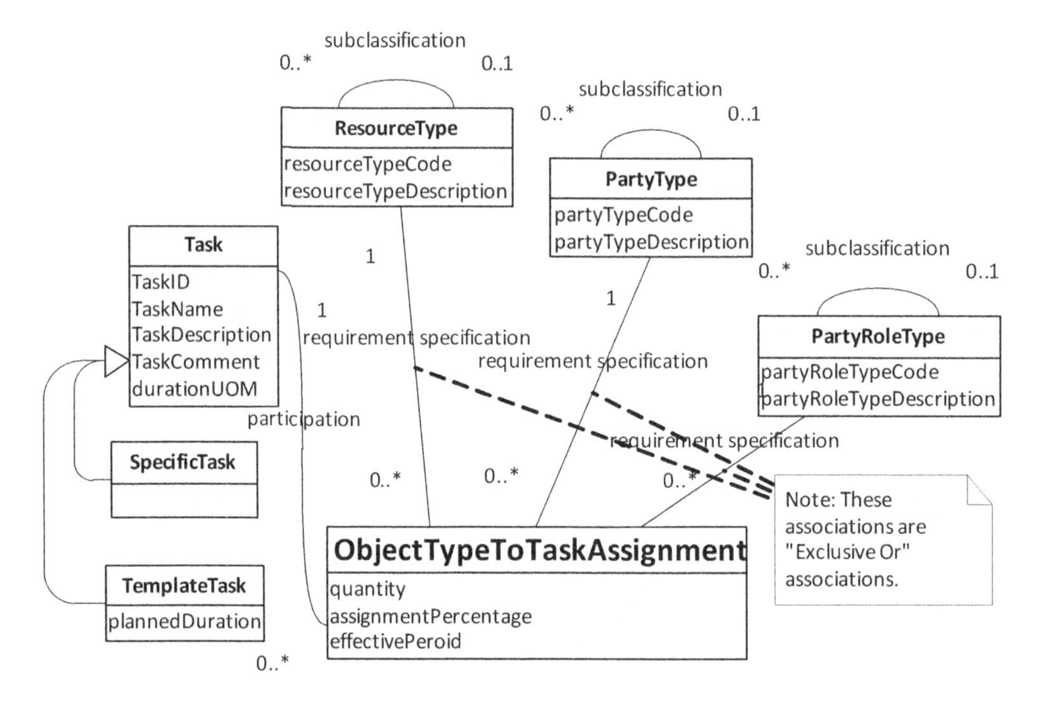

Figure 122: Object Types assigned to a Task

Note: Typically, Template Tasks will have Object Types assigned (for example "I want two Firefighters and one 4WD fire truck"). Conversely, Specific Tasks will typically have specific Objects assigned (for example "I want Alex, Brooke and that fire truck over there"). However, a Template Task can nominate that a specific Object is by default to be used, and a Specific Task can nominate the assignment of an Object Type.

Pattern: Product (tangible goods, intangible services)

Products are the things sold by companies. Pretty simple? Unfortunately there is some inconsistent usage of the word "product", even amongst data modelers.

Let's take an example. Acme Air sells three types of air conditioners; one model of evaporative cooler (model number "EC"), a small reverse-cycle model (model number "SRC"), and a large reverse-cycle model (model number "LRC"). When we speak to some modelers (and assuming a relational implementation), they will say Acme Air will have three rows in the "Product" table.

Acme Air is a pretty small outfit, and so far it has sold 100 evaporative coolers, 300 small reverse cycle air conditioners, and 500 large reverse cycle air conditioners. Every one of those 900 products sold has a unique serial number. Some modelers will say Acme Air will have 900 rows in the "Product" table. So, does the "Product" table have three rows, or 900?

David Hay, in his book "*Data Model Patterns*"[47] differentiates between these scenarios by calling the catalogue of product types "Product Type". That's pretty sensible, in my opinion. So in the above example, the catalogue of Product Types would have three entries. David also has an entry for product instances, which he simply calls "Product". I have no problem with that name as, within the context of David's patterns, he is crystal clear about the meaning.

Then we have Len Silverston, another of my favorite data model pattern authors. He names the entity defining product types as simply "Product". Oops. That's different

---

[47] Hay D. (1996) "*Data Model Patterns: Conventions of Thought*".

than David's use of the word "Product". Within Len's books on patterns, he, like David, is consistent and clear. Both are great resources, but they do have slight differences.

I've worked in the telecommunications industry, and years ago came across the TM Forum's standard information / data model (SID). They also were very clear and precise, but called the entity representing product types the "Product Specification" entity. So who is right? All models arguably have merit, and I don't want to make a ruling, but to differentiate, my light-weight model is as follows:

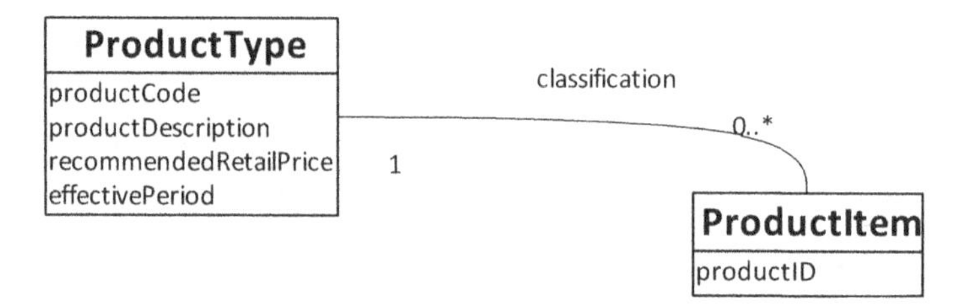

Figure 123: Product pattern core

For Acme Air, Product Type would have three entries, each instance representing one of the company's product types as clients might expect to find in the company's product catalogue. And Acme's Product Item would have 900 entries, each instance representing one product instance as it relates to one customer, for example Alex's Acme "evaporative cooler" model air conditioner with the serial number 12-34-56.

Len's Product model distinguishes between tangible (physical) goods such as an air conditioner, and intangible services such as the installation, or servicing, of the air conditioner. The extended model now looks like:

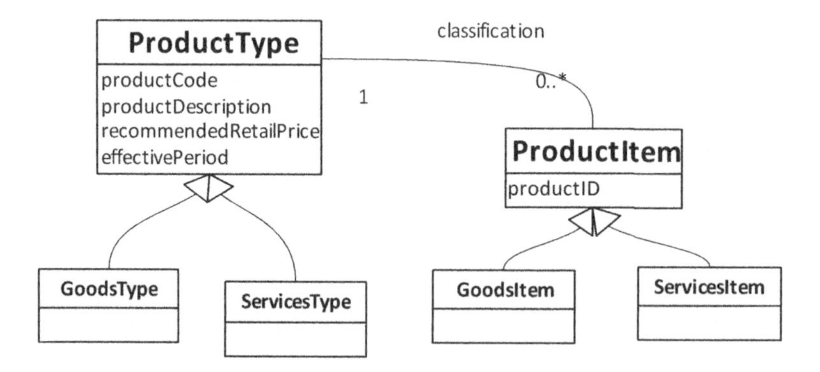

Figure 124: Pattern for Products as goods or services

If we look at Acme Air, we started with three Product Types, but Acme Air also sells two services – the installation of their air conditioners, and the servicing of those air conditioners. We now have five Product Types.

What the above model is saying is that one Product Type can be *either* one Goods Type (such as Acme Air's evaporative cooler), *or* one Services Type (such as servicing). That might be enough for some scenarios, but what if we want a more flexible model? If we look at a more complex scenario, we need more flexibility. For example, a telecommunications company might have the following amongst its range of product types:

- Mobile Phone XYZ: Comprised of one mobile phone handset (a goods type), a battery charger (another goods type), a missed-call answering facility (a service type), and 12 months international roaming (another service type).
- Basic Home Entertainment Pack: Comprised of one set-top-box (a goods type), and access to a library of golden-oldies movies (a service type).
- New Home Starters Pack: Comprised of two Mobile Phone XYZ product types plus one Basic Home Entertainment Pack product type.

The first two Product Types are each made up from multiple Goods Types and Services Types. The third Product Type is a package made up of other Product Types. A model to support this diversity follows.

Note:

- A Product Item can be made up from one or more tangible Goods Items and/or one or more intangible Services Items and/or one or more other Product Items.
- Similarly, a Product Type can be made up from one or more tangible Goods Types (as specified via the Product Goods Component many-to-many resolution class) and/or one or more intangible Services Types (as specified via the Product Services Component many-to-many resolution class) and/or one or more other Product Types (as specified via the Product Sub-product Component many-to-many resolution class).

- It is to be noted that one Goods Type (such as a type of set-top-box) can be included in the construction of multiple Product Types. Similarly, Service Types can be used again and again in the construction of varying Product Types. And of course, these flexibly constructed Product Types can themselves be re-packaged again and again to create bundled Product Types.

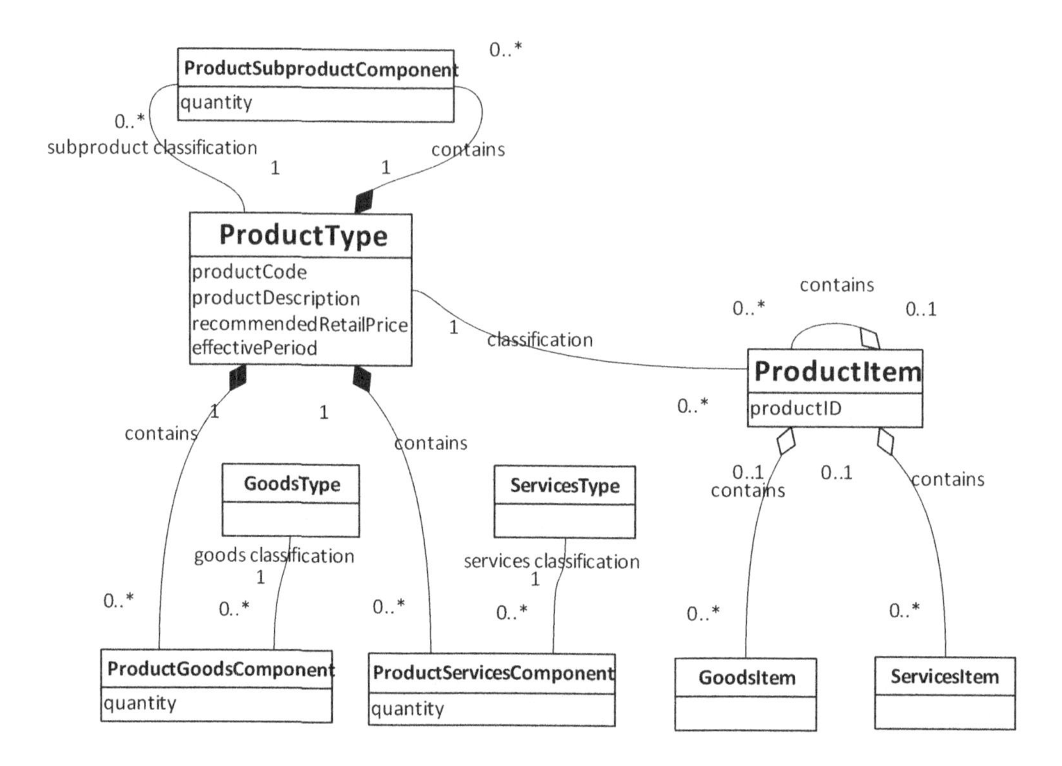

Figure 125: Pattern for Complex products comprising goods and/or services

That's a lot of flexibility for constructing a product catalogue.

Pattern: Location

This data model pattern represents data constructs typically found in a Geographic Information System (GIS) for mapping items to a position on the earth's surface. Such software is typically purchased as an off-the-shelf software component. We could develop our own GIS, but for most of us, this facility would be purchased rather than home-built. Nonetheless, this pattern is useful for inclusion in a high-level enterprise model as it represents concepts the business may need, even if its physical implementation is via a purchased solution.

In the wildfire emergency response scenario, recording data about locations is vital. What is the point at which a fire started? What line on a map represents the current fire front? What area has already been burned, and based on fire behavior predictions, what are is likely to be burned in the near future?

The Open Geospatial Consortium (OGC) has rich definitions for the structuring of data about geospatial locations. However, the following model may be a sufficient approximation of location data structures for top-down enterprise modeling.

There is a separation of concerns between the Geometry class which manages positioning of the location on a map (for example, the boundary of a shire council's area of responsibility), and the Geospatial Object class which records structured data (attributes and relationships) for the various types of mapped objects (for example, the shire council's name of the Council, a list of all contacts within the Council, statements on intended zoning changes, and so on).

The Geometry class is subclassed into Point (for example, the position where an event occurred), Line (for example, the position of a road or a river), and Polygon (for example, the area covered by the base of a building or defined by a land title). This can be extended to include 3-dimensional shapes also.

The model diagrams in this book use the UML notation, but usually only show the class and its attributes. For the Geometry class, the Get Implicit Proximity operation is included. This operation is noted to highlight the fact that a Geometry within a Geographic Information System (GIS) will have functions to determine one geospatial object's proximity in relation to other geospatial objects. Examples include determination of what it is contained within it, what it contains, what it shares a partial boundary with, and what it partially overlaps.

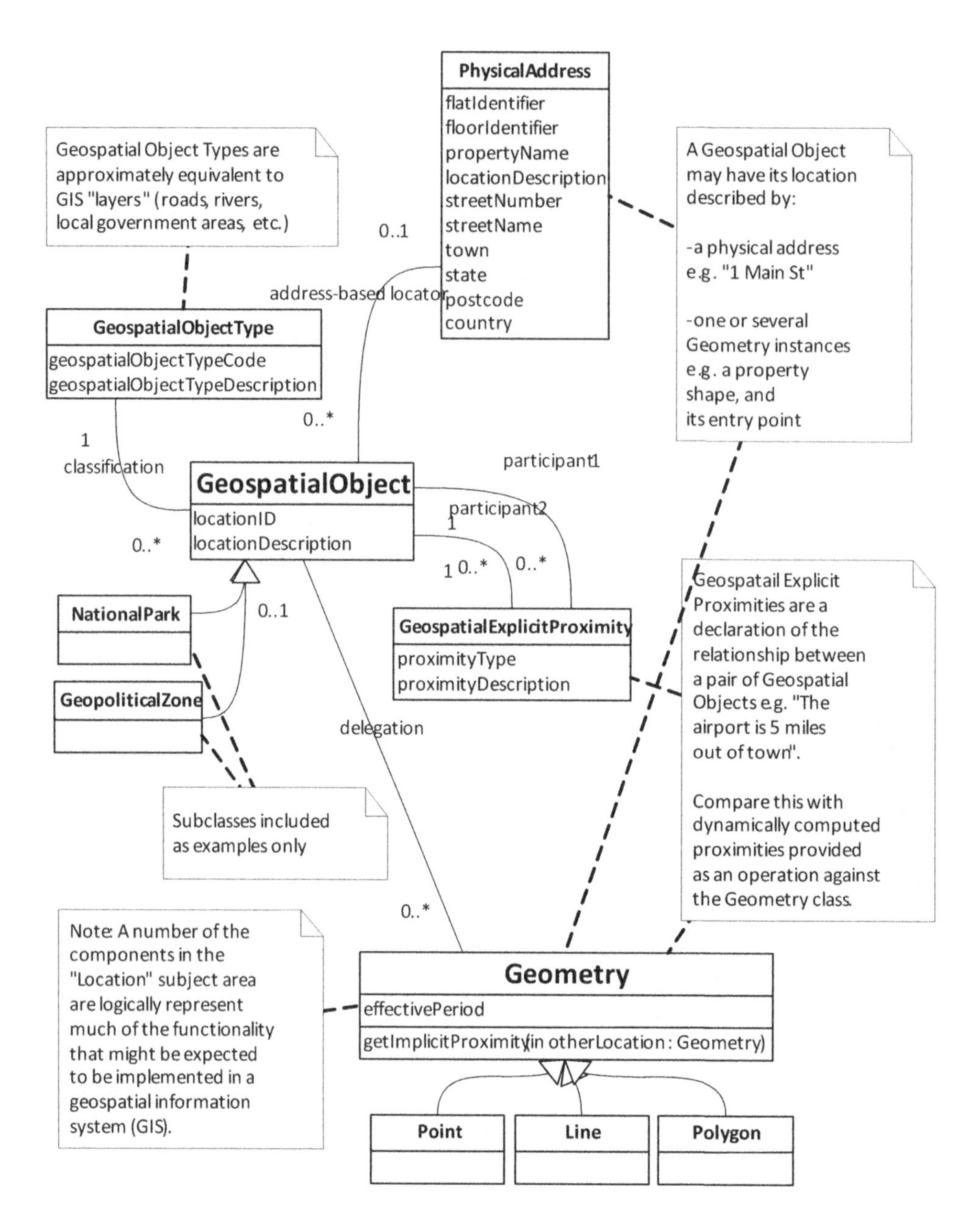

Figure 126: Location pattern

The Geospatial Object class captures structured data (for the shapes that can be presented on a map via the Geometry class). These Geospatial Objects are classified according to entries in the Geospatial Object Type class, which approximates the classification of "layers" on a map (the "roads" layer, the "rivers" layer, and so on). Where these different types of Geospatial Objects require their own attributes and/or associations, the Geospatial Object class may be subclassed – National Park and Geopolitical Zone are shown as examples.

The Geometry class had the Get Implicit Proximity operation to dynamically compute the proximity of one shape to another. In contrast, the Geospatial Object class delegates this responsibility to the associated Geospatial Explicit Geometry class to record manually determined proximities between a pair of Geospatial Objects. The Proximity Type attribute can record classifications such as "Complete containment", "Partial overlap", "Sharing of a partial boundary", or "Close". These are not necessarily precise, and these classifications may be supplemented by a Proximity Description such as "Proceed from the first object in a northerly direction until you encounter the black stump, then turn left for another 50 metres ..."!

Pattern: Document

This data model pattern represents data constructs typically found in a document / records management system, used to safely store and retrieve important documents. Even though such software is typically purchased as an off-the-shelf software component, this pattern is useful for inclusion in a high-level enterprise model as it represents concepts the business may need, even if its physical implementation is via a purchased solution.

Chapter 11 of Hay's *"Data Model Patterns"* book elaborates on the concept. My simplified version follows.

The Document class is responsible for managing storage of documents, be they paper-based Physical Documents, or Electronic Documents. Electronic Documents in turn may be Unstructured Electronic Documents (such as a smart phone video clip) or they can be Structured Electronic Documents that contain structured, machine-readable information (for example, in an XML document). The Document Format class records the type of storage form, and for some forms may correlate to typical file extensions ("doc", "jpg", "xls", etc.).

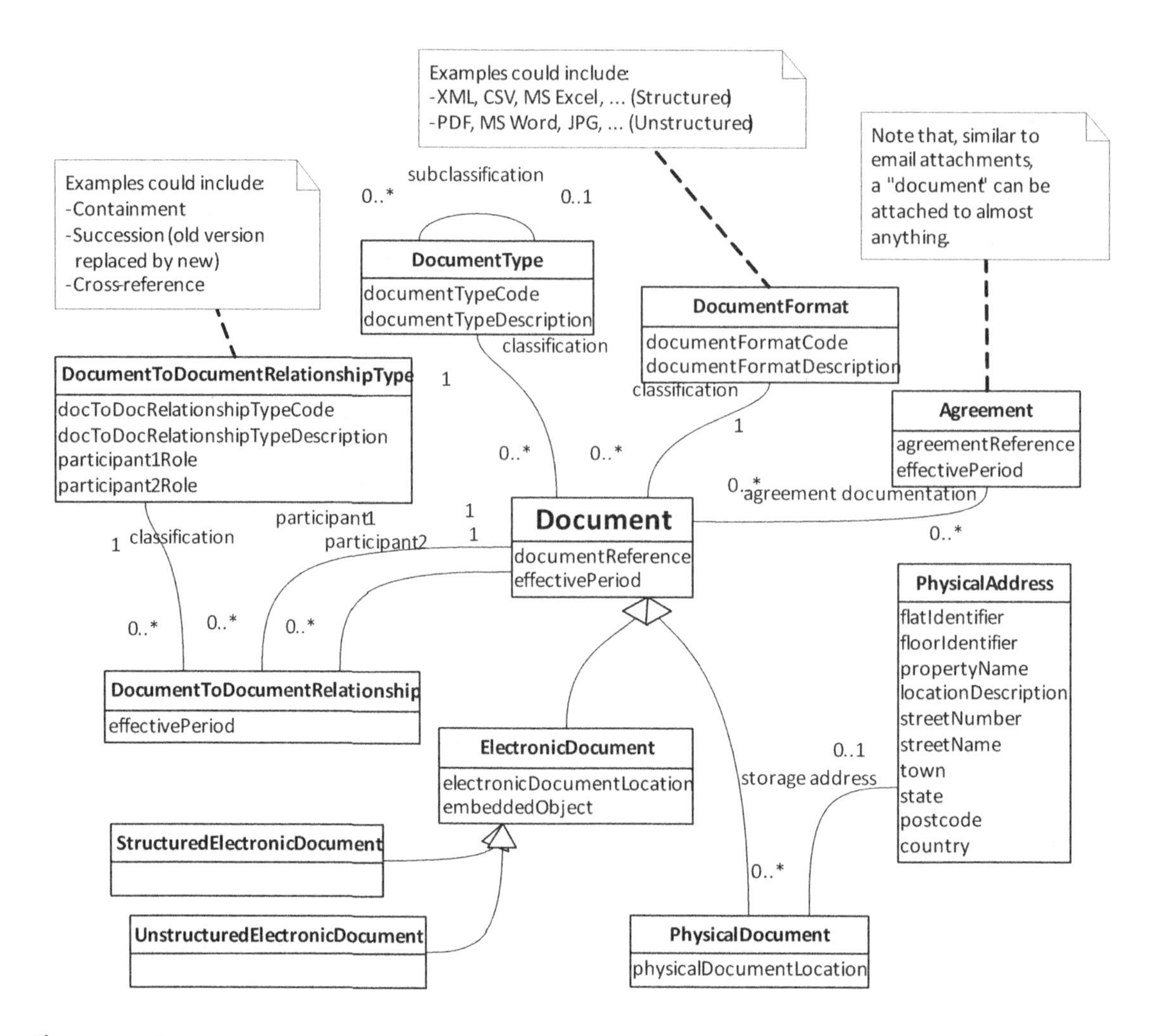

Figure 127: Document pattern

For Electronic Documents, they can either be stored in an Electronic Document Location (such as a URL, a drive and folder specification, ...), or they can be directly held as an Embedded Object, somewhat like an email can hold attachments. For Physical Documents, their storage location may optionally be defined via an associated Physical Address object.

The Document Type class classifies Documents according to their business role, for example an "Employment Contract", and another as a "Service Agreement".

Documents can be associated with other Documents, using the Document To Document Relationship class. Examples of the types of relationships can include Containment (where one Document contains another Document), Succession (where one now-obsolete version of a Document is replaced by a newer version Document), and Cross-Reference (where one Document simply notes the existence of a related Document). These allowable types of interrelationships are managed by the Document To Document Relationship Type class, which also specifies the role of each Document (for example, in the "Composition" relationship, the first participant may be labeled as the "Container" and the second the "Component").

Pattern: Account

This data model pattern represents data constructs typically found in an accounting package. Even though such software is typically purchased as an off-the-shelf software component, this pattern is useful for inclusion in a high-level enterprise model as it represents concepts the business may need, even if its physical implementation is via a purchased solution.

David Hay and Len Silverston offer multiple versions across their books. My model below is intended to present an easy-to-understand, light-weight simplification that may be a sufficient framework for high-level modeling.

Each instance in the Account class represents one account within one of the company's financial ledgers.

Subclasses of Accounts Payable and Accounts Receivable are shown as examples of "typing" of Accounts. Alternatively, the Account Type class can be used to logically represent types, and subtypes of Accounts.

The Account class has a self-referencing hierarchical relationship to enable Accounts to be defined as sub-Accounts of other consolidation Accounts.

Each instance in the Accounting Transaction class represents one accounting transaction such as an invoice issued or a payment received. Some of these types of Accounting Transactions may contain many "items". For example, an accounting transaction for a customer invoice may contain many invoice lines, each being an itemized charge as it relates to a discrete product purchase. Similarly, a payment might itemize the particulars of what is being paid. Each instance in the Accounting Transaction Item class represents one such item.

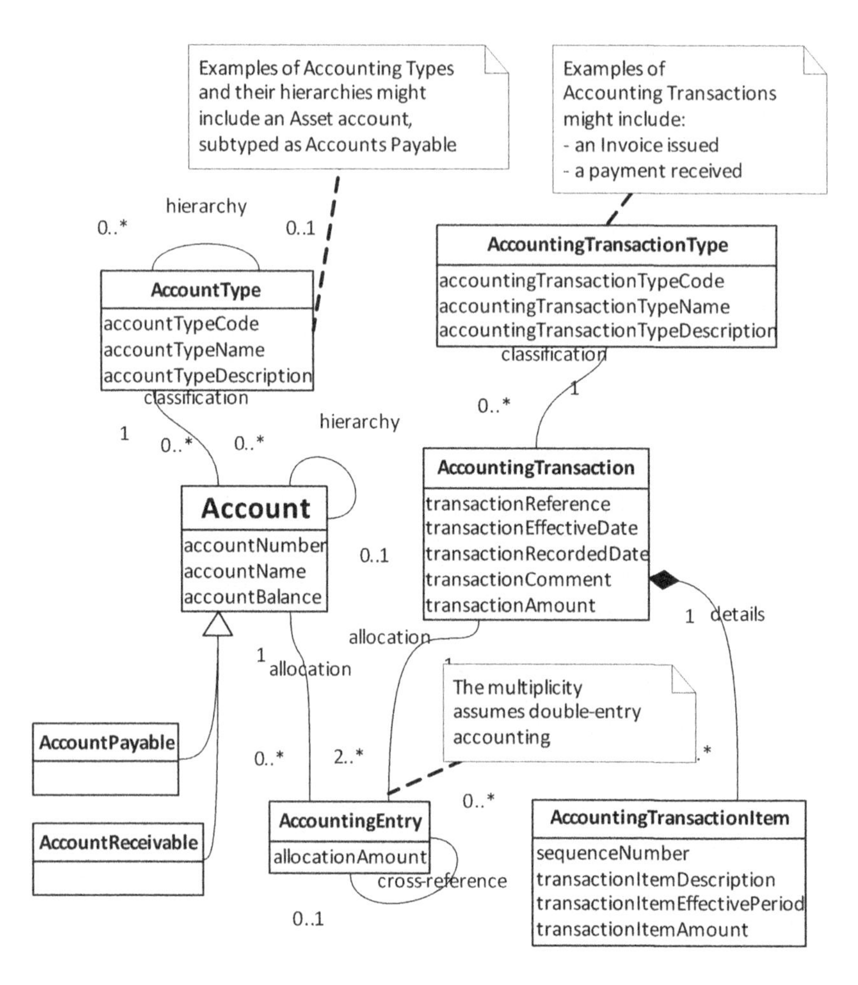

Figure 128: Account pattern core

The Accounting Transaction class attributes include:

- The Transaction Reference which optionally could record something such as an invoice number.
- The Transaction Recorded Date is the date the transaction was actually entered into a computer system.

- The Transaction Effective Date is the date that the transaction is deemed to be effective, not necessarily the date the transaction was recorded in a computer system.

Note that the single amount from an Accounting Transaction may be broken down into one or a set of debit amounts, and one or a set of credit amounts, for posting to Accounts, as defined via the associated Accounting Entry class. For example, an Accounting Transaction for $100.00 would have (for double entry accounting) at least two Accounting Entries, one as a debit and one as a credit. Further, these debit and/or credit Accounting Entries could be more fine-grained, for example allocating $60.00 to one Account and $40.00 to another.

There is a self-referencing relationship between Account Entries. This can be used, for example, to associate one Accounting Entry relating to an invoice to a matching payment Accounting Entry.

As shown below, by associating the Account pattern with the Party & Party Role patterns, we can incorporate a record of the parties, or parties in specific roles, involved with an account. For example, we could record who is the "Primary" account holder, the "Secondary" account holder, and maybe the "Guarantor" for a loan account, using the Participation Type attribute in the Account Participation class.

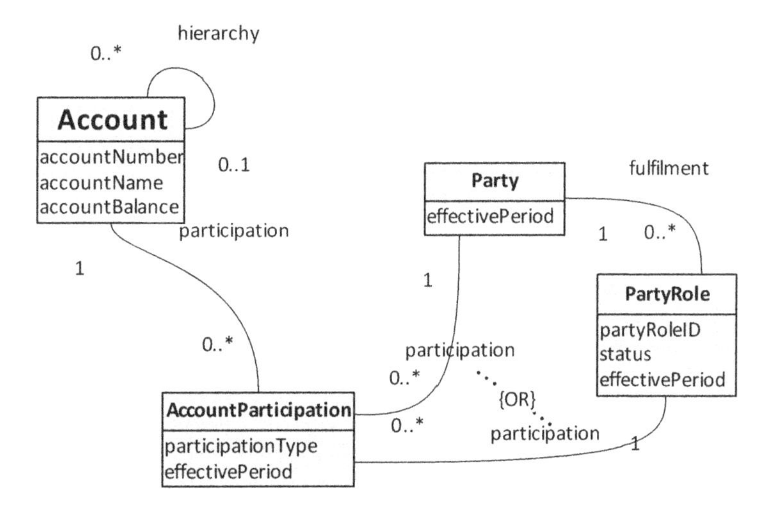

Figure 129: Account pattern and associated Parties

Pattern: Classification

The preceding patterns focus on what I have labeled the nine pillars of top-down big-picture modeling. They represent business concepts that non-technical people frequently speak about, so they are business-centric. It is important to note that they are also IT-centric in that they can certainly be implemented. These data model patterns are very effective at bridging the two worlds of business *and* IT.

There are also what I call "Utility" patterns. One example is for Units-of-Measure measure (kilometers and miles, kilograms and tons, liters and gallons ...), and their conversion routines. The business may want to know we can handle units-of-measure, but probably don't care how we do it.

One pattern that does get the attention of the business is the "Classification" pattern, which represents the code-&-description reference data sets typically encountered in Reference Data Management practices. Believe me, the business *is* interested in its code sets. It is just typically less interested in some of the elegant implementation aspects of this pattern. Often it is enough to let them know of the flexibility offered by this pattern, and they are satisfied. Nonetheless, a somewhat technical explanation of this pattern follows.

The "Classification" class is used to provide a generic and very flexible way of classifying "types" of things. For example, a commercial customer might be classified according to Australian & New Zealand Standard Industry Codes, some wildfires may be classified according to size and severity, employees may be classified according to formal competencies, and so on.

Silverston & Agnew's "*The Data Model Resource Book, Volume 3: Universal Patterns For Data Modeling*" presents a number of pattern variations in the chapter titled, "Types and Categories: The Classification of Data". The model below is a light-weight simplification that also reflects some of my own adaptations. It may be a sufficient framework for high-level modeling.

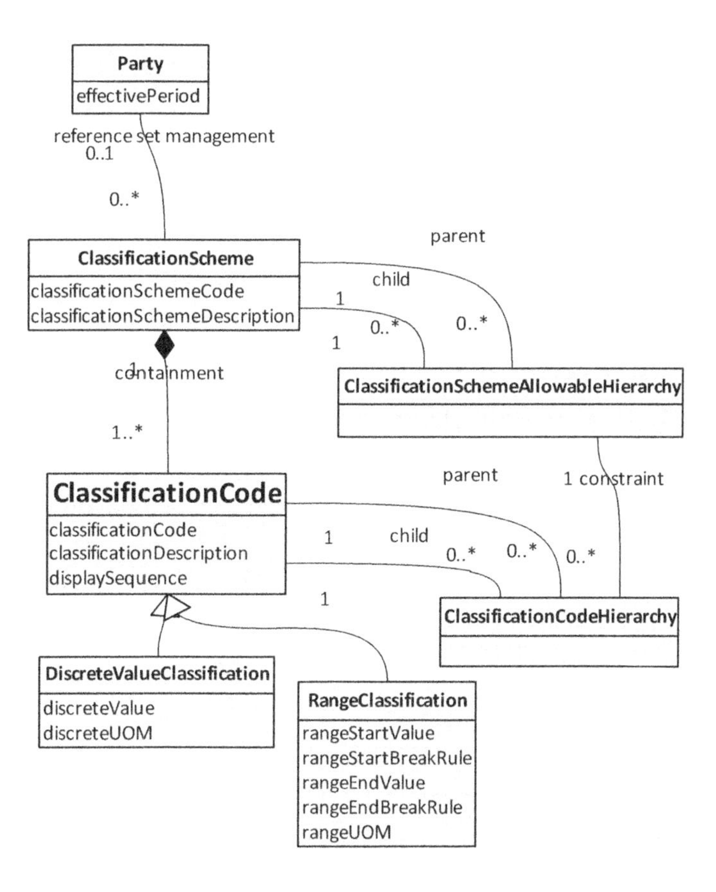

Figure 130: Classification pattern

The pattern starts with the Classification Scheme class. Across the enterprise, many classification schemes may exist. Examples could possibly include:

- Classification of customers by industry code (retail, manufacturing, ...)
- Classification of customers by sales area
- Classification of meters and valves on a factory floor by size, flow rate ranges, etc.
- Classification of vehicles by make, model, etc.

In the above list, "Industry Code", "Sales Area", the factory equipment's "Size" and "Flow Rate", and the vehicle's "Make" and "Model" are examples of Classification Schemes. Each instance in this class represents one such scheme.

For each Classification Scheme, the allowable codes need to be enumerated. For example, for the "Country" Classification Scheme there may be Classification Codes of "AUS" for Australia, not to be confused with "AUT" for Austria. This particular Classification Scheme may have its enumerations managed by one Party, in this case, the United Nations.

Two more examples of Classification Codes might be "Ford" and "Toyota" within the "Make" Classification Scheme, and "Mustang", "LandCruiser" and "Corolla" within the "Model" Classification Scheme. Here we have an interesting extension. "Mustang" is a Model for the "Ford" Make, and "Corolla" belongs to "Toyota". Here we have examples of where Classification Schemes may be sub-classified by yet other schemes.

To define these interrelationships, we begin with the Classification Scheme Allowable Hierarchy class. In the above example, it would identify the Classification Scheme of Make as an allowable "parent" to the "child" Classification Scheme of Model.

Sometimes there can be a sub-classification hierarchy within one code set. For example, in Australia the "Model" Classification Scheme may have "Commodore" as a model, but sub-classify this into "Commodore Executive", "Commodore Vacationer", etc. In this case, an instance in this Classification Scheme Allowable Hierarchy class would define the Classification Scheme of "Model" as an allowable "parent" to the "child" Classification Scheme of "Model" – a self-referencing relationship pointing back to the same Classification Scheme.

Once the allowable relationships between Classification Schemes are defined (for example, Make as parent of Model), instances of actual relationships (such as the "Ford" Make and the "Mustang" Model as its child) can be recorded in the Classification Code Hierarchy class.

The Classification Code class can record not only "code-&-description" data, but also specific values (refer to the Discrete Value Classification class), or ranges (refer to the Range Classification class). One example of use of such a feature might be the rating of cyclones / hurricanes / tornadoes where a level "3" might represent one range of wind speeds, and a level "4" another range. Where ranges are adjacent, the specification needs to nominate whether a boundary value belongs to one range or another. For example, if one wind speed is in the range of 50 to 100 kilometers per hour, and the adjacent range covers 100 to 150 kilometers per hour, which range does a speed of exactly 100 belong to? The attributes Range End Break Rule (for example, "less than") and Range Start Break Rule (for example, "greater than or equal to") clarify this detail.

Bibliography

Boehm B. & Turner T. (2003): *"Balancing Agility and Discipline"*

Fowler M. (1997): *"Analysis Patterns: Reusable Object Models"*

Gamma E., Helm R., Johnson R. & Vlissides J. (1995): "Design Patterns: Elements of Reusable Object-Oriented Software"

Hay D. (1996): *"Data Model Patterns: Conventions of Thought"*

Hay D. (2011): *"Enterprise Model Patterns: Describing the World"*

Hay D. (2018): *"Achieving Buzzword Compliance"*

Hultgren H (2012): *"Modeling the Agile Data Warehouse with Data Vault"*

Hoberman S., Burbank D., & Bradley C. (2009): *"Data Modeling for the Business"*

Linstedt D. (2011): *"Super Charge your Data Warehouse: Invaluable Data Modeling Rules to Implement Your Data Vault"*

Linstedt D. & Olschimke O. (2016): *"Building a Scalable Data Warehouse with Data Vault 2.0"*

Silverston L. (2001) *"The Data Model Resource Book, Volume 1: A library of Universal Data Models for All Enterprises"*

Silverston L. (2001): *"The Data Model Resource Book, Volume 2: A Library of Universal Data Models by Industry Types"*

Silverston L. & Agnew P. (2009): *"The Data Model Resource Book, Volume 3: Universal Patterns for Data Modeling"*

Simsion G. (2007): *"Data Modeling Theory and Practice"*

Index

Made in the USA
Las Vegas, NV
06 June 2023